IRIS

AFFAIRS

Edmund Burke

Edited by Matthew Arnold

NEW INTRODUCTION BY CONOR CRUISE O'BRIEN

THE CRESSET LIBRARY

London Melbourne Auckland Johannesburg

The Cresset Library

An imprint of Century Hutchinson Ltd

62–65 Chandos Place, London WC2N 4NW

Century Hutchinson Australia Pty Ltd
P O Box 496, 16–22 Church Street, Hawthorn,
Victoria 3122, Australia

Century Hutchinson New Zealand Ltd
P O Box 40–086, Glenfield, Auckland 10
New Zealand

Century Hutchinson South Africa (Pty) Ltd
P O Box 337, Berglvei 2012, South Africa

First published as *Letters, Speeches and Tracts on Irish Affairs*, 1881

This edition first published 1988

Made and printed in Great Britain by
Richard Clay Ltd, Bungay, Suffolk

ISBN 0 09 173177 1

CONTENTS.

INTRODUCTION to the Cresset Library edition

I

For most of the nineteenth century, thoughtful members of the upper and middle classes in Britain regarded the writings of Edmund Burke as a treasure-house of political wisdom. Liberals and conservatives were agreed on that point, though not entirely agreed as to where Burke's wisdom had most clearly revealed itself. Liberals valued most his writings on America and India, with their emphasis on respect for the principle of consent of the governed. Tories were naturally more impressed by his writings on what he significantly called, not the French Revolution but the Revolution in France – the point being that the revolution which began in France was an international one; he was warning against English Jacobins perhaps even more than against French ones (compare George Orwell's *Nineteen Eighty-four* which is as much a polemic against English sympathizers with Stalinism as it is against Stalinism itself).

Liberals might think that Edmund Burke might have gone too far in at least part of his polemic against the French Revolution; Tories might feel little enough enthusiasm, even retrospectively, for his arguments in favour of the American colonists. But on the whole there was a feeling, general among educated people, that broadly Burke had been right, both

about the American and French revolutions. Certainly, he had
shown a kind of prophetic power in that he had realized, earlier
and more clearly than his contemporaries, that what was taking
shape, both in America and in France, was something of world-
historical importance.

It was mainly on his writings about America and France
that Burke's great posthumous reputation rested, casting a long
shadow over British and European political thought especially
in the period 1814 to 1914.[1]

During the first eight decades of the nineteenth century
Burke's writing on Ireland — abundant, deeply considered,
deeply felt though they are — didn't seem particularly important
to English people. They didn't seem important, because Ireland
itself didn't seem important. But from 1880 on, for a period
of just over a decade, the Irish question, as it was called, came
to dominate and to convulse the politics of the United Kingdom.
This was due to an uneven and intermittent interaction between
forces making for different kinds of social and political change
in Ireland and in the rest of the then United Kingdom of Great
Britain and Ireland.

In Ireland, the social changes followed on, and were in large
part a consequence of, the great demographic changes following
on the great Famine of 1845 to 1848. In the Famine period
itself, about a million people had died and about a million
had emigrated to North America, mainly the United States.
Following those years a continued pattern of emigration had
been set, the population of Ireland continued to fall, while in
the United States the population of Irish origin continued to
expand, in numbers, in earning power and in influence. Many
— probably most — of these continued to have strong ties to
their relatives in Ireland, overwhelmingly of Catholic tenant-
farmer stock.

There were corresponding feelings of hostility, primarily towards the Irish landlords – mainly of Protestant stock – but also towards England, the Protestant power which had conquered the Catholic Irish and established the alien landlord system. Among the more politicized, there was a fixed belief that the Irish Famine had been 'man-made'; the result of calculated policies designed to exterminate a people; what we today would call genocide (this view, at least in its extreme forms, is now rejected by historians, but continues to influence the attitudes of certain kinds of political activists, notably the Provisional IRA and its supporters).

Associated with the 'man-made famine', but more deep seated, was a feeling of shame, about the passivity of the famine victims, who had gone 'like sheep to the slaughter'.

While the tendency of some twentieth-century political activists to equate the nineteenth-century Irish famine to the Holocaust of the European Jews nearly a hundred years later is a spurious piece of rhetoric, there is a genuine and close comparability between post-famine attitudes of Irish Catholic people – both in Ireland and in America – and post-Holocaust attitudes of twentieth-century Jews, especially in Israel and in America. In both cases there was a new and grim determination which could be expressed in two words: 'never again!'

As far as nineteenth-century Ireland was concerned, the moment of truth for the 'never again' people came at the end of the 1870s when a new famine seemed to loom ahead. The response to this was brilliantly innovative and became unprecedently successful. This was the movement known as 'the New Departure'.

The primary organ of the 'New Departure' was the Land League. In Ireland, the Land League, founded by Michael Davitt organized the tenant farmers to refuse rent and resist

eviction. In America, the Irish emigrants, at the call of John
Devoy and others, gave financial and propaganda support to
the Land League on a scale never available before to any Irish
movement. Both at Westminster and in Ireland Charles Stewart
Parnell emerged as the political leader of the whole movement.
His slogan 'keep a firm grip on your homesteads' summed up
the immediate object of the movement, and worked. Wherever
the Land League chose to concentrate its efforts, it succeeded
in ostracizing – and intimidating – the landlords and their
agents, to the accompaniment of enormous publicity. It was
the case of the County Mayo land agent, Captain Boycott –
which the British government chose for a conspicuously ridiculous showdown in 1880 – which gave the word 'boycott' to
the languages of the world.

By 1881, it had become apparent to the then Prime Minister,
William Ewart Gladstone, that the Irish land system had
become unworkable. Gladstone determined to introduce a
major piece of legislation which became the Land Act of 1881,
revolutionizing the Irish system of land tenure, and conceding
most of the tenant's demands. It was a signal victory for 'never
again'.

II

It was under the impact of the general turmoil caused by these
events that Matthew Arnold, poet, essayist, political authority
felt the need to bring together in one volume and present to
the public Edmund Burke's 'Letters Speeches and Tracts on
Irish Affairs'. Arnold's collection was compiled before Gladstone's Land Bill was introduced (7 April 1881), and went to
press shortly thereafter. Arnold had had the idea of making

such a collection at a time when British policies towards Ireland were being reassessed, and Arnold hoped that the study of Burke on Ireland would have a benign effect on the process of reassessment.[2] In Burke's words, which Arnold made his own in his preface, he hoped that Burke would 'set them on thinking'. In retrospect there is a deep irony in that. This is based, like much irony, on a hope that was *partially* fulfilled. For the greatest statesman of the Victorian age did indeed have his mind 'set on thinking' by Burke's writings on Ireland and the main result of Gladstone's thinking – the Home Rule Bill of 1886 – was to fill Matthew Arnold with the same revulsion and dismay as it inspired in most contemporary Englishmen, who had never been 'set on thinking' in this way.

How powerful an influence Burke's mind was exercising over Gladstone's at the time when Gladstone was moving towards his great decision on Home Rule may be seen in Morleys *Life of Gladstone* (London 1903; vol. 111 page 280). In late 1885 and early 1886 Gladstone was reading Burke 'nearly every day'. Gladstone wrote in his diary:

December 18 (1885) – read Burke; what a magazine of wisdom on Ireland and America.

January 9 – made many extracts from Burke – sometimes almost divine

We may easily imagine says Morley, how the heat from that profound and glowing furnace still further inflamed strong purposes and exhalted resolution in Mr. Gladstone.

One of Gladstone's former Cabinet colleagues, a conservative Whig, who knew his Burke, and also knew his Gladstone, was dismayed in this period to learn that Gladstone's reading Burke 'your *perfervidum ingenium Scoti*[3] does not need being touched with a live coal from that Irish altar'.

The man who feared the effects of a study of Burke ended up on the same side, practically speaking, as the man who warmly recommended the study in question: both against Home Rule for Ireland.

It is hard not to resist the conclusion that the man who was afraid of Burke, in the context of the time, had a clearer idea – or sounder intuition – of the forces at work than did the writer who collected and arranged 'Burke on Ireland', five years before the Home Rule Bill.

Arnold and Gladstone, although they came to reach conflicting conclusions set out from much the same point, as regards Burke on Ireland. They both believed that the Irish – specifically the Irish Catholics – had been much worse treated in the past than most Englishmen were aware and that a much more sympathetic approach was called for now. The question was: *how much* more sympathetic? It would appear that Arnold, at the time he prepared this collection for publication, did not realize how far Gladstone was preparing to go, even on the land settlement; let alone – on a longer perspective – on Home Rule. And 'Burke's wisdom' like that of the ancient oracles, is ambiguous. There are contradictions between the general emotional thrust of the body of his writings on Ireland and certain of his specific and programmatic utterances. Gladstone – and initially Arnold also – went along with the general thrust. Nor did they initially diverge, in any obvious way, on specifics. Both agreed with Burke's view that the connection between Britain and Ireland ought to be strengthened, not weakened. Gladstone came to hold that the connection would actually be strengthened by the concession of Home Rule – limited self-government within the Empire – as demanded by a large majority of the Irish electorate: a majority made up

almost entirely by an overwhelming majority of the Irish Catholic people. Arnold believed – passionately towards the end of
his life – that Home Rule would come to spell total separation
of Britain and Ireland. This was not a dispute that could be
resolved by an appeal to anything specific that Burke said. The
circumstances had changed drastically in the nearly ninety
years that had passed since Burke's death and no true Burkean
– and both Arnold and Gladstone were true Burkeans in their
own ways – could attempt to make light of circumstances. In
the *Reflections on the Revolution in France*, Burke had written:
'Circumstances (which with some gentlemen pass for nothing)
give in reality to every political principle its distinguishing colour
and discriminating effect. The circumstances are what render
every civil and political scheme beneficial or noxious to
mankind.'[4]

So specifics were not to be hoped for. Yet I think Gladstone's
bold enterprise was more in tune with the general spirit of
Burke's writing on Ireland than was Arnold's anxious and
cautious sympathy.[5]

Gladstone's attitude differed from that of Arnold – by the
mid 1880s – in being prepared to allow a great deal of weight
to the demands of a large majority of the Irish people – that
is, almost all the Catholics – even though these demands
appeared as absurdly exorbitant to many people in the United
Kingdom and to a compact and determined minority in Ireland
itself (especially in what is now Northern Ireland).

My guess is that Burke – had he been born in say 1829
rather than in 1729 – would have been likely to support
Gladstone's position, backed as it was, among the Irish Catholics, not only by the poor tenant-farmers, but by most middle-
class Catholics and the most influential members of the Catholic

hierarchy. That however is speculation. But as a matter of
practical influence both Gladstone and Argyle saw, though with
different feelings, the emotional impact of Burke's Irish writings
worked in the direction in which Gladstone decided to go. This
was because the bulk of Burke's Irish writings constitute a
great and memorable tract against Protestant ascendancy over
Catholics. By the late nineteenth century, the rigid caste-lines
which Burke had known in Ireland, especially in his youth, no
longer had the backing of the laws. But Protestant ascendancy
remained a social and economic fact and the main, and very
nearly the sole, upholders of the Union and opponents of Home
Rule in Ireland were the Protestants. An appeal to the high
authority of Burke, among the British ruling class, was among
other things a good way of having Irish Protestant opposition
discounted. The Irish Protestant record, as expounded by the
man who was then regarded as the greatest of British political
thinkers – and himself a Protestant of sorts – was made to tell
against the Irish Protestants of the late nineteenth century.
Thus, whatever Burke consciously thought and intended, the
influence of his Irish writings, in the late nineteenth century
and after, worked in favour of those who were seeking to
weaken, or at least attenuate, the British connection and tended
to undermine the position of the staunchest defenders of the
Union.

Matthew Arnold died on 14 April 1888, almost two years
after the introduction of the first Home Rule Bill. Perhaps
realizing that he had fallen into something of a trap over 'Burke
on Ireland', Arnold turned, near the end of his life, to a
significantly different body of Burke's writings: those on the
Revolution in France. This was the Burke of the Tories, who
led the fight against Home Rule. As Owen Dudley Edwards
puts it:

Increasingly Burke had been his great Mentor on Irish questions, and in 1881 he had faithfully edited Burke's *Letters, Speeches and Tracts of Irish Affairs*, the great storehouse of his own logic that Ireland must be given a sense of British concern for her welfare and an equal participation in the benefits of empire. Now he would turn to Burke again, to the Burke who broke remorselessly with old friends and party ties against the anarchy of the French Revolution and its British supporters and sympathizers. Was it was not just such anarchy that he saw in Ireland? and were it not just such treason to mankind to permit it to flourish? Burke had not seen an Ireland in arms, but he had seen the dangers that his Ireland might fall into the hands of designing enemies of civilization and history, of truth and culture. That time had now arrived.[6]

So Edmund Burke, in two different aspects of his thought and writing, is now enlisted on *both* sides of the great Home Rule controversy.[7]

Burke on Ireland was a patron saint to one side of the controversy, 'Burke on the French Revolution' to the other. Matthew Arnold, a Sorcerers Apprentice in political matters, began by conjuring up 'Burke on Ireland' and ended by taking refuge from 'Burke on Ireland' in the protecting and conserving shade of 'Burke on the French Revolution'.

'Setting people on thinking' is indeed a hazardous and unpredictable enterprise.

III

It is time to look at the Burke writings in themselves, as distinct from their impact or a later controversy. What follows is mainly intended to remove one or two difficulties which may stand between the modern reader and the full appreciation of the text.

There is first of all a technical difficulty. As the Cresset

Library text is not a new edition but a reprint of Arnold's
Selection and Arrangement, it has to follow Arnold's selection
and arrangement. As regards the selection, this does not present
any serious difficulty. It is true that the splendid modern
scholarly edition of Edmund Burke's letters[8] has brought to
light a considerable number of letters, alluding to Ireland as
well as to other subjects, which were not known to Burke's
nineteenth-century editors, and consequently not known to
Matthew Arnold either. However, Burke's major writings on
Ireland are in the present volume. These writings were intended
to influence public opinion in Burke's own day and they were
consequently either published or circulated in his life time and
were known to his nineteenth-century editors. Arnold wished
to present his nineteenth-century readers with Burke's principal
writings on this subject and was able to do so. So there is no
great problem about the selection.

As regards arrangement, Arnold set out to arrange chronologically Burke's relevant writings while separating the 'public'
from the 'private' letters. Actually he didn't manage to arrange
them all chronologically but there is only one deviation that
needs to be signalled here. The first letter to Sir Hercules
Langrishe (number V11 in this collection), dated 1792,
appears after a letter dated 1782 and before the letters dated
1780. The reader is advised to read this letter, not in its place
in this collection but immediately after the letter to John Merlott
(1780) and before the letter to William Smith (1795); that is
between numbers X and X1 of the present ordering.

This is not just fussing about chronological sequence, for its
own sake. It is important that this first letter to Sir Hercules
Langrishe should be read in its right order, because it happens
to occupy a pivotal position among Burke's writings on Ireland.

It is the first major letter on Ireland written after the beginning of the French Revolution. It should be read therefore as the beginning of a series which shows Burke as increasingly preoccupied — in relation to Ireland even more urgently than to the rest of the world — with the impact of the Revolution.

The reader is therefore recommended to read first all the pre-French Revolution items in the series, ending with number ten. A letter to John Merlott — but not including number seven. And then — having taken a pause for breath, as it were — to read the post-French Revolution items, beginning with the letter to Sir Hercules Langrishe (number X11).

I shall therefore consider first the pre-revolutionary section of the book and then the post-revolutionary. Burke's writings are in themselves extremely clear, but the modern reader is likely to need a little help, here and there, with the background. Matthew Arnold could assume, over a hundred years ago, that his readers would be familiar with the main features of Burke's biography (though not necessarily with his writings on Ireland). No such assumption of familiarity can be made today.

The principal items in the pre-revolutionary series, as far as Ireland is concerned are the 'Tracts on the Popery Laws' (number 1) and the 'letter to a Peer of Ireland on the Penal Laws against Irish Catholics' (number V1). These are to a great extent self-explanatory, as the object is to reach an English public with a clear account of the special and oppressive laws under which a majority of the subjects of the Crown in Ireland are being governed. Burke hoped — not altogether in vain — that if the educated public in England understood how Ireland was being governed, they would insist on reform. Compare in our own day the efforts of the Civil Rights movement, in Dixie in the 1950s and 1960s, to reach the northern American public

with its message about the peculiar institutions of the south.
Compare also the efforts of the Civil Rights movement in
Northern Ireland a little later to reach the British public with
a similar message about conditions for Catholics in Northern
Ireland under the Stormont System (1920–72).

The Penal Laws were in their greatest rigour in the first
half of the eighteenth century, and became progressively more
relaxed thereafter, partly through non-application of certain of
the more obviously obnoxious items in the code, and partly
through legislative reform. Throughout the eighteenth century,
however, only Protestants in Ireland enjoyed full legal rights
and the Irish Parliament throughout its existence – that is until
the passage of the Act of Union in 1800 – remained closed
to Catholics. Throughout Burke's boyhood, youth and early
manhood in Ireland, the penal laws were still in their heyday.
For Burke's complex personal relationship with the Ireland of
his youth, and the laws which governed it see section IV of
this introduction.

'The letter to a Peer of Ireland' figures in the modern edition
of the correspondence (Volume 1V pages 405 to 418) under
the heading 'to Viscount Kenmare'. Annotating this letter, the
editors of this volume make the following comment in relation
to the second paragraph on page 189 of this collection: 'Roman
Catholics had not been deprived of the franchise until 1728,
though after 1704 (2 Anne c. 6 – 'the ferocious act') they
could only vote if they took the vote of abjuration.' As this
shows, the Penal Laws continued to get *worse* for roughly the
first third of the century. 1728, the year in which Catholics,
as such, were stripped of the franchise, happened to be the
year before Burke was born. So Edmund Burke was born at
what may reasonably be regarded as the darkest hour of the
Penal Laws.

The second letter, that to Sir Charles Bingham has a certain irony about it, at least in the context of its nineteenth-century publication. In this letter, Burke opposes a proposal – which in the event came to nothing – to impose a special tax on landlords who, while owning land in Ireland, resided permanently in Britain. Burke was throughout his life an ardent defender of property rights, and in particular of landed property. As the question of land dominated everything else in 1881, when this collection was published, this letter tends to range Burke on the side of the landlords and against the people; whereas of course the general tendency of his much more numerous writings on the Penal Laws is to arouse sympathy for the Catholic people – tenant farmers – and to work against the Protestant landlords inheritors of iniquitous privilege. Another example of the difficulties inherent in 'setting people on thinking'.

The letter to Charles James Fox (number 111) is hardly of major importance; only the last three pages of it, from page 93 on, are about Ireland. These do however contain an important reflection which I shall quote later. This letter appears, and is annotated in the *Correspondence* (vol. 111 pages 380 to 388).

Items 1V and V should be considered together. The background is as follows: from 1774 to 1780 Burke was MP for Bristol. In the elections of 1780, Burke lost his seat. The two letters and the speech set out in 1V and V were part of the process of losing it.

Various sections of Burke's constituents had – as is usually the case – various grievances against him, but the most important grievances concerned Ireland. Influential people in Bristol objected to Burke's efforts in Parliament for the relaxation – and if possible removal – of the restrictions then in force on Irish trade with Britain and the colonies. Some of them also objected to his writings against the Penal Laws in Ireland. These objections, rather naturally tend to fuse, in a general idea that Burke seemed to be more interested in Ireland than in his own parliamentary constituency, Bristol.

In the letters and in the speech Burke takes remarkable high ground; I don't know that any elected representative since then, facing the possible loss of his seat, has addressed influential electors in that way (and small wonder, most practical politicians will say, since Burke lost his seat). The view that Burke here expounds, concerning the duties of an elected representative towards his electors has become a classic of political theory: one of those classics which evoke a theoretical admiration, out of proportion to their influence on conduct. In the present context, however, we need not concern ourselves too closely with the theoretical questions involved. What I think is most relevant here is the bearing which these transactions have, on our view of Burke's character in general, and specifically of the *seriousness* of his writings on Ireland.

Those who hate Burke – from Karl Marx to Sir Lewis Namier and beyond – generally depict Burke as a mere time-server, a man whose flowery language and fancy theories simply serve to distract attention from sordid self-interest in political practice. It is hard to reconcile that with what happened at Bristol. Nothing could be less time-serving than those letters and that speech. These constitute what a modern politician would call a 'suicide note'. They were not quite that; more a question of a self-inflicted and incapacitating wound. Burke was able to carry on with a parliamentary career for what a later age would call the 'rotten borough' of Malton, through the patronage of Lord Rockingham. Yet his political career can never be the same again. Up to 1780 he enjoys the status of the representative of a great commercial city. After 1780 he can he dismissed as the hanger-on of a great lord or – as Namier puts it – 'a racecourse acquaintance of the Marquis of Rockingham'. And Burke fully knew what he was risking. So far from being time-serving, these letters and that speech are even quixotic, both by the standards of his own time and by those of later times, including our own.

In respect of Burke's writings on Ireland, the British statements constitute what one might call 'the backing for the currency'. Bristol proves how serious Burke was about Ireland – on freedom of trade and Catholic rights – and how far he was prepared to place his views on Ireland ahead of his personal career. For there were no votes or power or money at all to be won, in the England of Burke's day, by going on about Ireland as Burke did. Very much the contrary. So if Burke had been the kind of person whom Marx, Namier and others represent, he would have shut up about Ireland, and got on with his promising career. But he did not shut up. It follows that his writings on Ireland deserve to be read with the attention and respect that should be commanded by great abilities used in the service of profound conviction.

Let us now consider Burke's *post*-French Revolution writing on Ireland: number V11 and numbers X to X1V inclusive, plus all the 'private letters' in the present collection.

The post-revolutionary material constitutes a much more compact body of writing than the pre-revolutionary material – which is of course spaced out over a much longer period of time – and I shall consider it as one body of writing, rather than under the separate heads.

Burke's response to the French Revolution was linked, from the beginning, to his position in relation to Ireland.[9]

Many, perhaps most, contemporary Englishmen had
welcomed the French Revolution in its early stages – roughly
from the summer of 1789 to the summer of 1791. The English
welcome for the French Revolution during this period was
founded on a general idea that the French were belatedly
following in the wake of the English and carrying out, simul-
taneously, their own rather crude equivalents of the English
Reformation and of England's Glorious Revolution. The French
Revolution was seen as stemming from a salutary process of
cumulative rejection of Popery. In this light, the Revolution –
which many Englishmen regarded as concluded in 1790 –
seemed on the whole a satisfactory conclusion of that process.

Even in the first few months after the fall of The Bastille
Edmund Burke showed himself much more sceptical about the
begignity of the Revolution than was the case with most of
his contemporaries. Then he became alarmed and incensed:
alarmed at the Revolution itself – a phenomenon whose epochal
nature he was, with Kant, among the first outside France to
comprehend – and incensed at the welcome which his English
contemporaries were complacently inclined to extend to that
phenomenon, through reflex anti-Popery. What put the match
to the fuse of Burke's prophetic indignation was a sermon
preached on 4 November 1789 by an eminent dissenting
minister the Rev. Richard Price. Dr Price saw the Revolution
as the outcome of 'A diffusion of knowledge which has under-
mined superstition and error.' Shortly after reading and
considering that sermon Burke started to work on the great
Tract which was published in November 1790 under the title
Reflections on the Revolution in France.

The 'Irish' writings we are now considering should be
considered as a follow-up on the earlier writings on Ireland,

but under conditions which had been radically changed, and to a great extent in Burke's favour, by the fact and development of the Revolution, and by the increasing impact of the *Reflections*. Burke's reputation increased enormously between the publication of the *Reflections* and his death seven years later. The accelerated course of the Revolution, especially from the summer of 1792 on bringing with it in rapid succession the deposition of the King, the September massacres, and the Terror — including the execution not only of the King and Queen but of moderate figures of the early phases of the Revolution — seemed to many Englishmen, from the King down, to constitute confirmation in full of Burke's case in the *Reflections*. The fact that Burke had been able to see the latency of all that so very early on, made him something of a prodigy in the eyes of ordinary Englishmen. But the greatest change of all, of course, is that from the beginning of 1793, England is at war with Revolutionary France. So expressions of sympathy with the French Revolution, which were socially acceptable in 1789 to 1790, and no worse than dubious in 1791 to 1792, had become treasonable in 1793. And at that time there was no subject of His Majesty whose credentials were more secure in relation to the revolution in France than Edmund Burke.

In his Irish writings, from 1792 to his death, Burke does his formidable best to make his enhanced authority,[10] in the changed circumstances, work to bring to an end the oppression of the Catholics of Ireland.

Put in a nutshell, the case that Burke makes in these writings is as follows:

The idea that the Pope is the great enemy is absurdly and dangerously out of date. The real enemies today are the Jacobins (whether in France or England or Ireland). The Jacobins are the Pope's enemies as well as yours. The Catholics everywhere are your natural allies, or potential allies. But the laws in force in Ireland continue to be so oppressive towards the Catholics that you are turning your potential allies into potential allies of the Jacobins.

In one form or another this line of argument is present on every page of what Burke writes about Ireland in this period. Take the following passage from the first letter to Sir Hercules Langrishe (pages 248 to 249) written while the King of France, after his attempted flight, was a prisoner of the Jacobins and on the verge of the deposition that would be followed by his execution:

As little shall I detain you with matters that can as little obtain admission into a mind like yours; such as the fear, or pretence of fear, that, in spite of your own power, and the trifling power of Great Britain, you may be conquered by the Pope; or that this commodious bugbear (who is of infinitely more use to those who pretend to fear, than to those who love him) will absolve His Majesty's subjects from their allegiance, and send over the Cardinal of York to rule you as his viceroy; or that, by the plenitude of his power, he will take that fierce tyrant, the King of the French, out of his jail, and arm that nation (which on all occasions treats His Holiness so very politely) with his bulls and pardons, to invade poor old Ireland, to reduce you to Popery and slavery, and to force the free-born, naked feet of your people into the wooden shoes of that arbitrary monarch. I do not believe that discourses of this kind are held, or that anything like them will be held, by any who walk about without a keeper. Yet I confess that, on occasions of this nature, I am the most afraid of the weakest reasoning, because they discover the strongest passions. These things will never be brought out in definite propositions. They would not prevent pity towards any persons; they would only cause it for those who were capable of talking in such a strain. But I know, and am sure, that such ideas as no man will distinctly produce to another, or hardly venture to bring in any plain shape to his own mind – he will utter in obscure, ill-explained doubts, jealousies, surmises, fears, and apprehensions; and that, in such a fog, they will appear to have a good deal of size, and will make an impression, when, if they were clearly brought forth and defined, they would meet with nothing but scorn and derison.

In its almost casual variety, and startling change of pace, the above is a highly characteristic specimen of Burke's style. It opens with a brisk barrage of heavy sarcasm; reminding us that Dr Johnson, who loved and admired Burke, had a poor opinion of his humour: 'Tis low, tis conceit.' But then it goes on in the passage opening with the words, 'Yet I confess', into a subtle and acute exploration of how prejudice works. And note here a fine example of the Burkean aphorism: 'I am the most afraid of the weakest reasonings, because they discover the strongest passions.'

While pressing the arguments for the rehabilitation of the Catholics, Burke is increasingly aware that time may be running out. He fears the movement of the United Irishmen, spreading Jacobin revolutionary ideas down from radicalized Protestants to a Catholic population with so little reason to love the status quo.

Considering the progress of the United Irish movement, Burke dictated from his sick bed, less than six months before his death, the 'Letter on the Affairs of Ireland' (number X1V in this collection). This letter headed 'To unknown' is dated 'February 1797' in the *Correspondence*, where it appears in Volume 1X pages 253 to 263. In the course of this letter, Burke says:

On the part of the Catholics (that is to say, of the body of the people of the kingdom of Ireland) it is a terrible alternative, either to submit to the yoke of declared and insulting enemies; or to seek a remedy in plunging themselves into the horrors and crimes of that Jacobinism, which unfortunately is not disagreeable to the principles and inclinations of, I am afraid, the majority of what we call the Protestants of Ireland. The Protestant part of that kingdom is represented by the British Government itself to be, by whole counties, in nothing less than open rebellion. I am sure that it is everywhere teeming with dangerous conspiracy.

I believe it will be found that though the principles of the Catholics, and the incessant endeavours of their clergy, have kept them from being generally infected with the systems of this time, yet, whenever their situation brings them nearer into contact with the Jacobin Protestants, they are more or less infected with their doctrines.

In a private letter written around the same time – December 1796 – Burke shows a degree of sympathy with rebellious Irish Catholics that would have been likely to surprise and disconcert British and international admirers of the great counter-revolutionary. The passage appears in the second letter to the Rev. Dr Hussey (the third of the 'private letters' in this collection). Hussey was a Catholic priest in Ireland and shared Burke's fears about the spread of United Irish ideas and the danger of rebellion. But it seems that Burke saw Hussey as inclined to go too far in recommending submissiveness. Burke wrote:

You state, what has long been but too obvious, that it seems the unfortunate policy of the hour to put to the far largest portion of the king's subjects in Ireland the desperate alternative between a thankless acquiescence under grievous oppression, or a refuge in Jacobinism, with all its horrors and all its crimes. You prefer the former dismal part of the choice. There is no doubt but that you would have reason, if the election of one of these evils was at all a security against the other. But they are things very alliable, and as closely connected as cause and effect. That Jacobinism which is speculative in its origin, and which arises from wantonness and fulness of bread, may possibly be kept under by firmness and prudence. The very levity of character which produces it may extinguish it. But Jacobinism, which arises from penury and irritation, from scorned loyalty and rejected allegiance, has much deeper roots. They take their nourishment from the bottom of human nature, and the unalterable constitution of things, and not from humour and caprice, or the opinions of the day about privileges and liberties. These roots will be shot into the depths of hell, and will at last raise up their proud tops to heaven itself. This radical evil may baffle the attempts of heads much wiser than those are, who, in the petulance and riot of their drunken power, are neither ashamed nor afraid to insult and provoke those whom it is their duty, and ought to be their glory, to cherish and protect.

So then, the little wise men of the west, with every hazard of this evil, are resolved to persevere in the manly and well-timed resolution of a war against Popery.

In the long term Burke's argument for the rehabilitation of Catholics and Catholicism exercised a significant influence over developments and policy, especially in the nineteenth century. But in the short run, Burke at the very end knew that he had failed and that Jacobin insurrection was on its way in Ireland.

Edmund Burke died on 9 July 1797. In the following year, the great Irish Rebellion broke out under the influence, and partly under the leadership of the United Irishmen. Although the rebellion had more mass support than any subsequent Irish insurrection and although the French sent a small expeditionary force the rebellion was ruthlessly crushed.[11]

IV

The careful reader is likely to be puzzled occasionally by the question of Burke's personal relation to his main subject matter: the condition of the Irish Catholic. Burke is something of a ventriloquist; we are not always sure what direction his voice is coming from.

For example Burke speaks of himself, more than once, as an Englishman (see pages 133 and 412). Burke was not in fact English, as the term was used either in his own time, or earlier, or later. He was born in Ireland of Irish parents and his anscestry, as far as is known, is entirely Irish and of native, settler stock. His English contemporaries do not take him to be English. John Wilkes said that Burke's oratory 'stank of whiskey and potatoes'; an ethnic eureka, if ever there was one. Later a more subtle critic, the great feminist Mary Wollstone-craft took exception to his usurpation of the pronoun 'we' meaning the English (it was also Mary Wollstonecraft who made a neat hit at the expense of Burke's grand manner: 'Gothick affability', she called it). Burke sat for English constituents in the mainly English parliament of Westminster and no doubt he was concerned to stress that in matters of state-craft he was speaking for the English generally and not for his 'little platoon', the Irish. But there is a certain awkward-ness, or uneasiness about his use of the word: Tracts which are characteristic of Burke, in one of his aspects.[12]

The question of where Burke's voice is coming from is most crucial in relation to his religion. Burke is writing about the Irish Catholics, a people to whom according to law, professed denomination and social convention, he did not belong. Edmund Burke was baptized into the Church of Ireland (in communion with the Church of England) and remained a professed member of that church to the end of his life, so far as is known.[13] According to the law, Edmund Burke was a member of that Irish Protestant Ascendancy which he so detested.

Hostile contemporaries were sceptical about Burke's Prot-estantism, and not without reason. His early years in public life in England are dogged by rumours that he was a crypto-

Catholic and throughout his life cartoonists continued to depict him in the garb of a Jesuit. And in fact his connections with the Irish Catholic people were about as close as it is possible to be without actually being an acknowledged Catholic.

Burke's mother, Mary Nangle, was and always remained a Catholic. The Nagles were a family of Catholic gentry in the Blackwater valley; one of them, Richard Nagle, had been Attorney-General to James II, and they all suffered, in varying degrees, from the ruin of the Jacobite cause. Burke's earliest schooling was at a Catholic and Gaelic speaking 'Hedge-school' near his Nagle relatives, and he always remained closely attached in his mother's side of the family.

About Edmund Burke's father, Richard Burke 'Almost nothing is certain' as the great Burke scholar, Thomas Copeland, has written. It seems probable, however that Richard Burke had been a Catholic who conformed to the Established Church in order to be allowed to practice the law: quite a common practice at the time, and one denounced by some Church of Ireland Bishops. Certainly a Richard Burke did confirm to the Established Church in 1722, seven years before Edmund Burke was born, and about the time Edmund Burke's father must have started his professional career. It is not certain that the Richard Burke who conformed was Edmund Burke's father. But there is a strong family tradition that it was. The eminent Irish genealogist, Basil O'Connell, referred to the view that Richard Burke, father of Edmund Burke, did conform as being 'the univocal tradition of the Statesman's Nagle collaterals, of whom the present writer is one'.[14] Personally, I have no hesitation in accepting the Nagle family tradition on this point. There was simply no reason to make it up; the transaction was nothing to boast about.

Against that probable background, consider the following

passage (p. 353 of this collection) from a letter of Edmund
Burke to his son Richard Burke, concerning the Oath of
Conformity required of Catholics, before they could enter the
professions.

Let three millions of people but abandon all that they and their
ancestors have been taught to believe sacred, and to forswear it
publicly in terms the most degrading, scurrilous, and indecent for
men of integrity and virtue, and to abuse the whole of their former
lives, and to slander the education they have received, – and nothing
more is required of them.

Later writers were to see Burke as a Liberal Protestant,
moved by a generous compassion for the Catholic under-class.
W. B. Yeats, in a fit of idealizing the Protestant Anglo-Irishry,
cited Burke among the heros of the Anglo Irish and stressed
the gratuitous and disinterested nature of his exertions on behalf
of Ireland: 'People of Burke and of Grattan . . . that gave
though free to refuse.'

It wasn't really like that. It was more like the case of a Jew
whose father had chosen assimilation, through conformity to
the Established Church, and who felt torn as a result. The
family position of Karl Marx was remarkably similar. Karl
Marx's father, the son of a Rabbi, conformed to the Lutheran
Church, so Karl was supposed to be a Lutheran.

Such situations do 'set people on thinking' but they don't
necessarily set them on thinking in the same ways or in the
same direction. Marx and Burke solved their problem in what
appear as diametrically opposing ways. But it was essentially
the same problem.

Burke, I believe, felt an abiding loyalty – and one which
cost him dear – to the people from whom he came, and from

whom he might seem to have defected. But it is a loyalty tinged with horror: a horror which can, though on rare occasions, take on a Swiftian intensity. There is a remarkable passage in the Guildhall speech – pages 149 to 150 in the present collection – in which Burke's horror of the Penal Laws and their consequences can hardly be distinguished from a horror of the people degraded by those laws:

In this situation men not only shrink from the frowns of a stern magistrate: but they are obliged to fly from their very species. The seeds of destruction are sown in civil intercourse, in social habitudes. The blood of wholesome kindred is infected. Their tables and beds are surrounded with snares. All the means given by Providence to make life safe and comfortable are perverted into instruments of terror and torment. This species of universal subserviency, that makes the very servant who waits behind your chair the arbiter of your life and fortune, had such a tendency to degrade and abase mankind, and to deprive them of that assured and liberal state of mind which alone can make us what we ought to be, that I vow to God I would sooner bring myself to put a man to immediate death for opinions I disliked, and so to get rid of the man and his opinions at once, than to fret him with a feverish being, tainted with the jail-distemper of a contagious servitude, to keep him above ground – an animated mass of putrefaction, corrupted himself, and corrupting all about him.

I don't know what the good burghers of Bristol, assembled in the Guildhall, can have made of all that. Certainly these words couldn't have contributed towards getting Burke re-elected as Member for Bristol, even if that had been on the cards on other grounds. But there is no passage in all Burke's writings on Ireland which so conveys the feeling of what it is like to live under such laws; and more especially the feeling of what it was like to *escape* living under them, by the skin of your teeth, or your father's teeth, and at no small psychic cost.

V

As we saw, the original architect of this collection, Matthew Arnold, hoped, by invoking Burke, to influence a great contemporary debate about Ireland. And Burke's writings operating on the mind of William Ewert Gladstone did indeed influence the contemporary debate in a direction which Arnold found so alarming that he re-invoked Burke, in order to cast out Burke (above section 11).

It may be tempting to try to relate Burke's writings on Ireland to our own late twentieth century debate about Ireland, such as it is. On the whole, this is a temptation that ought to be resisted. A hundred years ago it was natural for English gentlemen to appeal to Burke as an authority accepted both by Liberals and Conservatives. Today, no Prime Minister with a major practical decision to make would sit for hours as Gladstone did, reading Burke and taking notes. Tories do occasionally quote or misquote Burke, to lend a touch of class to an otherwise dreary speech, but that's about it. I doubt whether either Garret FitzGerald or Margaret Thatcher – the architects of the Anglo-Irish Agreement – have read much Burke and I don't know what effect he may have had on them if they have read him. Yet I feel that if they had read the essays contained in this collection, this would have fortified them in their feeling that they were doing the right thing. (I reach this conclusion with a certain mild dismay. I am an admirer of Edmund Burke, this side idolatry, and I have very deep reservations about the Anglo-Irish Agreement.)

In its essence, the Anglo-Irish Agreement constitutes a deal between Irish Catholics and the British at the expense of Irish Protestants in their 'Ulster' bastion.[15]

Yet Burke has also a word of advice which Irish Catholics might take to heart in the aftermath of the Anglo-Irish Agreement: 'Surely the State of Ireland ought for ever to teach parties moderation in their victories.'[18]

And those who would hope to move, under cover of that Agreement, gradually in the direction of a United Ireland would not find much warrant for that in Burke; assuming they wanted any. It was Burke's enemies, the United Irelanders, who thought and hoped in terms of an Irish nation, without distinction of religion, separate from Britain. Burke thought, and wrote of the Irish Catholics as a nation. That much at least is profoundly relevant today. The Irish Catholics are indeed a nation. The Ulster Protestants know they don't belong to that nation and don't want to be dominated by it (though of course they enjoyed dominating it, as long as they could). The Irish Catholics – while continuing to pay some lip-service to 'United Ireland' ideals – don't in their hearts regard the Ulster Protestants as belonging to the same nation with them either. What the Catholics want is their land back, which is what the Protestants want to stop the Catholics having. What we are witnessing is a kind of smouldering holy war over ancestral land, carried on under a cloud of confused and misleading slogans. There is nothing in any of that to surprise Edmund Burke. The holy war was already going on, and hundreds of years old, in his own day. After his day, and with some help from him, the balance shifted in favour of the Catholics. He would have had to welcome the shift in the balance, but surely not the continuation of the holy war *after* the shift in the balance.

However, it is not mainly for such relevance as it has to the Ireland of today that 'Burke on Ireland' is worth reading now. Burke is worth reading basically because he stretches the mind and imagination of his reader in unexpected and sometimes startling ways, as in some of the passages I have quoted and a great many others. Matthew Arnold's experience with Burke, in relation to practical politics, was almost comically disconcerting, like an exploding cigar. Yet at a deeper level and as a poet, Arnold is absolutely right: 'setting people on thinking' is indeed what it is all about. 'Burke on Ireland' will enrich the thinking of its careful reader in relation to whatever most deeply concerns that reader. It doesn't have to be Ireland, and in fact it is probably better if it is not Ireland, since Ireland in this connection involves the danger of a vain quest for literal prescriptions, and of consequent intellectual, moral and political entanglements.

So read Burke about Ireland, and then think about something else.

Conor Cruise O'Brien
1987

NOTES

1 If Burke's political wisdom was perhaps over-estimated up to the First World War, I believe it had been under-estimated since. I think the mere fact that he had had such a reputation for wisdom up to 1914 tended to discredit him thereafter. If the generation and the classes had brought the world into the disaster of the First World War had venerated Burke for his political wisdom, then the post-war generation decided, without reading him, that Burke must have been a fool or a fraud. They would have done better to read him.

2 The editor of the definitive edition of Arnold's prose works R. H. Super tells us: 'The idea of bringing out a selection of Burke's principal writings on Ireland was presumably Arnold's not his publishers. Proofs of the text began to reach him about April 20 1881. The Preface was not sent off until about May 10. The volume was published about June 4 at 65. As a publishing venture it was not a success.' *Prose Works of Matthew Arnold English Literature and Irish Politics*, p. 416.

3 Enthusiastic Scottish genius.

4 Pelican/Penguin books edition 1968–82.

5 The development of Arnold's attitudes towards Ireland is subtly and sensitively explored in an important essay, 'Matthew Arnold's Fight for Ireland', by Owen Dudley Edwards (in Robert Giddings (ed.), *Matthew Arnold Between Two Worlds*, Vision Press 1986). In the matter of Anglo/Irish relations, Arnold's influence was of little direct political significance. Culturally it was important as opening the way for a sympathetic hearing to the Irish Literary Revival of the 1890s.

6 'Matthew Arnold's Fight for Ireland', in R. Giddings (ed.), *Matthew Arnold Between Two Worlds*, p. 192.

7 'Burke on America' was an ally of 'Burke on Ireland', on the Gladstonian side. The idea was that just as Burke's wisdom in proposing timely concessions might have averted the American Revolution, so Gladstonian wisdom, inspired by Burke could avert revolution in Ireland. The Duke of Argyle had seen that identification looming up, and taken proportionate alarm.

8 *The correspondence of Edmund Burke*, under the general editorship of Thomas W. Copeland, Cambridge and Chicago, in ten volumes: 1958–.

9 See my Introduction *passim*, to the Pelican/Penguin edition of Burke's *Reflections on the Revolution in France*.

10 Burke, especially towards the end, denied having *any* political influence. True, his influence over political specifics was quite limited and – at least after 1795 – almost non-existent. But his influence over the general political 'climate of opinion', as we would now call it, in the mid 1790s, was probably greater than that of anybody else.

11 For a historical narrative of the Rising see Thomas Pakenham *The Year Of Liberty*: for a deeply researched fictional treatment see Thomas Flanagan *The Year of the French*. Both make absorbing reading.

12 Burke would have had a better title to the description 'British' had he chosen to use it, but I can't find that he ever did. The people most inclined to use the description 'British' about themselves were the Scots, and Burke clearly felt closer to the English than to the Scots. The Church of Ireland, in which Burke was baptized, was in communion with the Church of England, not the Church of

Scotland. The whole matter is tied in with the ambiguities of Burke's religious affiliation, discussed in the following section of the text.

13 I say 'so far as is known' because I should not be surprised if Mrs Burke, a devout Catholic, had a priest somewhere near at hand when Burke lay dying in Beaconsfield in early July 1797. There is, however, no evidence at all that this is so.

14 Journal of the Cork Historical and Archeological Society, LX, 192, July–December 1955.

15 The conclusion of the Agreement was accompanied by a great deal of verbiage about 'reconciling the two traditions' in Northern Ireland, but all that was cant, and of the hollowest description. The reality has been the Dublin–London deal. The general thrust of Burke's writings on Ireland is in the direction of some such deal. More to the point, at least emotionally, is the fact that the reminder of what Protestant Ascendancy was like, in the pages of Burke is such as to isolate the impoverished and frustrated heirs of that Ascendancy, in the Northern Ireland of today. This is particularly so when the heirs in question celebrate the memory of that Ascendancy, with reverberating nostalgia, in the months of July and August every year.

16 Letter to Charles James Fox, page 95 in this collection.

PREFACE.

Who now reads Bolingbroke? Burke once asked; and if the same question were at this day asked in respect to Burke himself, what would be the answer? Certainly not that he is read anything like as much as he deserves to be read. We English make far too little use of our prose classics,—far less than the French make of theirs. The place which a writer like Pascal, for instance, fills in French education, and in the minds of cultivated Frenchmen in general, how different is it from the place which Burke fills in our reading and thoughts, and how much larger! Shakespeare and Milton we are all supposed to know something of; but of none of our prose classics, I think, if we leave stories out of the account, such as are the *Pilgrim's Progress* and the *Vicar of Wakefield*, are we expected to have a like knowledge. Perhaps an exception is to be made for Bacon's *Essays*, but even of this I do not feel sure. Our grandfathers were bound to know their Addison, but for us the obligation has ceased; nor is that loss, indeed, a very serious matter. But to lose Swift and Burke out of our mind's circle of acquaintance is a loss

indeed, and a loss for which no conversance with contemporary prose literature can make up, any more than
conversance with contemporary poetry could make up
to us for unacquaintance with Shakespeare and Milton.
In both cases the unacquaintance shuts us out from
great sources of English life, thought, and language, and
from the capital records of its history and development, and leaves us in consequence very imperfect and
fragmentary Englishmen. It can hardly be said that
this inattention to our prose classics is due to their being
contained in collections made up of many volumes,—
collections dear and inaccessible. Their remaining
buried in such collections,—a fate so unlike that which
has been Rousseau's in France, or Lessing's in Germany,
—is rather the result of our inattention than its cause.
While they are so buried, however, they are in truth
almost inaccessible to the general public, and all occasions for rescuing and exhibiting representative speci-
mens of them should be welcomed and used.

Such an occasion offers itself, for Burke, in the
interest about Ireland which the present state of that
country compels even the most unwilling Englishman
to feel. Our neglected classic is by birth an Irishman;
he knows Ireland and its history thoroughly. "I have
studied it," he most truly says, "with more care than is
common." He is the greatest of our political thinkers
and writers. But his political thinking and writing has
more value on some subjects than on others; the value
is at its highest when the subject is Ireland. The writ-

ings collected in this volume cover a period of more
than thirty years of Irish history, and show at work all
the causes which have brought Ireland to its present
state. The tyranny of the grantees of confiscation ; of
the English garrison ; Protestant ascendency ; the reliance of the English Government upon this ascendency
and its instruments as their means of government ; the
yielding to menaces of danger and insurrection what was
never yielded to considerations of equity and reason ;
the recurrence to the old perversity of mismanagement
as soon as ever the danger was passed,—all these are
shown in this volume; the evils, and Burke's constant
sense of their gravity, his constant struggle to cure
them. The volume begins with the *Tracts on the Popery
Laws,* written probably between 1760 and 1765, when
that penal code, of which the monstrosity is not half
known to Englishmen, and may be studied by them
with profit in the *Tracts,* was still in force, and when
Irish trade was restricted, almost annulled, from jealousy
lest it should interfere with the trade of England. Then
comes the American war. In the pressure of difficulty
and danger, as that war proceeded, Lord North's Government proposed, in 1778, to conciliate Ireland by partly
withdrawing the restrictions on her trade. The commercial middle class,—the class with which a certain
school of politicians supposes virtue, abhorring nobles
and squires, to have taken refuge,—the men of Liverpool,
Manchester, Glasgow, and Bristol, were instantly in
angry movement, and forced the Minister to abandon his

propositions. The danger deepened; Spain joined herself
with France and America; the Irish volunteers appeared
in arms. Then, in 1779, the restrictions on Irish trade, of
which the partial withdrawal had been refused the year
before, were withdrawn altogether. But the irritation
of his constituents at his supporting this withdrawal,
and at his supporting a measure of relief to Catholics,
cost Burke his seat at Bristol. Meanwhile, the Irish
Parliament proceeded in establishing its independence
of that of Great Britain. Irish affairs were controlled
by Irish legislators ; the penal laws were relaxed, the
Catholics admitted to the franchise, though not to Parliament. The English Government had to govern Ireland through the Irish Legislature. But it persisted on
leaning upon that party in the Irish Legislature,—a Protestant Legislature, no doubt, but containing such patri-
otic and liberal Protestants as Grattan,—it persisted on
leaning upon that party which represented Protestant
ascendency and the rule of the grantees of confiscation in
its worst form. In 1789 came the French Revolution.
To remove the disabilities under which the Catholics of
Ireland still lay was a measure which commended itself
to all the best politicians at that time. The English
Government sent, in 1795, Burke's friend, Lord Fitzwilliam, as Viceroy to Ireland. Lord Fitzwilliam was
the declared friend of Catholic emancipation. It seemed
on the point of being granted, when the Irish Protestant
junto, as Burke calls it, prevailed with Mr. Pitt, and
Lord Fitzwilliam was recalled. In 1797 Burke died,

full of mournful apprehensions for the future ; in 1798 came the Irish Rebellion. But with the Rebellion we pass beyond the life of Burke, and beyond the period of Irish history covered by this volume.

The rapid summary just given of that history, from 1760 to 1797, will afford a sufficient clue to the writings and speeches which follow. Burke, let me observe in passing, greatly needs to be re-edited; indeed, he has never yet been properly edited at all. But all that I have attempted to do in the present volume is to arrange chronologically the writings and speeches on Irish affairs, which, in Burke's collected works, are now scattered promiscuously ; and to subjoin the most important of his private letters on the same subject, taken from the correspondence published in 1844 by the late Lord Fitzwilliam, the son of Burke's friend, the Irish Viceroy.[1] In my opinion, the importance of Burke's thoughts on the policy pursued in Ireland is as great now as when he uttered them, and when they were received, as he himself tells us, with *contempt*. "You do not suppose," said Mr. Bright the other day in the City,—"you do not suppose that the fourteen members of the Government spend days and weeks in the consideration of a measure such as the Irish Land Bill without ascertaining in connexion with it everything everybody else can know." Alas ! how many English Governments have been confident

---

[1] The copyright of these Letters belongs to Messrs. Rivington, and I have to thank them for their kindness in permitting me to print such as I needed for my purpose.

that they had ascertained in connexion with their Irish policy "everything everybody else could know!" Burke writes to Mrs. Crewe that a work of his has, he is told, "put people in a mood a little unusual to them—*it has set them on thinking.*" "One might have imagined," he adds, "that the train of events, as they passed before their eyes, might have done that!" Nevertheless, it does not; and so, he concludes, "Let them think now who never thought before!" In general, our Governments, however well informed, feel bound, it would seem, to adapt their policy to our normal mental condition, which is, as Burke says, a non-thinking one. Burke's paramount and undying merit as a politician is, that instead of accepting as fatal and necessary this non-thinking condition of ours, he battles with it, mends and changes it; he will not rest until he has "put people in a mood a little unusual with them," until he has "set them on thinking."

LETTERS, SPEECHES, AND TRACTS

ON

IRISH AFFAIRS.

I.

TRACTS relative to the LAWS AGAINST POPERY IN
IRELAND.[1]

CHAPTER I.

Fragments of a Tract on the Popery Laws.

THE PLAN.

I PROPOSE first to make an introduction, in order to
show the propriety of a closer inspection into the
affairs of Ireland; and this takes up the first chapter;
which is to be spent in this introductory matter, and
in stating the Popery Laws in general as one leading
cause of the imbecility of the country.

---

[1] The condition of the Roman Catholics in Ireland appears to have
engaged the attention of Mr. Burke at a very early period of his political life. It was probably soon after the year 1765, that he formed

B

Chap. II. states particularly the laws themselves in a plain and popular manner.

Chap. III. begins the remarks upon them, under the heads of, 1*st*, The object, which is a numerous people ; 2*dly*, Their means, a restraint on property ; 3*dly*, Their instruments of execution, corrupted morals ; which affect the national prosperity.

Chap. IV. The impolicy of those laws as they affect the national security.

Chap. V. Reasons by which the laws are supported, and answers to them.

the plan of a work upon that subject, the fragments of which are now given to the public. No title is prefixed to it in the original manuscript ; and the *Plan*, which it has been thought proper to insert here, was evidently designed merely for the convenience of the author. Of the first chapter some unconnected fragments only—too imperfect for publication—have been found. Of the second there is a considerable portion, perhaps nearly the whole ; but the copy from which it is printed is evidently a first rough draft. The third chapter, as far as it goes, is taken from a fair corrected copy ; but the end of the second part of the first head is left unfinished ; and the discussion of the second and third heads was either never entered upon, or the manuscript containing it has unfortunately been lost. What follows the third chapter appears to have been designed for the beginning of the fourth, and is evidently the first rough draft ; and to this we have added a fragment which appears to have been a part either of this or the first chapter.

CHAPTER II.

In order to lay this matter with full satisfaction before the reader, I shall collect into one point of view, and state as shortly and as clearly as I am able, the purport of these laws, according to the objects which they affect, without making at present any further observation upon them, but just what shall be necessary to render the drift and intention of the Legislature, and the tendency and operation of the laws, the more distinct and evident.

I shall begin with those which relate to the possession and inheritance of landed property in Popish hands. The first operation of those Acts upon this object was wholly to change the course of descent by the common law; to take away the right of primogeniture; and, in lieu thereof, to substitute and establish a new species of Statute Gavelkind. By this law, on the death of a Papist possessed of an estate in fee simple, or in fee tail, the land is to be divided by equal portions between all the male children; and those portions are likewise to be parcelled out, share and share alike, amongst the descendants of each son, and so to proceed in a similar distribution *ad infinitum*. From this regulation it was proposed that some important consequences should follow. First—By taking away the right of primogeniture, perhaps in the very first generation, certainly in the second, the families of

Papists, however respectable, and their fortunes, however considerable, would be wholly dissipated, and
reduced to obscurity and indigence, without any possibility that they should repair them by their industry
or abilities—being, as we shall see anon, disabled from
every species of permanent acquisition. Secondly—By
this law the right of testamentation was taken away,
which the inferior tenures had always enjoyed; and
all tenures from the 27th Hen. VIII. Thirdly—The
right of settlement was taken away, that no such persons should, from the moment the Act passed, be
enabled to advance themselves in fortune or connection by marriage—being disabled from making any
disposition in consideration of such marriage but what
the law had previously regulated; the reputable establishment of the eldest son, as representative of the
family, or to settle a jointure,—being commonly the
great object in such settlements,—which was the very
power which the law had absolutely taken away.

The operation of this law, however certain, might
be too slow. The present possessors might happen to
be long lived. The Legislature knew the natural
impatience of expectants, and upon this principle they
gave encouragement to children to anticipate the inheritance. For it is provided that the eldest son of
any Papist shall, immediately on his conformity, change
entirely the nature and properties of his father's legal
estate; if he before held in fee simple, or, in other
words, had the entire and absolute dominion over the

land, he is reduced to an estate for his life only, with all the consequences of the natural debility of that estate ; by which he becomes disqualified to sell, mortgage, charge (except for his life), or in any wise to do any act by which he may raise money for relief in his most urgent necessities. The eldest son, so conforming, immediately acquires—and in the life-time of his father—the permanent part,—what our law calls the reversion and inheritance of the estate ; and he discharges it by retrospect, and annuls every sort of voluntary settlement made by the father ever so long before his conversion. This he may sell or dispose of immediately, and alienate it from the family for ever.

Having thus reduced his father's estate, he may also bring his father into the Court of Chancery, where he may compel him to swear to the value of his estate ; and to allow him out of that possession (which had been before reduced to an estate for life), such an immediate annual allowance as the Lord Chancellor or Lord Keeper shall judge suitable to his age and quality.

This indulgence is not confined to the eldest son. The other children likewise, by conformity, may acquire the same privileges, and in the same manner force from their father an immediate and independent maintenance. It is very well worth remarking, that the statutes have avoided to fix any determinate age for these emancipating conversions ; so that the children, at any age—however incapable of choice in other

respects, however immature, or even infantile—are
yet considered sufficiently capable to disinherit their
parents, and totally to subtract themselves from their
direction and control, either at their own option, or by
the instigation of others.   By this law the tenure and
value of a Roman Catholic in his real property is not
only rendered extremely limited and altogether precarious, but the paternal power is in all such families
so enervated, that it may well be considered as entirely
taken away; even the principle upon which it is
founded seems to be directly reversed.   However, the
Legislature feared that enough was not yet done upon
this head; the Roman Catholic parent, by selling his
real estate, might in some sort preserve the dominion
over his substance and his family, and thereby evade
the operation of these laws, which intended to take
away both.   Besides, frequent revolutions and many
conversions had so broken the landed property of
Papists in that kingdom, that it was apprehended that
this law could have in a short time but a few objects
upon which it would be capable of operating.

To obviate these inconveniences another law was
made, by which the dominion of children over their
parents was extended universally throughout the whole
Popish part of the nation, and every child of every
Popish parent was encouraged to come into what is
called a Court of Equity to prefer a Bill against his
father, and compel him to confess, upon oath, the
quantity and value of his substance, personal as well

as real, of what nature soever, or howsoever it might
be employed ; upon which discovery the Court is empowered to seize upon and allocate, for the immediate
maintenance of such child or children, any sum not
exceeding a third of the whole fortune—and as to their
future establishment on the death of the father no
limits are assigned. The Chancery may, if it thinks fit,
take the whole property, personal as well as real, money,
stock in trade, etc., out of the power of the possessor,
and secure it in any manner they judge expedient for
that purpose ; for the Act has not assigned any sort of
limit with regard to the quantity which is to be
charged, or given any direction concerning the means
of charging and securing it—a law which supersedes
all observation.

But the law is still more extensive in its provision.
Because there was a possibility that the parent, though
sworn, might by false representations evade the discovery of the ultimate value of his estate, a new Bill
may be at any time brought by one, any, or all, of the
children for a further discovery ; his effects are to
undergo a fresh scrutiny, and a new distribution is to
be made in consequence of it.   So that the parent has
no security against perpetual inquietude and the re-
iteration of Chancery suits, but by (what is somewhat
difficult for human nature to comply with) fully, and
without reserve, abandoning his whole property to the
discretion of the Court to be disposed of in favour of
such children.

But is this enough, and has the parent purchased
his repose by such a surrender? Very far from it.
The law expressly, and very carefully, provides that
he shall not; before he can be secure from the persecution of his children, it requires another and a much
more extraordinary condition; the children are authorised, if they can find that their parent has by his industry, or otherwise, increased the value of his property
since their first Bill, to bring another, compelling a new
account of the value of his estate, in order to a new
distribution proportioned to the value of the estate at
the time of the new Bill preferred. They may bring
such Bills, *toties quoties*, upon every improvement of
his fortune, without any sort of limitation of time or
regard to the frequency of such Bills, or to the quantity
of the increase of the estate which shall justify the
bringing them. This Act expressly provides that he
shall have no respite from the persecution of his children, but by totally abandoning all thoughts of improvement and acquisition.

This is going a great way surely, but the laws in
question have gone much farther. Not satisfied with
calling upon children to revolt against their parents
and to possess themselves of their substance, there are
cases where the withdrawing of the child from his
father's obedience is not left to the option of the child
himself; for if the wife of a Roman Catholic should
choose to change her religion, from that moment she
deprives her husband of all management and direction

of his children, and even of all the tender satisfaction which a parent can feel in their society, and which is the only indemnification he can have for all his cares and sorrows; and they are to be torn for ever, at the earliest age, from his house and family; for the Lord Chancellor is not only authorised, but he is strongly required, to take away all his children from such Popish parent, to appoint where, in what manner, and by whom, they are to be educated; and the father is compelled to pay not for the ransom but for the deprivation of his children, and to furnish such a sum as the Chancellor thinks proper to appoint for their education to the age of eighteen years. The case is the same if the husband should be the conformist; though how the law is to operate in this case I do not see, for the Act expressly says that the child shall be taken from such Popish parent. And whilst such husband and wife cohabit it will be impossible to put it into execution without taking the child from one as well as from the other, and then the effect of the law will be, that if either husband or wife becomes Protestant, both are to be deprived of their children.

The paternal power thus being wholly abrogated, it is evident that by the last regulation the power of a husband over his wife is also considerably impaired, because, if it be in her power, whenever she pleases, to subtract the children from his protection and obedience, she herself by that hold inevitably acquires a power and superiority over her husband.

But she is not left dependent upon this oblique influence, for if in any marriage settlement the husband has reserved to him a power of making a jointure, and he dies without settling any, her conformity executes his powers, and executes them in as large extent as the Chancellor thinks fit. The husband is deprived of that coercive power over his wife which he had in his hands by the use he might make of the discretionary power reserved in the settlement.

But if no such power had been reserved, and no such settlement existed, yet if the husband dies leaving his conforming wife without a fixed provision by some settlement on his real estate, his wife may apply to Chancery, where she shall be allotted a portion from his leases and other personal estate not exceeding one-third of his whole clear substance. The laws in this instance, as well as in the former, have presumed that the husband has omitted to make all the provision which he might have done, for no other reason than that of her religion. If, therefore, she chooses to balance any domestic misdemeanours to her husband by the public merit of conformity to the Protestant religion, the law will suffer no plea of such misdemeanours to be urged on the husband's part, nor proof of that kind to be entered into. She acquires a provision totally independent of his favour, and deprives him of that source of domestic authority which the common law had left to him—that of rewarding or punishing, by a voluntary distribution of his effects,

what in his opinion was the good or ill behaviour of
his wife.

Thus the laws stand with regard to the property
already acquired, to its mode of descent, and to family
powers. Now as to the new acquisition of real property, and both to the acquisition and security of personal, the law stands thus :—

All persons of that persuasion are disabled from
taking or purchasing directly or by a trust, any lands,
any mortgage upon land, any rents or profits from
land, any lease, interest, or term of any land, any
annuity for life or lives, or years, or any estate whatsoever, chargeable upon, or which may in any manner
affect, any lands.

One exception, and one only, is admitted by the
statutes to the universality of this exclusion, viz. a
lease for a term not exceeding thirty-one years. But
even this privilege is charged with a prior qualification. This remnant of a right is doubly curtailed; 1st,
that on such a short lease, a rent not less than two-
thirds of the full improved yearly value, at the time
of the making it, shall be reserved during the whole
continuance of the term ; and 2dly, it does not extend
to the whole kingdom. This lease must also be in
possession, and not in reversion. If any lease is made,
exceeding either in duration or value, and in the smallest degree, the above limits, the whole interest is forfeited, and vested *ipso facto* in the first Protestant discoverer or informer. This discoverer, thus invested with

the property, is enabled to sue for it as his own right.
The Courts of Law are not alone open to him ; he may
(and this is the usual method) enter into either of the
Courts of Equity, and call upon the parties, and those
whom he suspects to be their trustees, upon oath, and
under the penalities of perjury, to discover against
themselves the exact nature and value of their estates
in every particular, in order to induce their forfeiture
on the discovery.   In such suits the informer is not
liable to those delays which the ordinary procedure of
those Courts throws into the way of the justest claimant ; nor has the Papist the indulgence which he allows
to the most fraudulent defendant—that of plea and
demurrer.   But the defendant is obliged to answer the
whole directly upon oath.   The rule of *favores ampli-
andi*, etc., is reversed by this Act, lest any favour should
be shown, or the force and operation of the law in any
part of its progress be enervated.   All issues to be
tried on this Act are to be tried by none but known
Protestants.

It is here unnecessary to state as a part of this
law what has been for some time generally understood
as a certain consequence of it.   The Act had expressly
provided that a Papist could possess no sort of estate
which might affect land (except as before excepted).
On this a difficulty did not unnaturally arise.   It is
generally known, a judgment being obtained or acknowledged for any debt since the Statute of Westm.
2, 13 Ed. I. c. 18, one half of the debtor's land is to

be delivered unto the creditor until the obligation is satisfied, under a writ called *Elegit*, and this writ has been ever since the ordinary assurance of the land, and the great foundation of general credit in the nation. Although the species of holding under this writ is not specified in the Statute, the received opinion, though not juridically delivered, has been, that if they attempt to avail themselves of that security, because it may create an estate, however precarious, in land, their whole debt or charge is forfeited, and becomes the property of the Protestant informer. Thus you observe, first, that by the express words of the law all possibility of acquiring any species of valuable property, in any sort connected with land, is taken away; and secondly, by the construction, all security for money is also cut off. No security is left, except what is merely personal, and which, therefore, most people, who lend money, would, I believe, consider as none at all.

Under this head of the acquisition of property, the law meets them in every road of industry, and in its direct and consequential provisions throws almost all sorts of obstacles in their way. For they are not only excluded from all offices in Church and State, which, though a just and necessary provision, is yet no small restraint in the acquisition; but they are interdicted from the Army and the Law in all its branches. This point is carried to so scrupulous a severity, that chamber practice, and even private conveyancing, the most voluntary agency, are prohibited to them under

the severest penalties, and the most rigid modes of
inquisition. They have gone beyond even this; for
every barrister, six clerk, attorney, or solicitor, is
obliged to take a solemn oath not to employ persons of
that persuasion; no, not as hackney clerks, at the
miserable salary of seven shillings a week. No trades-
man of that persuasion is capable, by any service or
settlement, to obtain his freedom in any town corporate;
so that they trade and work in their own native towns
as aliens, paying, as such, quarterage, and other charges
and impositions. They are expressly forbidden, in
whatever employment, to take more than two appren-
tices, except in the linen manufacture only.

In every state, next to the care of the life and
properties of the subject, the education of their youth
has been a subject of attention. In the Irish Laws
this point has not been neglected. Those who are
acquainted with the constitution of our Universities,
need not be informed that none but those who conform
to the Established Church can be at all admitted to
study there; and that none can obtain degrees in them
who do not previously take all the tests, oaths, and
declarations. Lest they should be enabled to supply
this defect by private academies and schools of their
own, the law has armed itself with all its terrors
against such a practice. Popish schoolmasters of every
species are proscribed by those Acts, and it is made
felony to teach even in a private family; so that
Papists are entirely excluded from an education in any

of our authorised establishments for learning at home.
In order to shut up every avenue to instruction, the
Act of King William in Ireland has added to this restraint by precluding them from all foreign education.
This Act is worthy of attention, on account of the
singularity of some of its provisions.   Being sent for
education to any Popish school or college abroad, upon
conviction, incurs (if the party sent has any estate of
inheritance) a kind of unalterable and perpetual outlawry.   The tender and incapable age of such a person,
his natural subjection to the will of others, his necessary
unavoidable ignorance of the Laws, stands for nothing
in his favour.   He is disabled to sue in Law or Equity;
to be guardian, executor, or administrator; he is
rendered incapable of any legacy or deed of gift; he
forfeits all his goods and chattels for ever, and he
forfeits for his life all his lands, hereditaments, offices,
and estate of freehold, and all trusts, powers, or interests
therein.

All persons concerned in sending them or maintaining them abroad, by the least assistance of money
or otherwise, are involved in the same disabilities, and
subjected to the same penalties.

The mode of conviction is as extraordinary as the
penal sanctions of this Act.   A Justice of Peace, upon
information that any child is sent away, may require
to be brought before him all persons charged or even
suspected of sending or assisting, and examine them
and other persons on oath concerning the fact.   If on

this examination he finds it *probable,* that the party
was sent contrary to this Act, he is then to bind over
the parties and witnesses in any sum he thinks fit—but
not less than £200—to appear and take their trial at
the next Quarter Sessions. Here the Justices are to
re-examine evidence, until they arrive, as before, to
what shall appear to them a probability. For the
rest, they resort to the accused ; if they can prove that
any person, or any money, or any bill of exchange, has
been sent abroad by the party accused, they throw the
proof upon him to show for what innocent purposes it
was sent ; and on failure of such proof he is subjected
to all the above-mentioned penalties. Half the forfeiture is given to the Crown ; the other half goes to
the informer.

It ought here to be remarked, that this mode of
conviction not only concludes the party has failed in
his expurgatory proof, but it is sufficient also to subject
to the penalties and incapacities of the law, the infant
upon whose account the person has been so convicted.
It must be confessed that the law has not left him
without some species of remedy in this case, apparently
of much hardship, where one man is convicted upon
evidence given against another, if he has the good fortune to live ; for, within a twelvemonth after his return,
or his age of twenty-one, he has a right to call for a new
trial, in which he also is to undertake the negative
proof, and to show by sufficient evidence, that he has
not been sent abroad against the intention of the Act.

If he succeeds in this difficult exculpation, and demonstrates his innocence to the satisfaction of the Court, he forfeits all his goods and chattels, and all the profits of his lands incurred and received before such acquittal ; but he is freed from all other forfeitures, and from all subsequent incapacities. There is also another method allowed by the law in favour of persons under such unfortunate circumstances, as in the former case for their innocence, in this upon account of their expiation ;—if within six months after their return, with the punctilious observation of many ceremonies, they conform to the Established Church, and take all the oaths and subscriptions,—the Legislature, in consideration of the incapable age in which they were sent abroad, of the merit of their early conformity, and to encourage conversions, only confiscates, as in the former case, the whole personal estate, and the profits of the real—in all other respects restoring and rehabilitating the party.

So far as to property and education. There remain some other heads upon which the Acts have changed the course of the common law ; and first, with regard to the right of self-defence, which consists in the use of arms. This, though one of the rights by the law of nature, yet is so capable of abuses, that it may not be unwise to make some regulations concerning them ; and many wise nations have thought proper to set several restrictions on this right, especially temporary ones, with regard to suspected persons, and on occasion of some imminent danger to the public from foreign invasion or domestic commotions.

But provisions, in time of trouble proper, and perhaps necessary, may become in time of profound peace a scheme of tyranny. The method which the Statute Law of Ireland has taken upon this delicate article, is, to get rid of all difficulties at once by an universal prohibition to all persons, at all times, and under all circumstances, who are not Protestants, of using or keeping any kind of weapons whatsoever. In order to enforce this regulation, the whole spirit of the common law is changed; very severe penalties are enjoined; the largest powers are vested in the lowest magistrates. Any two Justices of Peace, or magistrates of a town, with or without information, at their pleasure, by themselves, or their warrant, are empowered to enter and search the house of any Papist, or even of any other person, whom they suspect to keep such arms in trust for them. The only limitation to the extent of this power is, that the search is to be made between the rising and setting of the sun; but even this qualification extends no farther than to the execution of the Act in the open country; for in all cities and their suburbs, in towns corporate and market towns, they may, at their discretion, and without information, break open houses, and institute such search at any hour of the day or night. This I say they may do at their discretion, and it seems a pretty ample power in the hands of such magistrates. How-

ever, the matter does by no means totally rest on their
discretion. Besides the discretionary and occasional
search, the statute has prescribed one that is general
and periodical. It is to be made annually, by the
Warrant of the Justices at their Midsummer Quarter
Sessions, by the high and petty constables, or any
others whom they may authorise, and by all corporate
magistrates, in all houses of Papists, and every other,
where they suspect arms for the use of such persons to
be concealed, with the same powers, in all respects,
which attend the occasional search. The whole of
this regulation, concerning both the general and particular search, seems to have been made by a Legislature which was not at all extravagantly jealous of
personal liberty. Not trusting, however, to the activity
of the magistrate acting officially, the law has invited
all voluntary informers by considerable rewards, and
even pressed involuntary informers into this service by
the dread of heavy penalties. With regard to the latter
method, two Justices of Peace, or the magistrate of any
corporation, are empowered to summon before them
any persons whatsoever, to tender them an oath, by
which they oblige them to discover all persons who
have any arms concealed contrary to law. Their refusal, or declining to appear, or appearing, their refusal
to inform, subjects them to the severest penalties. If
peers or peeresses are summoned (for they may be
summoned by the bailiff of a corporation of six
cottages) to perform this honourable service, and

refuse to inform, the first offence is £300 penalty ; the second is *Premunire*—that is to say, imprisonment for life, and forfeiture of all their goods. Persons of an inferior order are, for their first offence, fined £30 ; for the second, they too are subjected to *Premunire*. So far as to involuntary; now as to voluntary informers. The law entitles them to half the penalty incurred by carrying or keeping arms ; for, on conviction of this offence, the penalty upon persons of whatever substance is the sum of £50 and a year's imprisonment, which cannot be remitted even by the Crown.

The only exception to this law is a license from the Lord Lieutenant and Council to carry arms, which, by its nature, is extremely limited, and I do not suppose that there are six persons now in the kingdom who have been fortunate enough to obtain it.

There remains, after this system concerning property and defence, to say something concerning the exercise of religion, which is carried on in all persuasions, but especially in the Romish, by persons appointed for that purpose. The law of King William and Queen Anne ordered all Popish parsons exercising ecclesiastical jurisdiction, all orders of monks and friars, and all priests not then actually in parishes, and to be registered, to be banished the kingdom, and if they should return from exile, to be hanged, drawn, and quartered. Twenty pounds reward is given for apprehending them. Penalty on harbouring and concealing.

As all the priests then in being and registered are

long since dead, and as these laws are made perpetual, every Popish priest is liable to the law.

The reader has now before him a tolerably complete view of the Popery Laws relative to property by descent or acquisition, to education, to defence, and to the free exercise of religion, which may be necessary to enable him to form some judgment of the spirit of the whole system, and of the subsequent reflections that are to be made upon it.

CHAPTER III.

PART I.

The system which we have just reviewed, and the manner in which religious influence on the public is made to operate upon the laws concerning property in Ireland, is in its nature very singular, and differs, I apprehend, essentially, and perhaps to its disadvantage, from any scheme of religious persecution now existing in any other country in Europe, or which has prevailed in any time or nation with which history has made us acquainted. I believe it will not be difficult to show that it is unjust, impolitic, and inefficacious; that it has the most unhappy influence on the prosperity, the morals, and the safety of that country; that this influence is not accidental, but has flowed as the necessary and direct consequence of the laws themselves, first on account of the object which they affect, and next by the quality of the greatest part of the instruments

they employ. Upon all these points, first upon the
general, and then on the particular, this question will
be considered with as much order as can be followed
in a matter of itself as involved and intricate as it is
important.

The first and most capital consideration with regard
to this, as to every object, is the extent of it; and here
it is necessary to premise,—this system of penalty and
incapacity has for its object no small sect or obscure
party, but a very numerous body of men—a body which
comprehends at least two-thirds of that whole nation; it
amounts to 2,800,000 souls—a number sufficient for the
materials constituent of a great people. Now it is
well worthy of a serious and dispassionate examination,
whether such a system, respecting such an object, be in
reality agreeable to any sound principles of legislation,
or any authorised definition of law; for if our reasons
or practices differ from the general informed sense of
mankind, it is very moderate to say that they are at
least suspicious.

This consideration of the magnitude of the object
ought to attend us through the whole inquiry; if it
does not always affect the reason, it is always decisive
on the importance of the question. It not only makes
in itself a more leading point, but complicates itself
with every other part of the matter, giving every error,
minute in itself, a character and significance from its
application. It is therefore not to be wondered at,
if we perpetually recur to it in the course of this Essay.

In the making of a new law it is undoubtedly the duty of the legislator to see that no injustice be done even to an individual; for there is then nothing to be unsettled, and the matter is under his hands to mould it as he pleases; and if he finds it untractable in the working, he may abandon it without incurring any new inconvenience. But in the question concerning the repeal of an old one, the work is of more difficulty, because laws, like houses, lean on one another, and the operation is delicate and should be necessary; the objection in such a case ought not to arise from the natural infirmity of human institutions, but from substantial faults which contradict the nature and end of law itself—faults not arising from the imperfection, but from the misapplication and abuse of our reason. As no legislators can regard the *minima* of equity, a law may in some instances be a just subject of censure, without being at all an object of repeal. But if its transgressions against common right and the ends of just government should be considerable in their nature and spreading in their effects—as this objection goes to the root and principle of the law—it renders it void in its obligatory quality on the mind, and therefore determines it as the proper object of abrogation and repeal so far as regards its civil existence. The objection here is, as we observed, by no means on account of the imperfection of the law. It is on account of its erroneous principle, for if this be fundamentally wrong, the more perfect the law is made the worse it becomes. It cannot be said to have the properties of genuine law even in its imperfections and defects. The true weakness and opprobrium of our best general constitutions is that they cannot provide beneficially for every particular case, and thus fill adequately to their intentions the circle of universal justice. But where the principle is faulty, the erroneous part of the law is the beneficial; and justice only finds refuge in those holes and corners which had escaped the sagacity and inquisition of the legislator. The happiness or misery of multitudes can never be a thing indifferent. A law against the majority of the people is in substance a law against the people itself; its extent determines its invalidity; it even changes its character as it enlarges its operation; it is not particular injustice, but general oppression, and can no longer be considered as a private hardship which might be borne, but spreads and grows up into the unfortunate importance of a national calamity.

Now, as a law directed against the mass of the nation has not the nature of a reasonable institution, so neither has it the authority; for in all forms of government the people is the true legislator; and whether the immediate and instrumental cause of the law be a single person or many, the remote and efficient cause is the consent of the people — either actual or implied— and such consent is absolutely essential to its validity. To the solid establishment of every law two things are essentially requisite : first, a proper and sufficient human power to declare and modify the matter of the

law; and next, such a fit and equitable constitution as
they have a right to declare and render binding. With
regard to the first requisite, the human authority, it is
their judgment they give up, not their right. The
people, indeed, are presumed to consent to whatever the
Legislature ordains for their benefit; and they are to
acquiesce in it though they do not clearly see into the
propriety of the means by which they are conducted to
that desirable end. This they owe as an act of homage
and just deference to a reason which the necessity of
Government has made superior to their own. But
though the means, and indeed the nature of a public
advantage, may not always be evident to the understanding of the subject, no one is so gross and stupid as
not to distinguish between a benefit and an injury. No
one can imagine then an exclusion of a great body of
men, not from favours, privileges, and trusts, but from
the common advantages of society, can ever be a thing
intended for their good, or can ever be ratified by any
implied consent of theirs. If, therefore, at least an
implied human consent is necessary to the existence
of a law, such a constitution cannot in propriety be a
law at all.

But if we could suppose that such a ratification was
made not virtually, but actually by the people not
representatively, but even collectively, still it would
be null and void. They have no right to make a law
prejudicial to the whole community, even though the
delinquents in making such an Act should be them-

selves the chief sufferers by it, because it would be
made against the principle of a superior law, which it
is not in the power of any community, or of the whole
race of man, to alter—I mean the will of Him who
gave us our nature, and in giving, impressed an invariable law upon it.   It would be hard to point out any
error more truly subversive of all the order and beauty,
of all the peace and happiness of human society, than
the position—that any body of men have a right to
make what laws they please; or that laws can derive
any authority from their institution merely, and independent of the quality of the subject-matter.   No arguments of policy, reason of State, or preservation of the
constitution, can be pleaded in favour of such a practice.
They may indeed impeach the frame of that constitution, but can never touch this immovable principle.
This seems to be indeed the doctrine which Hobbes
broached in the last century, and which was then so
frequently and so ably refuted.   Cicero exclaims with
the utmost indignation and contempt against such a
notion;[1] he considers it not only as unworthy of a
philosopher, but of an illiterate peasant; that of all
things this was the most truly absurd to fancy—that

---

[1] Cicero de Legibus, lib. prim. 15 and 16. O rem dignam, in quâ
non modo docti, verum etiam agrestes erubescant! Jam vero illud
stultissimum existimare omnia justa esse, quæ scita sunt in populorum
institutis aut legibus, etc.   Quod si populorum jussis, si principum
decretis, si sententiis judicum jura constituerentur, jus esset latroci-
nari, jus adulterare, jus testamenta falsa supponere, si hæc suffragiis
aut scitis multitudinis probarentur.

the rule of justice was to be taken from the constitutions of commonwealths, or that laws derived their authority from the statutes of the people, the edicts of princes, or the decrees of judges. If it be admitted that it is not the black letter and the king's arms that makes the law, we are to look for it elsewhere.

In reality there are two, and only two foundations of law, and they are both of them conditions without which nothing can give it any force—I mean equity and utility. With respect to the former, it grows out of the great rule of equality which is grounded upon our common nature, and which Philo, with propriety and beauty, calls the mother of justice. All human laws are, properly speaking, only declaratory; they may alter the mode and application, but have no power over the substance of original justice. The other foundation of law, which is utility, must be understood not of partial or limited, but of general and public utility, connected in the same manner with, and derived directly from our rational nature; for any other utility may be the utility of a robber, but cannot be that of a citizen, —the interest of the domestic enemy, and not that of a member of the commonwealth. This present equality can never be the foundation of statutes, which create an artificial difference between men, as the laws before us do, in order to induce a consequential inequality in the distribution of justice. Law is a mode of human action respecting society, and must be governed by the same rules of equity which govern every private action, and

so Tully considers it in his offices as the only utility
agreeable to that nature; *unum debet esse omnibus pro-*
positum, ut eadem sit utilitas unius cujusq; et univer-
sorum; quam si ad se quisq; rapiat, dissolvetur omnis
humana consortio.

If any proposition can be clear in itself, it is this,
that a law which shuts out from all secure and valuable
property the bulk of the people, cannot be made for the
utility of the party so excluded. This therefore is not
the utility which Tully mentions. But if it were true
(as it is not) that the real interest of any part of the
community could be separated from the happiness of
the rest, still it would afford no just foundation for a
statute providing exclusively for that interest at the expense of the other; because it would be repugnant to the
essence of law, which requires that it be made as much as
possible for the benefit of the whole. If this principle
be denied or evaded, what ground have we left to reason
on? We must at once make a total change in all our
ideas, and look for a new definition of law. Where to
find it I confess myself at a loss. If we resort to the
fountains of jurisprudence, they will not supply us
with any that is for our purpose. *Jus* (says Paulus)
pluribus modis dicitur; uno modo, cum id, quod semper
æquum et bonum est, Jus dicitur, ut est Jus naturale. This
sense of the word will not be thought, I imagine, very
applicable to our penal laws. *Altero modo, quod omni-*
bus aut pluribus in unâquâque civitate utile est, ut est
Jus civile. Perhaps this latter will be as insufficient,

and would rather seem a censure and condemnation of
the Popery Acts, than a definition that includes them;
and there is no other to be found in the whole digest,
neither are there any modern writers whose ideas of law
are at all narrower.

It would be far more easy to heap up authorities on
this article, than to excuse the prolixity and tediousness
of producing any at all in proof of a point which, though
too often practically denied, is in its theory almost self-
evident.   For Suarez, handling this very question, *utrum
de ratione et substantiâ Legis esse ut propter commune
bonum feratur,* does not hesitate a moment, finding no
ground in reason or authority to render the affirmative
in the least degree disputable.   *In quæstione ergo pro-
positâ* (says he) *nulla est inter authores controversia; sed
omnium commune est axioma de substantiâ et ratione
Legis esse, ut pro communi bono feratur; ita ut propter
illud præcipuè tradatur,* having observed in another place,
*contra omnem rectitudinem est bonum commune ad
privatum ordinare, seu totum ad partem propter ipsum
referre.*   Partiality and law are contradictory terms.
Neither the merits nor the ill deserts, neither the wealth
and importance, nor the indigence and obscurity of the
one part or of the other, can make any alteration in this
fundamental truth.   On any other scheme I defy any
man living to settle a correct standard, which may discriminate between equitable rule and the most direct
tyranny.   For if we can once prevail upon ourselves to
depart from the strictness and integrity of this principle,

in favour even of a considerable party, the argument
will hold for one that is less so, and thus we shall go on
narrowing the bottom of public right, until step by step
we arrive, though after no very long or very forced
deduction, at what one of our poets calls the *enormous
faith*—the faith of the many, created for the advantage
of a single person. I cannot see a glimmering of distinction to evade it, nor is it possible to allege any
reason for the proscription of so large a part of the
kingdom, which would not hold equally to support,
under parallel circumstances the proscription of the
whole.

I am sensible that these principles in their abstract
light will not be very strenuously opposed. Reason is
never inconvenient but when it comes to be applied.
Mere general truths interfere very little with the
passions. They can, until they are roused by a troublesome application, rest in great tranquillity side by side
with tempers and proceedings the most directly opposite
to them. Men want to be reminded who do not want
to be taught, because those original ideas of rectitude,
to which the mind is compelled to assent when they are
proposed, are not always as present to it as they ought
to be. When people are gone, if not into a denial, at
least into a sort of oblivion of those ideas, when they
know them only as barren speculations, and not as
practical motives for conduct, it will be proper to press
as well as to offer them to the understanding, and when
one is attacked by prejudices which aim to intrude

themselves into the place of law, what is left for us but
to vouch and call to warranty those principles of original
justice from whence alone our title to everything
valuable in society is derived ? Can it be thought to
arise from a superfluous vain parade of displaying
general and uncontroverted maxims, that we should
revert at this time to the first principles of law, when
we have directly under our consideration a whole
body of statutes, which I say are so many contradictions, which their advocates allow to be so many exceptions from those very principles ? Take them in the
most favourable light, every exception from the original
and fixed rule of equality and justice ought surely to be
very well authorised in the reason of their deviation,
and very rare in their use.   For if they should grow to
be frequent, in what would they differ from an abrogation of the rule itself? By becoming thus frequent,
they might even go farther, and establishing themselves
into a principle, convert the rule into the exception.
It cannot be dissembled that this is not at all remote
from the case before us, where the great body of the
people are excluded from all valuable property, where
the greatest and most ordinary benefits of society are
conferred as privileges, and not enjoyed on the footing
of common rights.

The clandestine manner in which those in power
carry on such designs is a sufficient argument of the
sense they inwardly entertain of the true nature of their
proceedings. Seldom is the title or preamble of the law

of the same import with the body and enacting part; but
they generally place some other colour uppermost, which
differs from that which is afterwards to appear, or at
least one that is several shades fainter.   Thus the penal
laws in question are not called laws to oblige men
baptized and educated in Popery to renounce their religion or their property; but are called laws to prevent
the growth of Popery; as if their purpose was only to
prevent conversions to that sect, and not to persecute a
million of people already engaged in it.   But of all the
instances of this sort of legislative artifice, and of the
principles that produced it, I never met with any which
made a stronger impression on me than that of Louis
XIV. in the revocation of the Edict of Nantes.   That
monarch had, when he made that revocation, as few
measures to keep with public opinion as any man.   In
the exercise of the most unresisted authority at home,
in a career of uninterrupted victory abroad, and in a
course of flattery equal to the circumstances of his
greatness in both these particulars, he might be supposed to have as little need as disposition to render any
sort of account to the world of his procedure towards
his subjects.   But the persecution of so vast a body of
men as the Huguenots was too strong a measure even for
the law of pride and power.   It was too glaring a contradiction even to those principles upon which persecution itself is supported.   Shocked at the naked attempt,
he had recourse, for a palliation of his conduct, to an
unkingly denial of the fact, which made against him.

In the preamble, therefore, to his Act of Revocation he
sets forth that the Edict of Nantes was no longer necessary, as the object of it (the Protestants of his kingdom)
were then reduced to a very small number. The refugees
in Holland cried out against this misrepresentation.
They asserted, I believe with truth, that this revocation
had driven 20,000 of them out of their country; and
that they could readily demonstrate there still remained
600,000 Protestants in France. If this were the fact
(as it was undoubtedly), no argument of policy could
have been strong enough to excuse a measure by which
800,000 men were despoiled, at one stroke, of so many
of their rights and privileges. Louis XIV. confessed
by this sort of apology, that if the number had been
large, the revocation had been unjust. But after all, is
it not most evident that this act of injustice, which let
loose on that monarch such a torrent of invective and
reproach, and which threw so dark a cloud over all the
splendour of a most illustrious reign, falls far short of
the case in Ireland ? The privileges which the Protestants of that kingdom enjoyed antecedent to this revocation were far greater than the Roman Catholics of
Ireland ever aspired to under a contrary establishment.
The number of their sufferers, if considered absolutely,
is not half of ours; if considered relatively to the body
of each community, it is not perhaps a twentieth part.
And then the penalties and incapacities which grew
from that revocation are not so grievous in their nature,
nor so certain in their execution, nor so ruinous by a

great deal to the civil prosperity of the State, as those
which we have established for a perpetual law in our
unhappy country. It cannot be thought to arise from
affectation, that I call it so. What other name can be
given to a country which contains so many hundred
thousands of human creatures reduced to a state of the
most abject servitude ?

In putting this parallel I take it for granted that we
can stand for this short time very clear of our party
distinctions. If it were enough by the use of an odious
and unpopular word to determine the question, it would
be no longer a subject of rational disquisition ; since
that very prejudice, which gives these odious names,
and which is the party charged for doing so, and for the
consequences of it, would then become the judge also.
But I flatter myself that not a few will be found who
do not think that the names of Protestant and Papist
can make any change in the nature of essential justice.
Such men will not allow that to be proper treatment to
the one of these denominations, which would be cruelty
to the other ; and which converts its very crime into
the instrument of its defence. They will hardly persuade
themselves that what was bad policy in France can be
good in Ireland, or that what was intolerable injustice
in an arbitrary monarch becomes, only by being more
extended and more violent, an equitable procedure in a
country professing to be governed by law. It is, however, impossible not to observe with some concern that
there are many also of a different disposition—a number

of persons whose minds are so formed that they find
the communion of religion to be a close and an endear-
ing tie, and their country to be no bond at all; to whom
common altars are a better relation than common habita-
tions, and a common civil interest; whose hearts are
touched with the distresses of foreigners, and are abundantly awake to all the tenderness of human feeling on
such an occasion, even at the moment that they
are inflicting the very same distresses, or worse, on
their fellow-citizens, without the least sting of compassion or remorse. To commiserate the distresses of
all men suffering innocently, perhaps meritoriously, is
generous, and very agreeable to the better part of our
nature—a disposition that ought by all means to be
cherished. But to transfer humanity from its natural
basis—our legitimate and homebred connections; to lose
all feeling for those who have grown up by our sides,
in our eyes, the benefit of whose cares and labours we
have partaken from our birth, and meretriciously to
hunt abroad after foreign affections, is such a disarrange-
ment of the whole system of our duties, that I do not
know whether benevolence so displaced is not almost
the same thing as destroyed, or what effect bigotry
could have produced that is more fatal to society. This
no one could help observing, who has seen our doors
kindly and bountifully thrown open to foreign sufferers
for conscience, whilst through the same ports were
issuing fugitives of our own, driven from their country
for a cause which to an indifferent person would seem

to be exactly similar, whilst we stood by, without any
sense of the impropriety of this extraordinary scene,
accusing, and practising injustice. For my part, there
is no circumstance in all the contradictions of our most
mysterious nature, that appears to be more humiliating
than the use we are disposed to make of those sad
examples which seem purposely marked for our correc-
tion and improvement. Every instance of fury and
bigotry in other men, one should think, would naturally
fill us with horror of that disposition. The effect, however, is directly contrary. We are inspired, it is true,
with a very sufficient hatred for the party, but with no
detestation at all of the proceeding. Nay, we are apt to
urge our dislike of such measures, as a reason for imitating them ; and, by an almost incredible absurdity,
because some powers have destroyed their country by
their persecuting spirit, to argue, that we ought to
retaliate on them by destroying our own. Such are the
effects, and such I fear has been the intention of those
numberless books which are daily printed and industriously spread, of the persecutions in other countries
and other religious persuasions. These observations,
which are a digression, but hardly, I think, can be considered as a departure from the subject, have detained
us some time ; we will now come more directly to our
purpose.

It has been shown, I hope with sufficient evidence,
that a Constitution against the interest of the many
is rather of the nature of a grievance than of a law ;

that of all grievances, it is the most weighty and
important; that it is made without due authority,
against all the acknowledged principles of jurisprudence,
against the opinions of all the great lights in that
science; and that such is the tacit sense even of those
who act in the most contrary manner. These points
are indeed so evident, that I apprehend the abettors of
the penal system will ground their defence on admission,
and not on a denial of them. They will lay it down as a
principle, that the Protestant religion is a thing beneficial for the whole community, as well in its civil interests as in those of a superior order. From thence they
will argue, that the end being essentially beneficial, the
means become instrumentally so; that these penalties
and incapacities are not final causes of the Law, but
only a discipline to bring over a deluded people to
their real interest; and therefore, though they may be
harsh in their operation, they will be pleasant in their
effects; and be they what they will, they cannot be
considered as a very extraordinary hardship, as it is in
the power of the sufferer to free himself when he
pleases; and that only by converting to a better religion,
which it is his duty to embrace, even though it were
attended with all those penalties from whence in
reality it delivers him: if he suffers, it is his own fault;
volenti non fit injuria.

I shall be very short without being, I think, the less
satisfactory in my answer to these topics, because they
never can be urged from a conviction of their validity,

and are indeed only the usual and impotent struggles of
those who are unwilling to abandon a practice which
they are unable to defend. First then, I observe that
if the principle of their final and beneficial intention be
admitted as a just ground for such proceedings, there
never was, in the blameable sense of the word, nor ever
can be, such a thing as a religious persecution in the
world. Such an intention is pretended by all men, who
all not only insist that their religion has the sanction of
Heaven, but is likewise, and for that reason, the best
and most convenient to human society. All religious
persecution, Mr. Bayle well observes, is grounded upon
a miserable *petitio principii.* You are wrong, I am
right ; you must come over to me, or you must suffer.
Let me add that the great inlet by which a colour for
oppression has entered into the world, is by one man's
pretending to determine concerning the happiness of
another, and by claiming a right to use what means he
thinks proper in order to bring him to a sense of it. It
is the ordinary and trite sophism of oppression. But
there is not yet such a convenient ductility in the human
understanding as to make us capable of being persuaded
that men can possibly mean the ultimate good of the
whole society by rendering miserable for a century
together the greater part of it, or that any one has such
a reversionary benevolence as seriously to intend the
remote good of a late posterity who can give up the
present enjoyment which every honest man must have
in the happiness of his contemporaries. Everybody is

satisfied that a conservation and secure enjoyment of
our natural rights is the great and ultimate purpose of
civil society, and that therefore all forms whatsoever of
Government are only good as they are subservient to
that purpose to which they are entirely subordinate.
Now, to aim at the establishment of any form of
Government by sacrificing what is the substance of it,
to take away, or at least to suspend the rights of nature
in order to an approved system for the protection of
them, and for the sake of that about which men must
dispute for ever—to postpone those things about which
they have no controversy at all, and this not in minute
and subordinate, but large and principal objects—is a
procedure as preposterous and absurd in argument as it
is oppressive and cruel in its effect. For the Protestant
religion, nor (I speak it with reverence, I am sure) the
truth of our common Christianity, is not so clear as this
proposition, that all men—at least the majority of men
in the society—ought to enjoy the common advantages
of it. You fall, therefore, into a double error ; first, you
incur a certain mischief for an advantage which is
comparatively problematical, even though you were sure
of obtaining it ; secondly, whatever the proposed advantage may be, were it of a certain nature, the attainment
of it is by no means certain, and such deep gaming for
stakes so valuable ought not to be admitted ; the risk
is of too much consequence to society. If no other
country furnished examples of this risk, yet our laws
and our country are enough fully to demonstrate the

fact; Ireland, after almost a century of persecution,
is at this hour full of penalties and full of Papists.
This is a point which would lead us a great way, but it
is only just touched here, having much to say upon it
in its proper place. So that you have incurred a certain
and an immediate inconvenience for a remote and for a
doubly uncertain benefit. Thus far, as to the argument
which would sanctify the injustice of these laws by the
benefits which are proposed to arise from them, and as
to that liberty which, by a new political chemistry, was
to be extracted out of a system of oppression.

Now, as to the other point, that the objects of these
laws suffer voluntarily, this seems to me to be an insult
rather than an argument. For, besides that it totally
annihilates every characteristic, and therefore every
faulty idea of persecution, just as the former does, it
supposes, what is fault in fact, that it is in a man's
moral power to change his religion whenever his convenience requires it. If he be beforehand satisfied that
your opinion is better than his, he will voluntarily
come over to you, and without compulsion, and then
your law would be unnecessary; but if he is not so
convinced, he must know that it is his duty in this
point to sacrifice his interest here to his opinion of his
eternal happiness, else he could have in reality no religion at all. In the former case, therefore, as your law
would be unnecessary, in the latter it would be persecuting—that is, it would put your penalty and his ideas
of duty in the opposite scales, which is, or I know not

what is, the precise idea of persecution. If, then, you require a renunciation of his conscience as a preliminary to his admission to the rights of society, you annex, morally speaking, an impossible condition to it. In this case, in the language of reason and jurisprudence, the condition would be void and the gift absolute ; as the practice runs, it is to establish the condition, and to withhold the benefit. The suffering is then not voluntary. And I never heard any other argument drawn from the nature of laws and the good of human society, urged in favour of those proscriptive statutes except those which have just been mentioned.

CHAPTER III.

PART II.

THE second head upon which I propose to consider those statutes with regard to their object, and which is the next in importance to the magnitude, and of almost equal concern in the inquiry into the justice of these laws, is its possession. It is proper to recollect that this religion, which is so persecuted in its members, is the old religion of the country and the once established religion of the State—the very same which had for centuries received the countenance and sanction of the laws, and from which it would at one time have been highly penal to have dissented. In proportion as mankind has become enlightened, the idea of religious

persecution, under any circumstances, has been almost
universally exploded by all good and thinking men.
The only faint shadow of difficulty which remains is
concerning the introduction of new opinions. Experience has shown that, if it has been favourable to the
cause of truth, it has not been always conducive to the
peace of society. Though a new religious sect should
even be totally free in itself from any tumultuous and
disorderly zeal, which, however, is rarely the case, it has
a tendency to create a resistance from the establishment
in possession productive of great disorders, and thus
becomes, innocently indeed, but yet very certainly, the
cause of the bitterest dissensions in the commonwealth.
To a mind not thoroughly saturated with the tolerating
maxims of the gospel, a preventive persecution on such
principles might come recommended by strong and
apparently no immoral motives of policy, whilst yet the
contagion was recent, and had laid hold but on a few
persons. The truth is, these politics are rotten and
hollow at bottom, as all that are founded upon any,
however minute a degree of positive injustice, must ever
be. But they are specious, and sufficiently so to delude
a man of sense and of integrity. But it is quite otherwise with the attempt to eradicate by violence a wide-
spreading and established religious opinion. If the
people are in an error, to inform them is not only fair
but charitable; to drive them is a strain of the most
manifest injustice. If not the right, the presumption at
least is ever on the side of possession. Are they mis-

taken? If it does not fully justify them, it is a great alleviation of guilt, which may be mingled with their misfortune, that the error is none of their forging; that they received it on as good a footing as they can receive your laws and your legislative authority, because it was handed down to them from their ancestors. The opinion may be erroneous, but the principle is undoubtedly right, and you punish them for acting upon a principle which, of all others, is perhaps the most necessary for preserving society—an implicit admiration and adherence to the establishments of their forefathers.

If, indeed, the legislative authority was on all hands admitted to be the ground of religious persuasion, I should readily allow that dissent would be rebellion. In this case it would make no difference whether the opinion was sucked in with the milk, or imbibed yesterday, because the same legislative authority which had settled could destroy it with all the power of a Creator over his creature. But this doctrine is universally disowned, and for a very plain reason. Religion, to have any force on men's understandings,—indeed, to exist at all,—must be supposed paramount to laws, and independent for its substance upon any human institution. Else it would be the absurdest thing in the world, an acknowledged cheat. Religion, therefore, is not believed because the laws have established it, but it is established because the leading part of the community have previously believed it to be true. As no water can rise higher than its spring, no establishment can have more

authority than it derives from its principle, and the
power of the Government can with no appearance of
reason go further coercively than to bind and hold down
those who have once consented to their opinions. The
consent is the origin of the whole. If they attempt to
proceed farther they disown the foundation upon which
their own establishment was built, and they claim a
religious assent upon mere human authority, which has
been just now shown to be absurd and preposterous, and
which they in fact confess to be so.

However, we are warranted to go thus far. The
people often actually do (and perhaps they cannot in
general do better) take their religion, not on the coercive,
which is impossible, but on the influencing authority of
their governors as wise and informed men. But if they
once take a religion on the word of the State, they
cannot in common sense do so a second time, unless
they have some concurrent reason for it. The prejudice
in favour of your wisdom is shaken by your change.
You confess that you have been wrong, and yet you
would pretend to dictate by your sole authority, whereas
you disengage the mind by embarrassing it. For why
should I prefer your opinion of to-day to your persuasion
of yesterday? If we must resort to prepossessions for
the ground of opinion, it is in the nature of man rather
to defer to the wisdom of times passed, whose weakness is not before his eyes, than to the present, of
whose imbecility he has daily experience. Veneration
of antiquity is congenial to the human mind. When,

therefore, an establishment would persecute an opinion in possession, it sets against it all the powerful prejudices of human nature. It even sets its own authority, when it is of most weight, against itself in that very circumstance in which it must necessarily have the least, and it opposes the stable prejudice of time against a new opinion founded on mutability—a consideration that must render compulsion in such a case the more grievous, as there is no security that, when the mind is settled in the new opinion, it may not be obliged to give place to one that is still newer, or even to a return of the old. But when an ancient establishment begins early to persecute an innovation, it stands upon quite other grounds, and it has all the prejudices and presumptions on its side. It puts its own authority, not only of compulsion, but prepossession, the veneration of past age, as well as the activity of the present time, against the opinion only of a private man or set of men. If there be no reason, there is at least some consistency in its proceedings. Commanding to constancy, it does nothing but that of which it sets an example itself. But an opinion at once new and persecuting is a monster, because in the very instant in which it takes a liberty of change, it does not leave to you even a liberty of perseverance.

Is then no improvement to be brought into society? Undoubtedly, but not by compulsion; but by encouragement; but by countenance, favour, privileges—which are powerful and are lawful instruments. The coercive authority of the State is limited to what is necessary

for its existence.   To this belongs the whole order of
Criminal Law.   It considers as crimes (that is, the
object of punishment) trespasses against those rules for
which society was instituted.   The law punishes delinquents—not because they are not good men, but
because they are intolerably wicked.   It does bear, and
must, with the vices and the follies of men until they
actually strike at the root of order.   This it does in
things actually moral.   In all matters of speculative
improvement the case is stronger, even where the matter
is properly of human cognisance.   But to consider an
averseness to improvement—the not arriving at perfection—as a crime, is against all tolerably correct jurisprudence ; for if the resistance to improvement should
be great and any way general, they would in effect give
up the necessary and substantial part in favour of the
perfection and the finishing.

But, say the abettors of our penal laws, this old
possessed superstition is such in its principles that
society, on its general principles, cannot subsist along
with it.   Could a man think such an objection possible
if he had not actually heard it made ?—an objection
contradicted not by hypothetical reasonings, but the
clear evidence of the most decisive facts.   Society not
only exists but flourishes at this hour, with this superstition, in many countries, under every form of Government—in some established, in some tolerated, in others
upon an equal footing.   And was there no civil society
at all in these kingdoms before the Reformation ?   To

say it was not as well constituted as it ought to be is
saying nothing at all to the purpose ; for that assertion
evidently regards improvement, not existence.   It certainly did then exist, and it as certainly then was at
least as much to the advantage of a very great part of
society as what we have brought in the place of it—
which is indeed a great blessing to those who have
profited by the change; but to all the rest as we have
wrought—that is by blending general persecution with
partial reformation—it is the very reverse.   We found
the people heretics and idolaters; we have, by way of
improving their condition, rendered them slaves and
beggars.   They remain in all the misfortune of their old
errors, and all the superadded misery of their recent
punishment.   They were happy enough—in their
opinion at least—before the change.   What benefits
society then had, they partook of them all.   They are
now excluded from those benefits, and so far as civil
society comprehends them, and as we have managed
the matter, our persecutions are so far from being
necessary to its existence, that our very Reformation is
made in a degree noxious.   If this be improvement,
truly I know not what can be called a depravation of
society.

   But as those who argue in this manner are perpetually
shifting the question, having begun with objecting—in
order to give a fair and public colour to their scheme—
to a toleration of those opinions as subversive of society
in general, they will surely end by abandoning the

broad part of the argument, and attempting to show
that a toleration of them is inconsistent with the established Government among us.   Now, though this
position be in reality as untenable as the other, it is not
altogether such an absurdity on the face of it.   All I
shall here observe is, that those who lay it down little
consider what a wound they are giving to that Establishment for which they pretend so much zeal.   However, as this is a consideration not of general justice
but of particular and national policy, and as I have
reserved a place expressly where it will undergo a
thorough discussion, I shall not here embarrass myself
with it, being resolved to preserve all the order in my
power in the examination of this important melancholy
subject.

However, before we pass from this point concerning
possession, it will be a relaxation of the mind not wholly
foreign to our purpose to take a short review of the
extraordinary policy which has been held with regard
to religion in that kingdom, from the time our ancestors
took possession of it.   The most able antiquaries are
of opinion, and Archbishop Usher (whom I reckon
amongst the first of them) has, I think, shown that a
religion, not very remote from the present Protestant
persuasion, was that of the Irish before the union of
that kingdom to the Crown of England.   If this was
not directly the fact, this at least seems very probable,
that Papal authority was much lower in Ireland than
in other countries.   This union was made under the

authority of an arbitrary grant of Pope Adrian, in order
that the Church of Ireland should be reduced to the
same servitude with those that were nearer to his See.
It is not very wonderful that an ambitious monarch
should make use of any pretence in his way to so considerable an object. What is extraordinary is, that for
a very long time—even quite down to the Reformation—
and in their most solemn acts, the kings of England
founded their title wholly on this grant. They called for
obedience from the people of Ireland, not on principles
of subjection, but as vassals and mean lords between
them and the Popes; and they omitted no measure of
force or policy to establish that papal authority with all
the distinguishing articles of religion connected with it,
and to make it take deep root in the minds of the
people. Not to crowd instances unnecessarily, I shall
select two; one of which is in print, the other on
record; the one a Treaty, the other an Act of Parliament. The first is the submission of the Irish chiefs to
Richard II., mentioned by Sir John Davis. In this
pact they bind themselves for the future to preserve
peace and allegiance to the kings of England, under
certain pecuniary penalties. But what is remarkable,
these fines were all covenanted to be paid into the
Apostolical Chamber, supposing the Pope as the
superior power, whose peace was broken and whose
majesty was violated in disobeying his governor. By
this time, so far as regarded England, the kings had
extremely abridged the papal power in many material

E

particulars; they had passed the Statute of Provisors; the Statute of Premunire; and indeed struck out of the Papal authority all things at least, that seemed to infringe on their temporal independence. In Ireland, however, their proceeding was directly the reverse: there they thought it expedient to exalt it at least as high as ever. For, so late as the reign of Edward IV., the following short but very explicit Act of Parliament was passed:—

IV. ED. Cap. 3.

An Act, whereby letters patent of pardon from the king to those that sue to Rome for certain bene-fices is void.   Rot. Parl.

Item, At the request of the Commons it is ordeyned and established, by authority of the said Parliament, that all maner letters patents of the king, of pardons or pardon granted by the king, or hereafter to be granted to any provisor, that claim any title by the bulls of the Pope to any maner benefices, where at the time of the impetrating of the said bulls of provision, the benefice is full of an incumbent, that then the said letters patents of pardon or pardons be void in law and of none effect.

.   .   .   .

When by every expedient of force and policy, by a

war of some centuries, by extirpating a number of the
old, and by bringing in a number of new people full of
those opinions, and intending to propagate them, they
had fully compassed their object, they suddenly took
another turn; commenced an opposite persecution,
made heavy laws, carried on mighty wars, inflicted
and suffered the worst evils, extirpated the mass of the
old, brought in new inhabitants; and they continue at
this day an oppressive system, and may for four hundred years to come, to eradicate opinions which, by the
same violent means they had been four hundred years
endeavouring by every means to establish. They compelled the people to submit, by the forfeiture of all
their civil rights, to the Pope's authority, in its most
extravagant and unbounded sense, as a giver of kingdoms; and now they refuse even to tolerate them in
the most moderate and chastised sentiments concerning
it. No country, I believe, since the world began, has
suffered so much on account of religion; or has been
so variously harassed both for Popery and for Protestantism.

It will now be seen, that, even if these laws could
be supposed agreeable to those of Nature in these particulars, on another and almost as strong a principle
they are yet unjust, as being contrary to positive compact, and the public faith most solemnly plighted. On
the surrender of Limerick, and some other Irish garrisons, in the war of the Revolution, the Lords Justices
of Ireland, and the commander-in-chief of the king's

forces, signed a capitulation with the Irish, which was
afterwards ratified by the king himself, by *Inspeximus*
under the great seal of England. It contains some
public articles relative to the whole body of the Roman
Catholics in that kingdom, and some with regard to the
security of the greater part of the inhabitants of five
counties. What the latter were, or in what manner
they were observed, is at this day of much less public
concern. The former are two, the 1st and the 9th.
The first is of this tenour. The Roman Catholics of
this kingdom (Ireland) shall enjoy such privileges, in
the exercise of their religion, as are consistent with the
laws of Ireland, or as they did enjoy in the reign of
King Charles II.; and their Majesties, as soon as their
affairs will permit them to summon a Parliament in
this kingdom, will endeavour to procure the said Roman
Catholics such further security in that particular as
may preserve them from any disturbance on account of
their religion. The ninth article is to this effect. The
oath to be administered to such Roman Catholics as
submit to their Majesties' Government, shall be the oath
aforesaid, and no other; viz. the oath of allegiance,
made by Act of Parliament in England, in the first year
of their then Majesties; as required by the second of the
articles of Limerick. Compare this latter article with
the penal laws, as they are stated in the second chapter, and judge whether they seem to be the public Acts
of the same power, and observe whether other oaths are
tendered to them, and under what penalties. Compare

the former with the same laws, from the beginning to
the end ; and judge whether the Roman Catholics have
been preserved, agreeably to the sense of the article,
from any disturbance upon account of their religion ;
or rather, whether on that account there is a single
right of nature, or benefit of society, which has not
been either totally taken away or considerably impaired.

But it is said that the Legislature was not bound
by this article, as it has never been ratified in Parliament. I do admit that it never had that sanction,
and that the Parliament was under no obligation to
ratify these articles by any express Act of theirs.
But still I am at a loss how they came to be the less
valid, on the principles of our constitution, by being
without that sanction. They certainly bound the
king and his successors. The words of the article do
this ; or they do nothing ; and so far as the Crown
had a share in passing those Acts, the public faith was
unquestionably broken. In Ireland such a breach on
the part of the Crown was much more unpardonable
in administration, than it would have been here. They
have in Ireland a way of preventing any Bill even from
approaching the Royal Presence, in matters of far less
importance than the honour and faith of the Crown,
and the well-being of a great body of the people. For,
besides that they might have opposed the very first
suggestion of it in the House of Commons, it could not
be framed into a Bill without the approbation of the

Council in Ireland.   It could not be returned to them
again without the approbation of the King and Council
here.   They might have met it again in its second
passage through that House of Parliament, in which it
was originally suggested, as well as in the other.   If
it had escaped them through all these mazes, it was
again to come before the Lord Lieutenant, who might
have sunk it by a refusal of the royal assent.   The
constitution of Ireland has interposed all those checks
to the passing of any constitutional Act, however
insignificant in its own nature.   But did the Administration in that reign avail themselves of any one of
those opportunities?   They never gave the Act of the
11th of Queen Anne the least degree of opposition in
any one stage of its progress.   What is rather the fact,
many of the Queen's servants encouraged it, recommended it, were, in reality, the true authors of its
passing in Parliament, instead of recommending and
using their utmost endeavour to establish a law directly
opposite in its tendency, as they were bound to do by
the express letter of the very first article of the Treaty
of Limerick.   To say nothing further of the Ministry,
who in this instance most shamefully betrayed the
faith of Government, may it not be a matter of some
degree of doubt, whether the Parliament, who do not
claim a right of dissolving the force of moral obligation,
did not make themselves a party in this breach of
contract, by presenting a Bill to the Crown in direct
violation of those Articles so solemnly and so recently

executed, which by the constitution they had full
authority to execute ?

It may be further objected that, when the Irish
requested the ratification of Parliament to those articles,
they did, in effect, themselves entertain a doubt concerning their validity without such a ratification.   To
this I answer, that the collateral security was meant to
bind the Crown, and to hold it firm to its engagements.
They did not, therefore, call it a *perfecting* of the
security, but an *additional* security, which it could
not have been, if the first had been void; for the
Parliament could not bind itself more than the Crown
had bound itself.   And if all had made but *one* security,
neither of them could be called *additional* with propriety or common sense.   But let us suppose that they
did apprehend there might have been something wanting in this security without the sanction of Parliament.
They were, however, evidently mistaken ; and this
surplusage of theirs did not weaken the validity of the
single contract, upon the known principle of law, *Non
solent, quæ abundant, vitiare scripturas.*   For nothing
is more evident than that the Crown was bound, and
that no Act can be made without the royal assent.
But the constitution will warrant us in going a great
deal farther, and in affirming that a treaty executed
by the Crown, and contradictory of no preceding law,
is full as binding on the whole body of the nation as
if it had twenty times received the sanction of Parliament ; because the very same constitution, which has

given to the Houses of Parliament their definite
authority, has also left in the Crown the trust of
making peace, as a consequence, and much the best
consequence, of the prerogative of making war. If the
peace was ill made, my Lord Galway, Coningsby, and
Porter, who signed it, were responsible; because they
were subject to the community. But its own contracts
are not subject to it. It is subject to them; and the
compact of the king acting constitutionally was the
compact of the nation.

Observe what monstrous consequences would result
from a contrary position. A foreign enemy has entered,
or a strong domestic one has arisen in the nation. In
such events the circumstances may be, and often have
been, such that a Parliament cannot sit. This was
precisely the case in that rebellion in Ireland. It will
be admitted also that their power may be so great as
to make it very prudent to treat with them, in order
to save effusion of blood, perhaps to save the nation.
Now, could such a treaty be at all made if your enemies, or rebels, were fully persuaded that, in these
times of confusion, there was no authority in the State
which could hold out to them an inviolable pledge for
their future security; but that there lurked in the
constitution a dormant but irresistible power, who
would not think itself bound by the ordinary subsisting
and contracting authority, but might rescind its acts
and obligations at pleasure? This would be a doctrine
made to perpetuate and exasperate war; and on that

principle it directly impugns the law of nations, which
is built upon this principle, that war should be softened
as much as possible, and that it should cease as soon
as possible between contending parties and communities.
The king has a power to pardon individuals. If the
king holds out his faith to a robber to come in on
a promise of pardon, of life and estate, and, in all
respects, of a full indemnity, shall the Parliament say
that he must, nevertheless, be executed, that his estate
must be forfeited, or that he shall be abridged of any
of the privileges which he before held as a subject?
Nobody will affirm it. In such a case the breach of
faith would not only be on the part of the king, who
assented to such an act, but on the part of the Parliament, who made it. As the king represents the whole
contracting capacity of the nation, so far as his prerogative (unlimited, as I said before, by any precedent
law) can extend, he acts as the national procurator on
all such occasions. What is true of a robber is true
of a rebel; and what is true of one robber or rebel is
as true—and it is a much more important truth—of
one hundred thousand.

To urge this part of the argument farther is indeed,
I fear, not necessary, for two reasons. First, that it
seems tolerably evident in itself; and next, that there
is but too much ground to apprehend that the actual
ratification of Parliament would, in the then temper of
parties, have proved but a very slight and trivial
security. Of this there is a very strong example in

the history of those very articles. For, though the
Parliament omitted in the reign of King William to
ratify the first and most general of them, they did actually confirm the second and more limited—that which
related to the security of the inhabitants of those five
counties which were in arms when the treaty was
made.

CHAPTER IV.

In the foregoing book we considered these laws in
a very simple point of view, and in a very general
one—merely as a system of hardship imposed on the
body of the community; and from thence and from
some other arguments inferred the general injustice of
such a procedure. In this we shall be obliged to be
more minute; and the matter will become more complex as we undertake to demonstrate the mischievous
and impolitic consequences, which the particular mode
of this oppressive system, and the instruments which
it employs, operating, as we said, on this extensive
object, produce on the national prosperity, quiet, and
security.

The stock of materials by which any nation is
rendered flourishing and prosperous, are its industry,
its knowledge or skill, its morals, its execution of
justice, its courage, and the national union in direct-
ing these powers to one point, and making them all
centre in the public benefit. Other than these I do

not know, and scarcely can conceive any means by which a community may flourish.

If we show that these penal laws of Ireland destroy not one only, but every one of these materials of public prosperity, it will not be difficult to perceive that Great Britain, whilst they subsist, never can draw from that country all the advantages to which the bounty of nature has entitled it.

To begin with the first great instrument of national happiness and strength—its industry—I must observe that although these penal laws do indeed inflict many hardships on those who are obnoxious to them, yet their chief, their most extensive and most certain operation is upon property. Those civil constitutions which promote industry are such as facilitate the acquisition, secure the holding, enable the fixing, and suffer the alienation of property. Every law which obstructs it in any part of its distribution is, in proportion to the force and extent of the obstruction, a discouragement to industry. For a law against property is a law against industry, the latter having always the former, and nothing else, for its object. Now as to the acquisition of landed property, which is the foundation and support of all the other kinds, the laws have disabled three-fourths of the inhabitants of Ireland from acquiring any estate of inheritance for life or years, or any charge whatsoever, on which two-thirds of the improved yearly value are not reserved for thirty years.

This confinement of landed property to one set of
hands, and preventing its free circulation through the
community, is a most leading article of ill policy,
because it is one of the most capital discouragements
to all that industry which may be employed on the
lasting improvement of the soil, or is any way conversant about land.   A tenure of thirty years is evidently no tenure upon which to build, to plant, to raise
enclosures, to change the nature of the ground, to make
any new experiment which might improve agriculture,
or to do anything more than what may answer the
immediate and momentary calls of rent to the landlord,
and leave subsistence to the tenant and his family.
The desire of acquisition is always a passion of long
views.   Confine a man to momentary possession, and
you at once cut off that laudable avarice which every
wise State has cherished as one of the first principles
of its greatness.   Allow a man but a temporary possession, lay it down as a maxim that he never can
have any other, and you immediately and infallibly
turn him to temporary enjoyments; and these enjoyments are never the pleasures of labour and free
industry, whose quality it is to famish the present
hours, and squander all upon prospect and futurity;
they are, on the contrary, those of a thoughtless, loiter-
ing, and dissipated life.   The people must be inevitably disposed to such pernicious habits merely from
the short duration of their tenure which the law has

allowed.   But it is not enough that industry is checked
by the confinement of its views; it is further discouraged by the limitation of its own direct object—
profit.   This is a regulation extremely worthy of our
attention, as it is not a consequential, but a direct discouragement to melioration, as directly as if the law
had said in express terms, " Thou shalt not improve."

But we have an additional argument to demonstrate
the ill policy of denying the occupiers of land any
solid property in it.   Ireland is a country wholly un-
planted.   The farms have neither dwelling-houses nor
good offices, nor are the lands almost anywhere provided with fences and communications; in a word, in
a very unimproved state.   The land-owner there never
takes upon him, as it is usual in this kingdom, to
supply all these conveniences, and to set down his
tenant in what may be called a completely furnished
farm.   If the tenant will not do it, it is never done.
This circumstance shows how miserably and peculiarly
impolitic it has been in Ireland to tie down the body
of the tenantry to short and unprofitable tenures.   A
finished and furnished house will be taken for any term,
however short; if the repair lies on the owner, the
shorter the better.   But no one will take one not only
unfurnished but half built, but upon a term which, on
calculation, will answer with profit all his charges.   It
is on this principle that the Romans established their
Emphyteusis, or fee-farm.   For though they extended

the ordinary term of their location only to nine years,
yet they encouraged a more permanent letting to
farm, with the condition of improvement, as well as of
annual payment, on the part of the tenant, where the
land had lain rough and neglected; and therefore
invented this species of engrafted holding in the later
times, when property came to be worse distributed by
falling into a few hands. This denial of landed property to the gross of the people has this further evil
effect in preventing the improvement of land; that it
prevents any of the property acquired in trade to be
re-gorged as it were upon the land. They must have
observed very little who have not remarked the bold
and liberal spirit of improvement which persons bred
to trade have often exerted on their land-purchases;
that they usually come to them with a more abundant
command of ready money than most landed men possess; and that they have in general a much better
idea, by long habits of calculative dealings, of the propriety of expending in order to acquire. Besides, such
men often bring their spirit of commerce into their
estates with them, and make manufactures take a root
where the mere landed gentry had perhaps no capital,
perhaps no inclination, and most frequently not sufficient knowledge to effect anything of the kind. By
these means what beautiful and useful spots have
there not been made about trading and manufacturing
towns, and how has agriculture had reason to bless
that happy alliance with commerce; and how miser-

able must that nation be whose frame of polity has disjointed the landing and the trading interests !

.   .   .   .   .

The great prop of this whole system is not pretended to be its justice or its utility, but the supposed danger to the State, which gave rise to it originally, and which, they apprehend, would return if this system were overturned.   Whilst, say they, the Papists of this kingdom were possessed of landed property, and of the influence consequent to such property, their allegiance to the Crown of Great Britain was ever insecure; the public peace was ever liable to be broken; and Protestants never could be a moment secure either of their properties or of their lives.   Indulgence only made them arrogant, and power daring; confidence only excited and enabled them to exert their inherent treachery; and the times which they generally selected for their most wicked and desperate rebellions were those in which they enjoyed the greatest ease and the most perfect tranquillity.

Such are the arguments that are used both publicly and privately in every discussion upon this point. They are generally full of passion and of error, and built upon facts which, in themselves, are most false. It cannot, I confess, be denied that those miserable performances which go about under the names of Histories of Ireland, do indeed represent those events after this manner; and they would persuade us, contrary to the known order of Nature, that indulgence

and moderation in governors is the natural incitement
in subjects to rebel.   But there is an interior History
of Ireland—the genuine voice of its records and monuments—which speaks a very different language from
these histories from Temple and from Clarendon.
These restore nature to its just rights, and policy to its
proper order; for they even now show to those who
have been at the pains to examine them—and they may
show one day to all the world—that these rebellions
were not produced by toleration but by persecution;
that they arose not from just and mild government,
but from the most unparalleled oppression.   These
records will be far from giving the least countenance
to a doctrine so repugnant to humanity and good sense
as that the security of any establishment, civil or religious, can ever depend upon the misery of those who
live under it, or that its danger can arise from their
quiet and prosperity.   God forbid that the history of
this or any country should give such encouragement
to the folly or vices of those who govern.   If it can
be shown that the great rebellions of Ireland have
arisen from attempts to reduce the natives to the state
to which they are now reduced, it will show that an
attempt to continue them in that state will rather be
disadvantageous to the public peace than any kind of
security to it.   These things have, in some measure,
begun to appear already, and as far as regards the
argument drawn from former rebellions, it will fall
readily to the ground.   But, for my part, I think the

real danger to every state is, to render its subjects
justly discontented; nor is there in politics or science
any more effectual secret for their security than to
establish in their people a firm opinion that no change
can be for their advantage.   It is true that bigotry and
fanaticism may, for a time, draw great multitudes of
people from a knowledge of their true and substantial
interest.   But upon this I have to remark three things;
first, that such a temper can never become universal,
or last for a long time.   The principle of religion is
seldom lasting; the majority of men are in no persuasion bigots; they are not willing to sacrifice on
every vain imagination that superstition or enthusiasm
holds forth, or that even zeal and piety recommend, the
certain possession of their temporal happiness.   And if
such a spirit has been at any time roused in a society,
after it has had its paroxysm it commonly subsides
and is quiet, and is even the weaker for the violence
of its first exertion; security and ease are its mortal
enemies.   But secondly, if anything can tend to revive
and keep it up, it is to keep alive the passions of men
by ill usage.   This is enough to irritate even those
who have not a spark of bigotry in their constitution
to the most desperate enterprises; it certainly will inflame, darken, and render more dangerous, the spirit of
bigotry in those who are possessed by it.   Lastly, by
rooting out any sect, you are never secure against the
effects of fanaticism; it may arise on the side of the
most favoured opinions; and many are the instances

F

wherein the established religion of a state has grown
ferocious and turned upon its keeper, and has often
torn to pieces the civil establishment that had cherished
it, and which it was designed to support; France—
England—Holland.

But there may be danger of wishing a change,
even where no religious motive can operate; and
every enemy to such a state comes as a friend to the
subject; and where other countries are under terror,
they begin to hope.

This argument *ad verecundiam* has as much force
as any such have. But I think it fares but very
indifferently with those who make use of it; for they
would get but little to be proved abettors of tyranny
at the expense of putting me to an inconvenient
acknowledgment. For if I were to confess that there
are circumstances in which it would be better to
establish such a religion   .   .   .   .

.   .   .   .

With regard to the Pope's interest. This foreign
chief of their religion cannot be more formidable to us
than to other Protestant countries. To conquer that
country for himself is a wild chimera; to encourage
revolt in favour of foreign princes is an exploded idea
in the politics of that Court. Perhaps it would be
full as dangerous to have the people under the conduct
of factious pastors of their own as under a foreign
ecclesiastical court.

.   .   .   .

In the second year of the reign of Queen Elizabeth were enacted several limitations in the acquisition or the retaining of property, which had—so far as regarded any general principles—hitherto remained untouched under all changes.

These Bills met no opposition either in the Irish Parliament or in the English Council, except from private agents, who were little attended to; and they passed into laws with the highest and most general applauses, as all such things are, in the beginning, not as a system of persecution, but as masterpieces of the most subtle and refined politics. And to say the truth, these laws—at first view—have rather an appearance of a plan of vexatious litigation and crooked law chicanery, than of a direct and sanguinary attack upon the rights of private conscience, because they did not affect life, at least with regard to the laity; and making the Catholic opinions rather the subject of civil regulations than of criminal prosecutions, to those who are not lawyers and read these laws, they only appear to be a species of jargon. For the execution of criminal law has always a certain appearance of violence. Being exercised directly on the persons of the supposed offenders, and commonly executed in the face of the public, such executions are apt to excite sentiments of pity for the sufferers, and indignation against those who are employed in such cruelties—being seen as single acts of cruelty, rather than as ill general principles of government. But the operation of the laws

in question being such as common feeling brings home
to every man's bosom, they operate in a sort of comparative silence and obscurity; and though their
cruelty is exceedingly great, it is never seen in a
single exertion, and always escapes commiseration,
being scarce known, except to those who view them
in a general—which is always a cold and phlegmatic
—light. The first of these laws being made with so
general a satisfaction, as the chief governors found
that such things were extremely acceptable to the
leading people in that country, they were willling
enough to gratify them with the ruin of their fellow-
citizens; they were not sorry to divert their attention
from other inquiries, and to keep them fixed to this, as
if this had been the only real object of their national
politics; and for many years there was no speech
from the throne which did not, with great appearance
of seriousness, recommend the passing of such laws;
and scarce a session went over without in effect passing some of them, until they have by degrees grown to
be the most considerable head in the Irish Statute
Book. At the same time, giving a temporary and
occasional mitigation to the severity of some of the
harshest of those laws, they appeared in some sort the
protectors of those whom they were in reality destroying by the establishment of general constitutions
against them. At length, however, the policy of this
expedient is worn out; the passions of men are cooled;
those laws begin to disclose themselves, and to pro-

duce effects very different from those which were
promised in making them; for crooked counsels are
ever unwise; and nothing can be more absurd and
dangerous than to tamper with the natural foundations of society, in hopes of keeping it up by certain
contrivances.

II.

A LETTER to Sir Charles Bingham, Bart., on the Irish Absentee Tax.[1]

Dear Sir,

I am much flattered by your very obliging letter, and the rather because it promises an opening to our future correspondence.   This may be my only indemnification for very great losses.   One of the most odious parts of the proposed Absentee Tax is its tendency to separate friends, and to make as ugly breaches in private society as it must make in the unity of the great political body. I am sure that much of the satisfaction of some circles in London will be lost by it.   Do you think that our friend Mrs. Vesey will suffer her husband to vote for a tax that is to destroy the evenings at Bolton Row ?   I trust we shall have other supporters of the same sex,

---

1 From authentic documents found with the copy of this letter among Mr. Burke's papers, it appears that in the year 1773 a project of imposing a tax upon all proprietors of landed estates in Ireland, whose ordinary residence should be in Great Britain, had been adopted and avowed by his Majesty's ministers at that time.   A remonstrance against this measure, as highly unjust and impolitic, was presented to the ministers by several of the principal Irish absentees, and the project was subsequently abandoned.

equally powerful and equally deserving to be so, who will not abandon the common cause of their own liberties and our satisfactions. We shall be barbarised on both sides of the water if we do not see one another now and then. *We* shall sink into surly, brutish Johns, and *you* will degenerate into wild Irish. It is impossible that we should be the wiser or the more agreeable; certainly we shall not love one another the better for this forced separation which our ministers, who have already done so much for the dissolution of every other sort of good connection, are now meditating for the further improvement of this too well united empire. Their next step will be to encourage all the colonies—about thirty separate Governments—to keep their people from all intercourse with each other and with the mother country. A gentleman of New York or Barbadoes will be as much gazed at as a strange animal from Nova Zembla or Otaheite, and those rogues, the travellers, will tell us what stories they please about poor old Ireland.

In all seriousness (though I am a great deal more than half serious in what I have been saying), I look upon this projected tax in a very evil light. I think it is not advisable; I am sure it is not necessary; and as it is not a mere matter of finance, but involves a political question of much importance, I consider the principle and precedent as far worse than the thing itself. You are too kind in imagining I can suggest anything new upon the subject. The objections to it

are very glaring, and must strike the eyes of all those
who have not their reasons for shutting them against
evident truth. I have no feelings or opinions on this
subject which I do not partake with all the sensible
and informed people that I meet with. At first I
could scarcely meet with any one who could believe
that this scheme originated from the English Government. They considered it not only as absurd, but as
something monstrous and unnatural. In the first
instance it strikes at the power of this country, in the
end, at the union of the whole empire. I do not mean
to express, most certainly I do not entertain in my
mind, anything invidious concerning the superintend-
ing authority of Great Britain. But if it be true that
the several bodies which make up this complicated mass
are to be preserved as one empire, an authority sufficient to preserve that unity, and by its equal weight
and pressure to consolidate the various parts that compose it, must reside somewhere ;—that somewhere can
only be in England. Possibly any one member distinctly taken might decide in favour of that residence
within itself, but certainly no member would give its
voice for any other except this. So that I look upon
the residence of the supreme power to be settled here
not by force or tyranny, or even by mere long usage,
but by the very nature of things and the joint consent
of the whole body.

If all this be admitted, then without question this
country must have the sole right to the Imperial

Legislation, by which I mean that law which regulates
the polity and economy of the several parts, as they
relate to one another and to the whole.   But if any of
the parts, which (not for oppression but for order) are
placed in a subordinate situation, will assume to themselves the power of hindering or checking the resort of
their municipal subjects to the centre, or even to any
other part of the empire, they arrogate to themselves
the imperial rights, which do not, which cannot, belong
to them, and, so far as in them lies, destroy the happy
arrangement of the entire empire.

A free communication, by *discretionary residence*, is
necessary to all the other purposes of communication.
For what purpose are the Irish and Plantation laws
sent hither, but as means of preserving this sovereign
constitution ?   Whether such a constitution was originally right or wrong, this is not the time of day to
dispute.   If any evils arise from it, let us not strip it
of what may be useful in it.   By taking the English
Privy Council into your Legislature, you obtain a new,
a further, and, possibly, a more liberal consideration of
all your acts.   If a local Legislature shall by oblique
means tend to deprive any of the people of this benefit,
and shall make it penal to them to follow into England
the laws which may affect them, then the English
Privy Council will have to decide upon your acts
without those lights that may enable them to judge
upon what grounds you made them, or how far they
ought to be modified, received, or rejected.

To what end is the ultimate appeal in judicature
lodged in this kingdom, if men may be disabled from
following their suits here, and may be taxed into an
absolute *denial of justice?* You observe, my dear sir,
that I do not assert that, in all cases, two shillings will
necessarily cut off this means of correcting legislative
and judicial mistakes, and thus amount to a denial of
justice.   I might indeed state cases in which this very
quantum of tax would be fully sufficient to defeat this
right.   But I argue not on the case, but on the principle, and I am sure the principle implies it.   They
who may restrain, may prohibit.   They who may impose two shillings, may impose ten shillings, in the
pound; and those who may condition the tax to six
months' annual absence, may carry that condition to
six weeks, or even to six days, and thereby totally
defeat the wise means which have been provided for
extensive and impartial justice, and for orderly, well-
poised, and well-connected government.

What is taxing the resort to and residence in any
place, but declaring that your connection with that
place is a grievance?   Is not such an Irish tax as is
now proposed a virtual declaration that England is a
foreign country, and a renunciation on your part of the
principle of *common naturalisation*, which runs through
this whole empire?

Do you, or does any Irish gentleman, think it a
mean privilege that, the moment he sets his foot upon
this ground, he is to all intents and purposes an

Englishman ?   You will not be pleased with a law, which by its operation tends to disqualify you from a seat in this Parliament; and if your own virtue or fortune, or if that of your children, should carry you or them to it, should you like to be excluded from the possibility of a peerage in this kingdom ?   If in Ireland we lay it down as a maxim, that a residence in Great Britain is a political evil, and to be discouraged by penal taxes, you must necessarily reject all the privileges and benefits which are connected with such a residence.

I can easily conceive that a citizen of Dublin, who looks no farther than his counter, may think that Ireland will be repaid for such a loss by any small diminution of taxes, or any increase in the circulation of money, that may be laid out in the purchase of claret or groceries in his corporation.   In such a man an error of that kind, as it would be natural, would be excusable.   But I cannot think that any educated man, any man who looks with an enlightened eye on the interest of Ireland, can believe that it is not highly for the advantage of Ireland that this Parliament, which, whether right or wrong, whether we will or not, will make some laws to bind Ireland, should always have in it some persons, who, by connection, by property, or by early prepossessions and affections, are attached to the welfare of that country.   I am so clear upon this point, not only from the clear reason of the thing, but from the constant course of my observation, by now

having sat eight sessions in Parliament, that I declare
it to you, as my sincere opinion, that (if you must do
either the one or the other) it would be wiser by far,
and far better for Ireland, that some new privileges
should attend the estates of Irishmen, members of the
two Houses here, than that their characters should
be stained by penal impositions, and their properties
loaded by unequal and unheard-of modes of taxation.
I do really trust that, when the matter comes a little to
be considered, a majority of our gentlemen will never
consent to establish such a principle of disqualification
against themselves and their posterity, and, for the sake
of gratifying the schemes of a transitory Administration
of the Cockpit or the Castle, or in compliance with the
lightest part of the most vulgar and transient popularity,
fix so irreparable an injury on the permanent interest
of their country.

This law seems, therefore, to me to go directly
against the fundamental points of the legislative and
judicial constitution of these kingdoms, and against
the happy communion of their privileges. But there
is another matter in the tax proposed, that contradicts
as essentially a very great principle necessary for preserving the union of the various parts of a State ;
because it does, in effect, discountenance mutual intermarriage and inheritance—things that bind countries
more closely together than any laws or constitutions
whatsoever. Is it right that a woman who marries
into Ireland, and perhaps well purchases her jointure

or her dower there, should not after her husband's death have it in her choice to return to her country and her friends without being taxed for it ?

If an Irish heiress should marry into an English family, and that great property in both countries should thereby come to be united in this common issue, shall the descendant of that marriage abandon his natural connection, his family interests, his public and his private duties, and be compelled to take up his residence in Ireland ?   Is there any sense or any justice in it, unless you affirm that there should be no such intermarriage and no such mutual inheritance between the natives ?   Is there a shadow of reason that because a Lord Rockingham, a Duke of Devonshire, a Sir George Saville, possess property in Ireland, which has descended to them without any act of theirs, they should abandon their duty in Parliament, and spend the winters in Dublin ? or, having spent the Session in Westminster, must they abandon their seats and all their family interests in Yorkshire and Derbyshire, and pass the rest of the year in Wicklow, in Cork, or Tyrone ?

See what the consequence must be from a municipal legislature considering itself as an unconnected body, and attempting to enforce a partial residence.   A man may have property in more parts than two of this empire.   He may have property in Jamaica and in North America, as well as in England and Ireland.   I know some that have property in all of them.   What

shall we say to this case? After the poor distracted
citizen of the whole empire has, in compliance with
your partial law, removed his family, bid adieu to his
connections, and settled himself quietly and snug in a
pretty box by the Liffey, he hears that the Parliament
of Great Britain is of opinion that all English estates
ought to be spent in England, and that they will tax
him double if he does not return. Suppose him, then
(if the nature of the two laws will permit it), providing
a flying camp, and dividing his year as well as he can
between England and Ireland, and at the charge of
two town-houses and two country-houses in both
kingdoms; in this situation he receives an account
that a law is transmitted from Jamaica, and another
from Pennsylvania, to tax absentees from these provinces, which are impoverished by the European residence of the possessors of their lands. How is he to
escape this *ricochet* cross-firing of so many opposite
batteries of police and regulation? If he attempts to
comply, he is likely to be more a citizen of the
Atlantic Ocean and the Irish Sea than of any of these
countries. The matter is absurd and ridiculous; and
while ever the idea of mutual marriages, inheritances,
purchases, and privileges subsist, can never be carried
into execution with common sense or common justice.

I do not know how gentlemen of Ireland reconcile
such an idea to their own liberties, or to the natural
use and enjoyment of their estates. If any of their
children should be left in a minority, and a guardian

should think, as many do (it matters not whether
properly or no), that his ward had better be educated
in a school or university here than in Ireland, is he
sure that he can justify the bringing a tax of ten per
cent, perhaps twenty, on his pupil's estate, by giving
what, in his opinion, is the best education in general,
or the best for that pupil's particular character and
circumstances?   Can he justify his sending him to
travel—a necessary part of the higher style of education, and, notwithstanding what some narrow writers
have said, of great benefit to all countries, but very
particularly so to Ireland ?   Suppose a guardian, under
the authority or pretence of such a tax of police, had
prevented our dear friend, Lord Charlemont, from going
abroad, would he have lost no satisfaction ?   Would
his friends have lost nothing in the companion ?   Would
his country have lost nothing in the cultivated taste
with which he has adorned it in so many ways ?   His
natural elegance of mind would undoubtedly do a great
deal ; but I will venture to assert, without the danger
of being contradicted, that he adorns his present residence in Ireland much the more for having resided a
long time out of it.   Will Mr. Flood himself think he
ought to have been driven by taxes into Ireland, whilst
he prepared himself by an English education to understand and to defend the rights of the subject in Ireland,
or to support the dignity of Government there according as his opinions, or the situation of things, may lead
him to take either part upon respectable principles ?

I hope it is not forgot that an Irish Act of Parliament sends its youth to England for the study of the Law, and compels a residence in the Inns of Court here for some years. Will you send out with one breath and recall with another? This Act plainly provides for that intercourse which supposes the strictest union in laws and policy, in both which the intended tax supposes an entire separation.

It would be endless to go into all the inconveniences this tax will lead to in the conduct of private life and the use of property. How many infirm people are obliged to change their climate whose life depends upon that change? How many families straitened in their circumstances are there, who from the shame, sometimes from the utter impossibility otherwise of retrenching, are obliged to remove from their country in order to preserve their estates in their families? You begin, then, to burthen these people precisely at the time when their circumstances of health and fortune render them rather objects of relief and commiseration.

I know very well that a great proportion of the money of every subordinate country will flow towards the metropolis. This is unavoidable. Other inconveniences too will result to particular parts; and why? Why, because they are particular parts; each a member of a greater, and not a whole within itself. But those members are to consider whether these inconveniences are not fully balanced—perhaps more than balanced—by the united strength of a great and compact body. I am sensible, too, of a difficulty that will be started against the application of some of the principles which I reason upon to the case of Ireland. It will be said that Ireland, in many particulars, is not bound to consider itself as a part of the British body, because this country in many instances is mistaken enough to treat you as foreigners, and draws away your money by absentees without suffering you to enjoy your natural advantages in trade and commerce. No man living loves restrictive regulations of any kind less than myself; at best, nine times in ten, they are little better than laborious and vexatious follies. Often, as in your case, they are great oppressions as well as great absurdities. But still an injury is not always a reason for retaliation, nor is the folly of others with regard to us a reason for imitating it with regard to them. Before we attempt to retort we ought to consider whether we may not injure ourselves even more than our adversary, since, in the contest who shall go the greatest length in absurdity, the victor is generally the greatest sufferer. Besides, when there is an unfortunate emulation in restraints and oppressions, the question of *strength* is of the highest importance. It little becomes the feeble to be unjust. Justice is the shield of the weak, and when they choose to lay this down, and fight naked in the contest of mere power, the event will be what must be expected from such imprudence.

G

I ought to beg your pardon for running into this
length. You want no arguments to convince you on
this subject, and you want no resources of matter to
convince others. I ought, too, to ask pardon for having
delayed my answer so long, but I received your letter
on Tuesday in town, and I was obliged to come to
the country on business. From the country I write
at present, but this day I shall go to town again. I
shall see Lord Rockingham, who has spared neither
time nor trouble in making a vigorous opposition to
this inconsiderate measure. I hope to be able to send
you the papers, which will give you information of
the steps he has taken. He has pursued this business
with the foresight, diligence, and good sense with
which he generally resists unconstitutional attempts of
Government. A life of disinterestedness, generosity,
and public spirit, are his titles to have it believed that
the effect which the Tax may have upon his private
property is not the sole nor the principal motive to
his exertions. I know he is of opinion that the opposition in Ireland ought to be carried on with that
spirit, as if no aid was expected from this country; and
here, as if nothing would be done in Ireland, many
things have been lost by not acting in this manner.

I am told that you are not likely to be alone in
the generous stand you are to make against this unnatural monster of Court popularity. It is said Mr.
Hussey—who is so very considerable at present, and who
is everything in expectation—will give his assistance.

I rejoice to see (that very rare spectacle) a good mind, a great genius, and public activity united together, and united so early in life. By not running into every popular humour he may depend upon it the popularity of his character will wear the better.

> Non ponebat enim rumores ante salutem ;
> Ergo postque magisque viri nunc gloria claret.

Adieu, my dear sir. Give my best respects to Lady Bingham ; and believe me, with great truth and esteem,—Your most obedient and most humble Servant,

EDM. BURKE.

BEACONSFIELD, *30th October* 1773.

To Sir Chas. Bingham.

III.

A LETTER to the HONOURABLE CHARLES JAMES FOX.

MY DEAR CHARLES,

I AM on many accounts exceedingly pleased with
your journey to Ireland. I do not think it was possible to dispose better of the interval between this and
the meeting of Parliament. I told you as much in
the same general terms by the post. My opinion of
the infidelity of that conveyance hindered me from
being particular. I now sit down with malice prepense to kill you with a very long letter, and must
take my chance for some safe method of conveying
the dose. Before I say anything to you of the place
you are in, or the business of it—on which, by the
way, a great deal might be said—I will turn myself to
the concluding part of your letter from Chatsworth.

You are sensible that I do not differ from you in
many things, and most certainly I do not dissent from
the main of your doctrine concerning the heresy of
depending upon contingencies. You must recollect
how uniform my sentiments have been on that subject.

I have ever wished a settled plan of our own, founded
in the very essence of the American business, wholly
unconnected with the events of the war, and framed
in such a manner as to keep up our credit and maintain our system at home, in spite of anything which
may happen abroad.   I am now convinced, by a long
and somewhat vexatious experience, that such a plan
is absolutely impracticable.   I think with you that
some faults in the constitution of those whom we must
love and trust, are among the causes of this impractica-
bility; they are faults, too, that one can hardly wish
them perfectly cured of, as I am afraid they are intimately connected with honest, disinterested intentions,
plentiful fortunes, assured rank, and quiet homes.   A
great deal of activity and enterprise can scarcely ever
be expected from such men, unless some horrible
calamity is just over their heads, or unless they suffer
some gross personal insults from power, the resentment
of which may be as unquiet and stimulating a principle
in their minds as ambition is in those of a different
complexion.   To say the truth, I cannot greatly blame
them.   We live at a time when men are not repaid
in fame for what they sacrifice in interest or repose.

On the whole, when I consider of what discordant,
and particularly of what fleeting materials the Opposition has been all along composed, and at the same
time review what Lord Rockingham has done, with
that and with his own shattered constitution for these
last twelve years, I confess I am rather surprised that

he has done so much and persevered so long, than
that he has felt now and then some cold fits, and that
he grows somewhat languid and desponding at last.
I know that he and those who are much prevalent
with him—though they are not thought so much devoted
to popularity as others—do very much look to the
people; and more than I think is wise in them, who
do so little to guide and direct the public opinion.
Without this they act indeed; but they act as it were
from compulsion, and because it is impossible, in their
situation, to avoid taking some part. All this it is
impossible to change, and to no purpose to complain of.

As to that popular humour, which is the medium
we float in, if I can discern anything at all of its
present state, it is far worse than I have ever known,
or could ever imagine it. The faults of the people are
not popular vices—at least they are not such as grow
out of what we used to take to be the English temper
and character. The greatest number have a sort of a
heavy, lumpish acquiescence in Government, without
much respect or esteem for those that compose it. I
really cannot avoid making some very unpleasant
prognostics from this disposition of the people. I
think many of the symptoms must have struck you;
I will mention one or two that are to me very remarkable. You must know that at Bristol we grow,
as an election interest, and even as a party interest,
rather stronger than we were when I was chosen.
We have just now a majority in the corporation. In

this state of matters what, think you, have they done ?
They have voted their freedom to Lord Sandwich and
Lord Suffolk !—to the first at the very moment when
the American privateers were domineering in the Irish
Sea, and taking the Bristol traders in the Bristol
Channel ;—to the latter when his remonstrances on
the subject of captures were the jest of Paris and of
Europe.   This fine step was taken, it seems, in honour
of the zeal of these two profound statesmen in the
prosecution of John the Painter—so totally negligent
are they of everything essential, and so long and so
deeply affected with trash the most low and contemptible ; just as if they thought the merit of Sir John
Fielding was the most shining point in the character
of great ministers in the most critical of all times, and,
of all others, the most deeply interesting to the commercial world !   My best friends in the Corporation
had no other doubts on the occasion than whether it
did not belong to me, by right of my representative
capacity, to be the bearer of this auspicious compliment.   In addition to this, if it could receive any
addition, they now employ me to solicit as a favour of
no small magnitude, that after the example of New-
castle they may be suffered to arm vessels for their
own defence in the Channel.   Their memorial, under
the seal of Merchant's Hall, is now lying on the table
before me.   Not a soul has the least sensibility on
finding themselves now for the first time obliged to
act as if the community were dissolved, and after

enormous payments towards the common protection, each part was to defend itself as if it were a separate State.

I don't mention Bristol as if that were the part farthest gone in this mortification. Far from it; I know that there is rather a little more life in us than in any other place. In Liverpool they are literally almost ruined by this American War; but they love it as they suffer from it. In short, from whatever I see, and from whatever quarter I hear, I am convinced that everything that is not absolute stagnation is evidently a party spirit very adverse to our politics and to the principles from whence they arise. There are manifest marks of the resurrection of the Tory party. They no longer criticise, as all disengaged people in the world will, on the acts of Government; but they are silent under every evil, and hide and cover up every ministerial blunder and misfortune with the officious zeal of men who think they have a party of their own to support in power. The Tories do universally think their power and consequence involved in the success of this American business. The clergy are astonishingly warm in it; and what the Tories are when embodied and united with their natural head, the Crown, and animated by their clergy, no man knows better than yourself. As to the Whigs, I think them far from extinct. They are, what they always were (except by the able use of opportunities), by far the weakest party in this country. They have

not yet learned the application of their principles to
the present state of things ; and as to the dissenters,
the main effective part of the Whig strength, they are
—to use a favourite expression of our American cam-
paign style—" not all in force." They will do very
little, and, as far as I can discern, are rather intimidated than provoked at the denunciations of the Court
in the Archbishop of York's sermon. I thought that
sermon rather imprudent when I first saw it ; but it
seems to have done its business.

In this temper of the people I do not wholly wonder
that our Northern friends look a little towards events.
In war, particularly, I am afraid it must be so. There
is something so weighty and decisive in the events of
war, something that so completely overpowers the
imagination of the vulgar, that all counsels must, in a
great degree, be subordinate to and attendant on them.
I am sure it was so in the last war very eminently.
So that, on the whole, what with the temper of the
people, the temper of our own friends, and the domineering necessities of war, we must quietly give up all
ideas of any settled, preconcerted plan. We shall be
lucky enough, if, keeping ourselves attentive and alert,
we can contrive to profit of the occasions as they arise;
though I am sensible that those who are best provided
with a general scheme are fittest to take advantage of
all contingencies. However, to act with any people
with the least degree of comfort, I believe we must
contrive a little to assimilate to their character. We

must gravitate towards them, if we would keep in the same system, or expect that they should approach towards us.   They are indeed worthy of much concession and management.   I am quite convinced that they are the honestest public men that ever appeared in this country, and I am sure that they are the wisest by far of those who appear in it at present.   None of those who are continually complaining of them, but are themselves just as chargeable with all their faults, and have a decent stock of their own into the bargain. They (our friends) are, I admit, as you very truly represent them, but indifferently qualified for storming a citadel.   After all, God knows whether this citadel is to be stormed by them, or by anybody else, by the means they use, or by any means.   I know that as they are, abstractedly speaking, to blame, so there are those who cry out against them for it, not with a friendly complaint as we do, but with the bitterness of enemies.   But I know, too, that those who blame them for want of enterprise have shown no activity at all against the common enemy; all their skill and all their spirit have been shown only in weakening, dividing, and indeed destroying their allies.   What they are and what we are is now pretty evidently experienced; and it is certain that partly by our common faults, but much more by the difficulties of our situation, and some circumstances of unavoidable misfortune, we are in little better than a sort of *cul-de-sac*.   For my part, I do all I can to give ease to my mind in this strange

position. I remember, some years ago, when I was
pressing some points with great eagerness and anxiety,
and complaining with great vexation to the Duke of
Richmond of the little progress I make, he told me
kindly, and I believe very truly, that though he was
far from thinking so himself, other people could not be
persuaded I had not some latent private interest in
pushing these matters, which I urged with an earnestness so extreme, and so much approaching to passion.
He was certainly in the right. I am thoroughly resolved to give, both to myself and to my friends, less
vexation on these subjects than hitherto I have done;
—much less indeed.

If *you* should grow too earnest, you will be still
more inexcusable than I was. Your having entered
into affairs so much younger ought to make them too
familiar to you to be the cause of much agitation, and
you have much more before you for your work. Do
not be in haste. Lay your foundations deep in public
opinion. Though (as you are sensible) I have never
given you the least hint of advice about joining yourself in a declared connection with our Party, nor do I
now; yet as I love that Party very well, and am clear
that you are better able to serve them than any man I
know, I wish that things should be so kept as to leave
you mutually very open to one another in all changes
and contingencies; and I wish this the rather, because,
in order to be very great, as I am anxious that you
should be (always presuming that you are disposed to

make a good use of power), you will certainly want
some better support than merely that of the Crown.
For I much doubt whether, with all your parts, you
are the man formed for acquiring real interior favour
in this Court, or in any ; I therefore wish you a firm
ground in the country; and I do not know so firm
and so sound a bottom to build on as our Party.
Well, I have done with this matter ; and you think
I ought to have finished it long ago.   Now I turn to
Ireland.

Observe that I have not heard a word of any news
relative to it from thence or from London ; so that I
am only going to state to you my conjectures as to
facts, and to speculate again on these conjectures.   I
have a strong notion that the lateness of our meeting
is owing to the previous arrangements intended in
Ireland.   I suspect they mean that Ireland should
take a sort of lead, and act an efficient part in this
war, both with men and money.   It will sound well,
when we meet, to tell us of the active zeal and loyalty
of the people of Ireland, and contrast it with the
rebellious spirit of America.   It will be a popular
topic—the perfect confidence of Ireland in the power
of the British Parliament.   From thence they will
argue the little danger, which any dependency of the
Crown has to apprehend from the enforcement of that
authority.   It will be, too, somewhat flattering to the
country gentlemen, who might otherwise begin to be
sullen, to hold out that the burthen is not wholly to

rest upon them, and it will pique our pride to be told
that Ireland has cheerfully stepped forward ; and when
a dependant of this kingdom has already engaged
itself in another year's war, merely for our dignity,
how can we, who are Principals in the quarrel, hold
off ? This scheme of policy seems to me so very
obvious, and is likely to be of so much service to the
present system, that I cannot conceive it possible they
should neglect it, or something like it.   They have
already put the people of Ireland to the proof.   Have
they not born the Earl of Buckinghamshire ? the person
who was employed to move the fiery Committee in the
House of Lords, in order to stimulate the Ministry to
this war ; who was in the chair ; and who moved
the Resolutions.

It is within a few days of eleven years since I
was in Ireland, and then after an absence of two.
Those who have been absent from any scene for even
a much shorter time, generally lose the true practical
notion of the country, and of what may or may not be
done in it.   When I knew Ireland it was very different
from the state of England, where Government is a vast
deal, the Public something, but Individuals comparatively very little.   But if Ireland bears any resemblance to what it was some years ago, neither Government nor public opinion can do a great deal ; almost
the whole is in the hands of a few leading people.
The populace of Dublin, and some parts in the North,
are in some sort an exception.   But the Primate, Lord

Hillsborough, and Lord Hertford, have great sway in
the latter, and the former may be considerable or not,
pretty much as the Duke of Leinster pleases. On the
whole, the success of the Government usually depended
on the bargain made with a very few men. The resi-
dent Lieutenancy may have made some change, and
given a strength to Government which formerly, I
know, it had not; still, however, I am of opinion, the
former state, though in other hands perhaps, and in
another manner, still continues. The house you are
connected with is grown into a much greater degree of
power than it had, though it was very considerable at
the period I speak of. If the D. of L. takes a popular
part, he is sure of the city of Dublin, and he has a
young man attached to him, who stands very forward
in Parliament, and in profession, and, by what I hear,
with more goodwill and less envy than usually attends
so rapid a progress. The movement of one or two
principal men, if they manage the little popular strength
which is to be found in Dublin and Ulster, may do a
great deal—especially when money is to be saved and
taxes to be kept off. I confess I should despair of
your succeeding with any of them, if they cannot be
satisfied that every job which they can look for on
account of carrying this measure, would be just as sure
to them for their ordinary support of Government.
They are essential to Government, which at this time
must not be disturbed, and their neutrality will be
purchased at as high a price as their alliance, offen-

sive and defensive. Now, as by supporting they may
get as much as by betraying their country, it must be
a great leaning to turpitude that can make them take
a part in this war. I am satisfied that if the Duke of
Leinster and Lord Shannon could act together, this
business would not go on; or if either of them took
part with Ponsonby, it would have no better success.
Hutchinson's situation is much altered since I saw you.
To please Tisdall, he had been in a manner laid aside
at the Castle. It is now to be seen whether he prefers
the gratification of his resentment and his appetite for
popularity—both of which are strong enough in him—
to the advantages which his independence gives him of
making a new bargain and accumulating new offices on
his heap. Pray do not be asleep in this scene of action;
at this time, if I am right, the principal. The Protestants of Ireland will be, I think, in general backward; they form infinitely the greatest part of the landed
and the monied interests, and they will not like to pay.
The Papists are reduced to beasts of burthen; they will
give all they have—their shoulders—readily enough if
they are flattered. Surely the state of Ireland ought
for ever to teach parties moderation in their victories.
People crushed by law have no hopes but from power.
If laws are their enemies, they will be enemies to laws;
and those who have much to hope and nothing to lose
will always be dangerous, more or less. But this is
not our present business. If all this should prove a
dream, however, let it not hinder you from writing to

me and telling me so.　You will easily refute, in your conversation, the little topics which they will set afloat; such as, that Ireland is a boat and must go with the ship; that if the Americans contended only for their liberties it would be different; but since they have declared independence, and so forth.

You are happy in enjoying Townsend's company. Remember me to him.　How does he like his private situation in a country where he was the son of the sovereign ?　Mrs. Burke and the two Richards salute you cordially.

E. B.

BEACONSFIELD, *8th October* 1777.

IV.

TWO LETTERS from Mr. Burke, to Gentlemen in
the City of Bristol; on the Bills depending in
Parliament relative to the Trade of Ireland,
1778.[1]

*To Samuel Span, Esq., Master of the Society of
Merchants Adventurers of Bristol.*

Sir,

I am honoured with your letter of the 13th, in
answer to mine, which accompanied the resolutions of
the House relative to the trade of Ireland.

You will be so good as to present my best respects
to the Society, and to assure them, that it was alto-

---

[1] These were propositions introduced by Lord North for removing
certain restrictions on the trade of Ireland. They were at first well
received on both sides of the House, as being founded in justice, and a
liberal policy required by the circumstances of the time. Subsequently,
the jealousy of the English manufacturers and traders was so strongly
expressed, and so much influenced the conduct of many of the representatives of those interests in Parliament, that in the bill giving effect
to the propositions it was thought necessary, towards the end of the
session, to give up most of the advantages originally intended for
Ireland.

H

gether unnecessary to remind me of the interest of the constituents. I have never regarded anything else since I had a seat in Parliament. Having frequently and maturely considered that interest, and stated it to myself in almost every point of view, I am persuaded that, under the present circumstances, I cannot more effectually pursue it than by giving all the support in my power to the propositions which I lately transmitted to the hall.

The fault I find in the scheme is,—that it falls extremely short of that liberality in the commercial system, which, I trust, will one day be adopted. If I had not considered the present resolutions merely as preparatory to better things, and as a means of showing, experimentally, that justice to others is not always folly to ourselves, I should have contented myself with receiving them in a cold and silent acquiescence. Separately considered, they are matters of no very great importance. But they aim, however imperfectly, at a right principle. I submit to the restraint to appease prejudice; I accept the enlargement, so far as it goes, as the result of reason and of sound policy.

We cannot be insensible of the calamities which have been brought upon this nation by an obstinate adherence to narrow and restrictive plans of government. I confess, I cannot prevail on myself to take them up precisely at a time when the most decisive experience has taught the rest of the world to lay them down. The propositions in question did not originate from me, or from my particular friends. But when things are so right in themselves, I hold it my duty not to inquire from what hands they come. I opposed the American measures upon the very same principle on which I support those that relate to Ireland. I was convinced that the evils which have arisen from the adoption of the former would be infinitely aggravated by the rejection of the latter.

Perhaps gentlemen are not yet fully aware of the situation of their country, and what its exigencies absolutely require. I find that we are still disposed to talk at our ease, and as if all things were to be regulated by our good pleasure. I should consider it as a fatal symptom, if, in our present distressed and adverse circumstances, we should persist in the errors which are natural only to prosperity. One cannot indeed sufficiently lament the continuance of that spirit of delusion by which, for a long time past, we have thought fit to measure our necessities by our inclinations. Moderation, prudence, and equity are far more suitable to our condition than loftiness, and confidence, and rigour. We are threatened by enemies of no small magnitude, whom, if we think fit, we may despise, as we have despised others; but they are enemies who can only cease to be truly formidable by our entertaining a due respect for their power. Our danger will not be lessened by our shutting our eyes to it; nor will our force abroad be increased by rendering ourselves feeble and divided at home.

There is a dreadful schism in the British nation. Since we are not able to re-unite the empire, it is our business to give all possible vigour and soundness to those parts of it which are still content to be governed by our councils. Sir, it is proper to inform you that our measures *must be healing*. Such a degree of strength must be communicated to all the members of the State, as may enable them to defend themselves and to co-operate in the defence of the whole. Their temper, too, must be managed, and their good affections cultivated. They may then be disposed to bear the load with cheerfulness, as a contribution towards what may be called with truth and propriety, and not by an empty form of words, *a common cause*. Too little dependence cannot be had, at this time of day, on names and prejudices. The eyes of mankind are opened; and communities must be held together by an evident and solid interest. God forbid that our conduct should demonstrate to the world that Great Britain can, in no instance whatsoever, be brought to a sense of rational and equitable policy, but by coercion and force of arms.

I wish you to recollect with what powers of concession, relatively to commerce, as well as to legislation, His Majesty's Commissioners to the united colonies have sailed from England within this week. Whether these powers are sufficient for their purposes, it is not now my business to examine. But we all know that our resolutions in favour of Ireland are trifling and

insignificant when compared with the concessions to
the Americans. At such a juncture I would implore
every man who retains the least spark of regard to
the yet remaining honour and security of this country
not to compel others to an imitation of their conduct,
or by passion and violence to force them to seek, in
the territories of the separation, that freedom, and
those advantages which they are not to look for whilst
they remain under the wings of their ancient Government.

After all, what are the matters we dispute with so
much warmth ? Do we in these resolutions *bestow*
anything upon Ireland ? Not a shilling. We only
consent to *leave* to them, in two or three instances, the
use of the natural faculties which God has given to
them and to all mankind. Is Ireland united to the
Crown of Great Britain for no other purpose than that
we should counteract the bounty of Providence in her
favour ?—and in proportion as that bounty has been
liberal that we are to regard it as an evil, which is
to be met with in every sort of corrective ? To say
that Ireland interferes with us, and therefore must be
checked, is, in my opinion, a very mistaken and a very
dangerous principle. I must beg leave to repeat what
I took the liberty of suggesting to you in my last
letter, that Ireland is a country in the same climate
and of the same natural qualities and productions with
this, and has consequently no other means of growing
wealthy in herself, or, in other words, of being useful

to us, but by doing the very same things which we do, for the same purposes. I hope that in Great Britain we shall always pursue, without exception, *every* means of prosperity ; and of course, that Ireland *will* interfere with us in something or other ; for either, in order to *limit* her, we *must restrain* ourselves, or we must fall into that shocking conclusion, that we are to keep our yet remaining dependency, under a general and indiscriminate restraint, for the mere purpose of oppression. Indeed, sir, England and Ireland may flourish together. The world is large enough for us both. Let it be our care not to make ourselves too little for it.

I know it is said that the people of Ireland do not pay the same taxes, and therefore ought not in equity to enjoy the same benefits with this. I had hopes that the unhappy phantom of a compulsory *equal taxation* had haunted us long enough. I do assure you, that until it is entirely banished from our imaginations (where alone it has, or can have any existence), we shall never cease to do ourselves the most substantial injuries. To that argument of equal taxation I can only say that Ireland pays as many taxes as those who are the best judges of her powers are of opinion she can bear. To bear more she must have more ability ; and, in the order of nature, the advantage must *precede* the charge. This disposition of things being the law of God, neither you nor I *can* alter it. So that if you will have more help from Ireland you

must *previously* supply her with more means. I believe it will be found that if men are suffered freely to
cultivate their natural advantages, a virtual equality
of contribution will come in its own time, and will
flow by an easy descent through its own proper and
natural channels. An attempt to disturb that course,
and to force nature, will only bring on universal discontent, distress, and confusion.

You tell me, sir, that you prefer a union with
Ireland to the little regulations which are proposed in
Parliament. This union is a great question of State,
to which, when it comes properly before me in my
parliamentary capacity, I shall give an honest and
unprejudiced consideration. However, it is a settled
rule with me, to make the most of my *actual situation ;*
and not to refuse to do a proper thing because there is
something else more proper, which I am not able to
do. This union is a business of difficulty, and, on
the principles of your letter, a business impracticable.
Until it can be matured into a feasible and desirable
scheme, I wish to have as close a union of interest
and affection with Ireland as I can have ; and that, I
am sure, is a far better thing than any nominal
union of government.

France, and indeed most extensive empires which,
by various designs and fortunes, have grown into one
great mass, contain many provinces that are very different from each other in privileges and modes of
government ; and they raise their supplies in different

ways, in different proportions, and under different
authorities; yet none of them are for this reason curtailed of their natural rights; but they carry on trade
and manufactures with perfect equality. In some
way or other the true balance is found, and all of
them are poised and harmonised. How much have
you lost by the participation of Scotland in all your
commerce? The external trade of England has more
than doubled since that period; and I believe your
internal (which is the most advantageous) has been
augmented at least fourfold. Such virtue there is in
liberality of sentiment, that you have grown richer
even by the partnership of poverty.

If you think that this participation was a loss,
commercially considered, but that it has been com-
pensated by the share which Scotland has taken in
defraying the public charge—I believe you have
not very carefully looked at the public accounts.
Ireland, sir, pays a great deal more than Scotland;
and is perhaps as much and as effectually united to
England as Scotland is. But if Scotland, instead of
paying little, had paid nothing at all, we should be
gainers, not losers, by acquiring the hearty co-operation
of an active, intelligent people, towards the increase of
the common stock; instead of our being employed in
watching and counteracting them, and their being employed in watching and counteracting us, with the
peevish and churlish jealousy of rivals and enemies on
both sides.

I am sure, sir, that the commercial experience of
the merchants of Bristol will soon disabuse them of
the prejudice, that they can trade no longer, if countries
more lightly taxed are permitted to deal in the same
commodities at the same markets.   You know that,
in fact, you trade very largely where you are met by
the goods of all nations.   You even pay high duties
on the import of your goods, and afterwards undersell
nations less taxed at their own markets; and where
goods of the same kind are not charged at all.   If it
were otherwise you could trade very little.   You know
that the price of all sorts of manufacture is not a great
deal enhanced (except to the domestic consumer) by
any taxes paid in this country.   This I might very
easily prove.

The same consideration will relieve you from the
apprehension you express with relation to sugars, and
the difference of the duties paid here and in Ireland.
Those duties affect the interior consumer only; and
for obvious reasons, relative to the interest of revenue
itself, they must be proportioned to his ability of payments; but in all cases in which sugar can be an
object of commerce, and therefore (in this view) of rival-
ship, you are sensible that you are at least on a par
with Ireland.   As to your apprehensions concerning
the more advantageous situation of Ireland, for some
branches of commerce (for it is so but for some), I
trust you will not find them more serious.   Milford
Haven, which is at your door, may serve to show you

that the mere advantage of ports is not the thing which shifts the seat of commerce from one part of the world to the other.   If I thought you inclined to take up this matter on local considerations, I should state to you that I do not know any part of the kingdom so well situated for an advantageous commerce with Ireland as Bristol; and that none would be so likely to profit of its prosperity as our city. But your profit and theirs must concur.   Beggary and bankruptcy are not the circumstances which invite to an intercourse with that or with any country; and I believe it will be found invariably true that the superfluities of a rich nation furnish a better object of trade than the necessities of a poor one.   It is the interest of the commercial world that wealth should be found everywhere.

The true ground of fear in my opinion is this, that Ireland, from the vicious system of its internal polity, will be a long time before it can derive any benefit from the liberty now granted, or from anything else. But, as I do not vote advantages in hopes that they may not be enjoyed, I will not lay any stress upon this consideration.   I rather wish that the Parliament of Ireland may, in its own wisdom, remove these impediments and put their country in a condition to avail itself of its natural advantages.   If they do not, the fault is with them and not with us.

I have written this long letter in order to give all possible satisfaction to my constituents with regard to the part I have taken in this affair. It gave me inexpressible concern to find that my conduct had been a cause of uneasiness to any of them. Next to my honour and conscience, I have nothing so near and dear to me as their approbation. However, I had much rather run the risk of displeasing than of injuring them—if I am driven to make such an option. You obligingly lament that you are not to have me for your advocate; but if I had been capable of acting as an advocate in opposition to a plan so perfectly consonant to my known principles and to the opinions I had publicly declared on a hundred occasions, I should only disgrace myself without supporting, with the smallest degree of credit or effect, the cause you wished me to undertake. I should have lost the only thing which can make such abilities as mine of any use to the world now or hereafter—I mean that authority which is derived from an opinion that a member speaks the language of truth and sincerity, and that he is not ready to take up or lay down a great political system for the convenience of the hour; that he is in Parliament to support his opinion of the public good, and does not form his opinion in order to get into Parliament or to continue in it. It is in a great measure for your sake that I wish to preserve this character. Without it I am sure I should be ill able to discharge, by any service, the smallest part of that debt of gratitude and affection which I owe you for the great and honourable trust you have reposed in me.—I am, with the highest regard and esteem, sir, your most obedient and humble servant,

E. B.

BEACONSFIELD,
    23d April 1778.

To Messrs. —— and Co., Bristol.

GENTLEMEN,

IT gives me the most sensible concern to find that my vote on the resolutions relative to the trade of Ireland has not been fortunate enough to meet with your approbation. I have explained at large the grounds of my conduct on that occasion in my letters to the Merchants Hall; but my very sincere regard and esteem for you will not permit me to let the matter pass without an explanation which is particular to yourselves, and which, I hope, will prove satisfactory to you.

You tell me that the conduct of your late member is not much wondered at; but you seem to be at a loss to account for mine; and you lament that I have taken so decided a part *against* my constituents.

This is rather a heavy imputation. Does it then really appear to you that the propositions to which you refer are, on the face of them, so manifestly wrong, and so certainly injurious to the trade and manufactures of Great Britain—and particularly to yours—that no man could think of proposing or supporting

them, except from resentment to you, or from some
other oblique motive? If you suppose your late
member, or if you suppose me, to act upon other
reasons than we choose to avow, to what do you
attribute the conduct of the *other* members, who in
the beginning almost unanimously adopted those
resolutions? To what do you attribute the strong
part taken by the ministers, and along with the ministers, by several of their most declared opponents?
This does not indicate a ministerial job, a party
design, or a provincial or local purpose. It is therefore not so absolutely clear that the measure is
wrong, or likely to be injurious to the true interests
of any place, or any person.

The reason, gentlemen, for taking this step at this
time is but too obvious and too urgent. I cannot
imagine that you forget the great war which has been
carried on with so little success (and, as I thought,
with so little policy) in America; or that you are not
aware of the other great wars which are impending.
Ireland has been called upon to repel the attacks of
enemies of no small power, brought upon her by
councils in which she has had no share. The very
purpose and declared object of that original war, which
has brought other wars and other enemies on Ireland,
was not very flattering to her dignity, her interest, or
to the very principle of her liberty. Yet she submitted patiently to the evils she suffered from an

attempt to subdue to *your* obedience, countries whose
very commerce was not open to her.   America was to
be conquered in order that Ireland should *not* trade
thither, whilst the miserable trade which she is permitted to carry on to other places has been torn to
pieces in the struggle.   In this situation, are we
neither to suffer her to have any real interest in our
quarrel, or to be flattered with the hope of any future
means of bearing the burdens which she is to incur
in defending herself against enemies which we have
brought upon her?

I cannot set my face against such arguments.   Is it
quite fair to suppose that I have no other motive for
yielding to them but a desire of acting *against* my
constituents?   It is for *you*, and for *your* interest, as
a dear, cherished, and respected part of a valuable
whole, that I have taken my share in this question.
You do not, you cannot suffer by it.   If honesty be
true policy with regard to the transient interest of
individuals, it is much more certainly so with regard
to the permanent interest of communities.   I know
that it is but too natural for us to see our own *certain*
ruin in the *possible* prosperity of other people.   It is
hard to persuade us that everything which is *got* by
another is not *taken* from ourselves.   But it is fit that
we should get the better of these suggestions, which
come from what is not the best and soundest part of
our nature, and that we should form to ourselves a way

of thinking more rational, more just, and more religious.   Trade is not a limited thing; as if the objects
of mutual demand and consumption could not stretch
beyond the bounds of our jealousies.   God has given
the earth to the children of men, and He has undoubtedly, in giving it to them, given them what
is abundantly sufficient for all their exigencies—not a
scanty, but a most liberal provision for them all.   The
Author of our nature has written it strongly in that
nature, and has promulgated the same law in His
written word, that man shall eat his bread by his
labour; and I am persuaded that no man, and no
combination of men, for their own ideas or their particular profit, can, without great impiety, undertake to
say that he *shall not* do so; that they have no sort of
right either to prevent the labour, or to withhold the
bread.   Ireland having received no *compensation*,
directly or indirectly, for any restraints on their trade,
ought not, in justice or common honesty, to be made
subject to such restraints.   I do not mean to impeach
the right of the Parliament of Great Britain to make
laws for the trade of Ireland.   I only speak of what
laws it is right for Parliament to make.

It is nothing to an oppressed people to say that in
part they are protected at our charge.   The military
force which shall be kept up in order to cramp the
natural faculties of a people, and to prevent their
arrival to their utmost prosperity, is the instrument of

their servitude, not the means of their protection. To protect men, is to forward, and not to restrain, their improvement. Else what is it more than to avow to them and to the world that you guard them from others only to make them a prey to yourself ? This fundamental nature of protection does not belong to free, but to all governments ; and is as valid in Turkey as in Great Britain. No government ought to own that it exists for the purpose of checking the prosperity of its people, or that there is such a principle involved in its policy.

Under the impression of these sentiments (and not as wanting every attention to my constituents which affection and gratitude could inspire), I voted for these bills which give you so much trouble. I voted for them, not as doing complete justice to Ireland, but as being something less unjust than the general prohibition which has hitherto prevailed. I hear some discourse as if in one or two paltry duties on materials Ireland had a preference ; and that those who set themselves against this act of scanty justice assert that they are only contending for an *equality*. What equality ? Do they forget that the whole woollen manufacture of Ireland, the most extensive and profitable of any, and the natural staple of that kingdom, has been in a manner so destroyed by restrictive laws of ours, and (at our persuasion, and on our promises) by restrictive laws of *their own*, that in a few years, it is probable, they will not be able to wear a coat of their own fabric ?   Is this equality ?   Do gentlemen forget that the understood faith upon which they were persuaded to such an unnatural act has not been kept, and that a linen-manufacture has been set up and highly encouraged against them ?   Is this equality ? Do they forget the state of the trade of Ireland in beer —so great an article of consumption—and which now stands in so mischievous a position with regard to their revenue, their manufacture, and their agriculture ?   Do they find any equality in all this ?   Yet, if the least step is taken towards doing them common justice in the slightest article for the most limited markets, a cry is raised as if we were going to be ruined by partiality to Ireland.

Gentlemen, I know that the deficiency in these arguments is made up (not by you, but by others) by the usual resource on such occasions—the confidence in military force and superior power.   But that ground of confidence, which at no time was perfectly just, or the avowal of it tolerably decent, is at this time very unseasonable.   Late experience has shown that it cannot be altogether relied upon ; and many, if not all of our present difficulties, have arisen from putting our trust in what may very possibly fail, and if it should fail, leaves those who are hurt by such a reli- ance without pity.   Whereas honesty and justice, reason and equity, go a very great way in securing prosperity to those who use them ; and, in case of

I

failure, secure the best retreat, and the most honourable consolations.

It is very unfortunate that we should consider those as rivals whom we ought to regard as fellow-labourers in a common cause. Ireland has never made a single step in its progress towards prosperity by which you have not had a share, and perhaps the greatest share, in the benefit. That progress has been chiefly owing to her own natural advantages and her own efforts, which, after a long time, and by slow degrees, have prevailed in some measure over the mischievous systems which have been adopted. Far enough she is still from having arrived even at an ordinary state of perfection, and if our jealousies were to be converted into politics as systematically as some would have them, the trade of Ireland would vanish out of the system of commerce. But, believe me, if Ireland is beneficial to you, it is so not from the parts in which it is restrained, but from those in which it is left free, though not left unrivalled. The greater its freedom the greater must be your advantage. If you should lose in one way, you will gain in twenty.

Whilst I remain under this unalterable and powerful conviction, you will not wonder at the *decided* part I take. It is my custom so to do when I see my way clearly before me, and when I know that I am not misled by any passion or any personal interest, as in this case I am very sure I am not. I find that disagreeable things are circulated among my constituents, and I wish my sentiments, which form my justification, may be equally general with the circulation against me. I have the honour to be, with the greatest regard and esteem, Gentlemen, your most obedient and humble servant,   E. B.

WESTMINSTER, *May* 2, 1778.

V

Mr. BURKE'S SPEECH at the Guildhall, in Bristol, previous to the late Election in that City, upon Certain Points Relative to his Parliamentary Conduct. 1780.

Mr. Mayor and Gentlemen,

I am extremely pleased at the appearance of this large and respectable meeting. The steps I may be obliged to take will want the sanction of a considerable authority; and in explaining any thing which may appear doubtful in my public conduct, I must naturally desire a very full audience.

I have been backward to begin my canvass. The dissolution of the Parliament was uncertain; and it did not become me, by an unseasonable importunity, to appear diffident of the fact of my six years' endeavours to please you. I have served the city of Bristol honourably; and the city of Bristol had no reason to think that the means of honourable service to the public were become indifferent to me.

I found on my arrival here that three gentlemen had been long in eager pursuit of an object which but two of us can obtain. I found that they had all met with encouragement. A contested election, in such a city as this, is no light thing. I paused on the brink of the precipice. These three gentlemen, by various merits and on various titles, I made no doubt were worthy of your favour. I shall never attempt to raise myself by depreciating the merits of my competitors. In the complexity and confusion of these cross pursuits, I wished to take the authentic public sense of my friends upon a business of so much delicacy. I wished to take your opinion along with me ; that if I should give up the contest at the very beginning, my sur-render of my post may not seem the effect of incon-stancy, or timidity, or anger, or disgust, or indolence, or any other temper unbecoming a man who has engaged in the public service. If, on the contrary, I should undertake the election, and fail of success, I was full as anxious that it should be manifest to the whole world, that the peace of the city had not been broken by my rashness, presumption, or fond conceit of my own merit.

I am not come by a false and counterfeit show of deference to your judgment, to seduce it in my favour. I ask it seriously and unaffectedly. If you wish that I should retire, I shall not consider that advice as a censure upon my conduct, or an alteration in your sentiments, but as a rational submission to the circumstances of affairs. If, on the contrary, you should think it proper for me to proceed on my

canvass, if you will risk the trouble on your part,
I will risk it on mine. My pretensions are such as
you cannot be ashamed of, whether they succeed or
fail.

If you call upon me, I shall solicit the favour of
the city upon manly ground. I come before you with
the plain confidence of an honest servant in the equity
of a candid and discerning master. I come to claim
your approbation,—not to amuse you with vain apologies,
or with professions still more vain and senseless. I
have lived too long to be served by apologies, or to
stand in need of them. The part I have acted has
been in open day ; and to hold out to a conduct
which stands in that clear and steady light for all its
good and all its evil,—to hold out to that conduct the
paltry winking tapers of excuses and promises—I
never will do it. They may obscure it with their
smoke ; but they never can illumine sunshine by
such a flame as theirs.

I am sensible that no endeavours have been left
untried to injure me in your opinion. But the use of
character is to be a shield against calumny. I could
wish, undoubtedly (if idle wishes were not the most
idle of all things), to make every part of my conduct
agreeable to every one of my constituents. But in so
great a city, and so greatly divided as this, it is weak
to expect it.

In such a discordancy of sentiments, it is better to
look to the nature of things than to the humours of

men.   The very attempt towards pleasing everybody
discovers a temper always flashy, and often false and
insincere.   Therefore, as I have proceeded straight
onward in my conduct, so I will proceed in my
account of those parts of it which have been most
excepted to.   But I must first beg leave just to hint
to you that we may suffer very great detriment by
being open to every talker.   It is not to be imagined
how much of service is lost from spirits full of
activity and full of energy, who are pressing, who
are rushing forward, to great and capital objects, when
you oblige them to be continually looking back.
Whilst they are defending one service, they defraud
you of a hundred.   Applaud us when we run ; con-
sole us when we fall ; cheer us when we recover ; but
let us pass on—for God's sake, let us pass on.

Do you think, gentlemen, that every public act in
the six years since I stood in this place before you—
that all the arduous things which have been done
in this eventful period, which has crowded into a few
years' space the revolutions of an age, can be opened
to you on their fair grounds in half an hour's conversation.

But it is no reason, because there is a bad mode
of inquiry, that there should be no examination at
all.   Most certainly it is our duty to examine ; it
is our interest too.   But it must be with discretion ;
with an attention to all the circumstances, and to all
the motives : like sound judges, and not like cavilling

pettifoggers and quibbling pleaders, prying into flaws and hunting for exceptions. Look, gentlemen, to the *whole tenor* of your member's conduct. Try whether his ambition or his avarice have justled him out of the straight line of duty ; or whether that grand foe of the offices of active life, that master-vice in men of business, a degenerate and inglorious sloth, has made him flag and languish in his course ? This is the object of our inquiry. If our member's conduct can bear this touch, mark it for sterling. He may have fallen into errors ; he must have faults ; but our error is greater, and our fault is radically ruinous to ourselves, if we do not bear, if we do not even applaud, the whole compound and mixed mass of such a character. Not to act thus is folly ; I had almost said it is impiety. He censures God, who quarrels with the imperfections of man.

Gentlemen, we must not be peevish with those who serve the people. For none will serve us whilst there is a court to serve, but those who are of a nice and jealous honour. They who think everything, in comparison of that honour, to be dust and ashes, will not bear to have it soiled and impaired by those for whose sake they make a thousand sacrifices to preserve it immaculate and whole. We shall either drive such men from the public stage, or we shall send them to the court for protection : where, if they must sacrifice their reputation, they will at least secure their interest. Depend upon it, that the lovers of freedom will be free.

None will violate their conscience to please us, in order afterwards to discharge that conscience, which have violated, by doing us faithful and affectionate service. If we degrade and deprave their minds by servility, it will be absurd to expect that they who are creeping and abject towards us, will ever be bold and incorruptible assertors of our freedom, against the most seducing and the most formidable of all powers. No! human nature is not so formed; nor shall we improve the faculties or better the morals of public men by our possession of the most infallible receipt in the world for making cheats and hypocrites.

Let me say with plainness, I who am no longer in a public character, that if by a fair, by an indulgent, by a gentlemanly behaviour to our representatives, we do not give confidence to their minds and a liberal scope to their understandings ; if we do not permit our members to act upon a *very* enlarged view of things ; we shall at length infallibly degrade our national representation into a confused and scuffling bustle of local agency. When the popular member is narrowed in his ideas and rendered timid in his proceedings, the service of the crown will be the sole nursery of statesmen. Among the frolics of the court it may at length take that of attending to its business. Then the monopoly of mental power will be added to the power of all other kinds it possesses. On the side of the people there will be nothing but impotence : for ignorance is impotence ; narrowness of mind is impotence ;

timidity is itself impotence, and makes all other qualities that go along with it, impotent and useless.

At present it is the plan of the court to make its servants insignificant. If the people should fall into the same humour, and should choose their servants on the same principles of mere obsequiousness, and flexibility, and total vacancy or indifference of opinion in all public matters, then no part of the State will be sound; and it will be in vain to think of saving it.

I thought it very expedient at this time to give you this candid counsel; and with this counsel I would willingly close, if the matters which at various times have been objected to me in this city concerned only myself and my own election. These charges I think, are four in number;—my neglect of a due attention to my constituents, the not paying more frequent visits here;—my conduct on the affairs of the first Irish trade acts;—my opinion and mode of proceeding on Lord Beauchamp's debtors bills;—and my votes on the late affairs of the Roman Catholics. All of these (except perhaps the first) relate to matters of very considerable public concern; and it is not lest you should censure me improperly, but lest you should form improper opinions on matters of some moment to you, that I trouble you at all upon the subject. My conduct is of small importance.

With regard to the first charge, my friends have spoken to me of it in the style of amicable expostulation; not so much blaming the thing, as lamenting the effects. Others, less partial to me, were less kind in

assigning the motives. I admit there is a decorum
and propriety in a member of Parliament's paying a
respectful court to his constituents. If I were conscious to myself that pleasure or dissipation, or low
unworthy occupations, had detained me from personal
attendance on you, I would readily admit my fault
and quietly submit to the penalty. But, gentlemen, I
live at a hundred miles distance from Bristol ; and
at the end of a session I come to my own house,
fatigued in body and in mind, to a little repose, and
to a very little attention to my family and my private
concerns. A visit to Bristol is always a sort of
canvass ; else it will do more harm than good. To
pass from the toils of a session to the toils of a canvass, is the farthest thing in the world from repose.
I could hardly serve you *as I have done*, and court you
too. Most of you have heard that I do not very
remarkably spare myself in *public* business ; and in
the *private* business of my constituents I have done
very nearly as much as those who have nothing else
to do. My canvass of you was not on the 'change, nor
in the county meetings, nor in the clubs of this city :
It was in the House of Commons ; it was at the
Custom-house ; it was at the Council ; it was at the
Treasury ; it was at the Admiralty. I canvassed you
through your affairs, and not your persons. I was not
only your representative as a body ; I was the agent,
the solicitor of individuals ; I ran about wherever your
affairs could call me ; and in acting for you I often

appeared rather as a ship broker, than as a Member of Parliament. There was nothing too laborious, or too low for me to undertake. The meanness of the business was raised by the dignity of the object. If some lesser matters have slipped through my fingers it was because I filled my hands too full; and, in my eagerness to serve you, took in more than any hands could grasp. Several gentlemen stand round me who are my willing witnesses; and there are others who, if they were here, would be still better; because they would be unwilling witnesses to the same truth. It was in the middle of a summer residence in London, and in the middle of a negotiation at the Admiralty for your trade, that I was called to Bristol; and this late visit, at this late day, has been possibly in prejudice to your affairs.

Since I have touched upon this matter, let me say, gentlemen, that if I had a disposition, or a right to complain, I have some cause of complaint on my side. With a petition of this city in my hand, passed through the corporation without a dissenting voice—a petition in unison with almost the whole voice of the kingdom (with whose formal thanks I was covered over)—while I laboured on no less than five bills for a public reform, and fought against the opposition, of great abilities and of the greatest power, every clause and every word of the largest of those bills, almost to the very last day of a very long session;—all this time a canvass in Bristol was as calmly carried on as if I

were dead.   I was considered as a man wholly out of
the question.   Whilst I watched, and fasted, and
sweated in the House of Commons—by the most easy
and ordinary arts of election, by dinners and visits, by
" How do you do's," and " My worthy friends," I was
to be quietly moved out of my seat—and promises
were made, and engagements entered into, without any
exception or reserve, as if my laborious zeal in my
duty had been a regular abdication of my trust.

To open my whole heart to you on this subject, I
do confess, however, that there were other times
besides the two years in which I did visit you when I
was not wholly without leisure for repeating that mark
of my respect.   But I could not bring my mind to see
you.   You remember that, in the beginning of this
American war (that era of calamity, disgrace, and
downfall, an era which no feeling mind will ever
mention without a tear for England), you were greatly
divided ; and a very strong body, if not the strongest,
opposed itself to the madness which every art and
every power were employed to render popular in order
that the errors of the rulers might be lost in the
general blindness of the nation.   This opposition continued until after our great but most unfortunate
victory at Long Island.   Then all the mounds and
banks of our constancy were borne down at once ; and
the frenzy of the American war broke in upon us
like a deluge.   This victory, which seemed to put an
immediate end to all difficulties, perfected us in that

spirit of domination which our unparalleled prosperity
had but too long nurtured. We had been so very
powerful and so very prosperous, that even the humblest
of us were degraded into the vices and follies of kings.
We lost all measure between means and ends ; and
our headlong desires became our politics and our
morals. All men who wished for peace, or retained
any sentiments of moderation, were overborne or
silenced ; and this city was led by every artifice (and
probably with the more management because I was
one of your members) to distinguish itself by its zeal
for that fatal cause. In this temper of your and of
my mind, I should have sooner fled to the extremities
of the earth than have shown myself here. I, who
saw in every American victory (for you have had a
long series of these misfortunes) the germ and seed of
the naval power of France and Spain, which all our
heat and warmth against America was only hatching
into life,—I should not have been a welcome visitant
with the brow and the language of such feelings.
When, afterwards, the other face of your calamity was
turned upon you, and showed itself in defeat and
distress, I shunned you full as much. I felt sorely
this variety in our wretchedness ; and I did not wish
to have the least appearance of insulting you with that
show of superiority which, though it may not be
assumed, is generally suspected in a time of calamity,
from those whose previous warnings have been despised. I could not bear to show you a representative

whose face did not reflect that of his constituents ; a
face that could not joy in your joys and sorrow in
your sorrows.   But time at length has made us all of
one opinion ; and we have all opened our eyes on the
true nature of the American war, to the true nature of
all its successes and all its failures.

In that public storm too I had my private feelings.   I had seen blown down and prostrate on the
ground several of those houses to whom I was chiefly
indebted for the honour this city has done me.   I
confess that, whilst the wounds of those I loved were
yet green, I could not bear to show myself in pride
and triumph in that place into which their partiality
had brought me, and to appear at feasts and rejoicings
in the midst of the grief and calamity of my warm
friends, my zealous supporters, my generous bene-
factors.   This is a true, unvarnished, undisguised state
of the affair.   You will judge of it.

This is the only one of the charges in which I
am personally concerned.   As to the other matters
objected against me, which in their turn I shall
mention to you, remember once more I do not mean
to extenuate or excuse.   Why should I, when the
things charged are among those upon which I found
all my reputation ?   What would be left to me, if I
myself was the man, who softened, and blended, and
diluted, and weakened, all the distinguishing colours
of my life, so as to leave nothing distinct and determinate in my whole conduct ?

It has been said, and it is the second charge, that
in the questions of the Irish trade I did not consult
the interest of my constituents; or, to speak out
strongly, that I rather acted as a native of Ireland
than as an English member of Parliament.

I certainly have very warm good wishes for the
place of my birth.   But the sphere of my duties is
my true country.   It was, as a man attached to your
interests, and zealous for the conservation of your
power and dignity, that I acted on that occasion, and
on all occasions.   You were involved in the American
war.   A new world of policy was opened, to which it
was necessary we should conform, whether we would
or not; and my only thought was how to conform to
our situation in such a manner as to unite to this
kingdom, in prosperity and in affection, whatever
remained of the empire.   I was true to my old, standing, invariable principle, that all things which came
from Great Britain should issue as a gift of her
bounty and beneficence, rather than as claims recovered against a struggling litigant; or, at least, that if
your beneficence obtained no credit in your concessions, yet that they should appear the salutary
provisions of your wisdom and foresight; not as
things wrung from you with your blood by the cruel
gripe of a rigid necessity.   The first concessions, by
being (much against my will) mangled and stripped of
the parts which were necessary to make out their just
correspondence and connection in trade, were of no

use. The next year a feeble attempt was made to bring the thing into better shape. This attempt (countenanced by the minister) on the very first appearance of some popular uneasiness, was, after a considerable progress through the House, thrown out by *him*.[1]

What was the consequence? The whole kingdom of Ireland was instantly in a flame. Threatened by foreigners, and, as they thought, insulted by England, they resolved at once to resist the power of France, and to cast off yours. As for us, we were able neither to protect nor to restrain them. Forty thousand men were raised and disciplined without commission from the Crown. Two illegal armies were seen with banners displayed at the same time and in the same country. No executive magistrate, no judicature in Ireland would acknowledge the legality of the army which bore the king's commission; and no law, or appearance of law, authorised the army commissioned by itself. In this unexampled state of things, which the least error, the least trespass on the right or left, would have hurried down the precipice into an abyss of blood and confusion, the people of Ireland demand a freedom of trade with arms in their hands. They interdict all commerce between the two nations. They deny all new supply in the House of Commons, although in time of war. They stint the trust of the old revenue, given for two years to all the king's predecessors, to six months. The British Parlia-

[1] See note prefixed to *Two Letters to Gentlemen in Bristol.*

K

ment, in a former session, frightened into a limited
concession by the menaces of Ireland, frightened out of
it by the menaces of England, were now frightened
back again, and made a universal surrender of all
that had been thought the peculiar, reserved, uncom-
municable rights of England:—the exclusive commerce
of America, of Africa, of the West Indies—all the
enumerations of the acts of navigation—all the manufactures—iron, glass, even the last pledge of jealousy
and pride, the interest hid in the secret of our hearts,
the inveterate prejudice moulded into the constitution
of our frame, even the sacred fleece itself—all went
together.[1]   No reserve; no exception; no debate; no
discussion.   A sudden light broke in upon us all.   It
broke in, not through well-contrived and well-disposed
windows, but through flaws and breaches; through the
yawning chasms of our ruin.   We were taught wisdom by humiliation.   No town in England presumed
to have a prejudice, or dared to mutter a petition.
What was worse, the whole Parliament of England,
which retained authority for nothing but surrenders,
was despoiled of every shadow of its superintendence.
It was, without any qualification, denied in theory, as
it had been trampled upon in practice.   This scene of
shame and disgrace has, in a manner, whilst I am
speaking, ended by the perpetual establishment of a
military power in the dominions of this Crown, without consent of the British Legislature,[2] contrary to the

---

[1] In 1779.   [2] Irish Perpetual Mutiny Act.

policy of the Constitution, contrary to the declaration
of right : and by this your liberties are swept away
along with your supreme authority——and both linked
together from the beginning, have, I am afraid, both
together perished for ever.

What ! gentlemen, was I not to foresee, or foreseeing, was I not to endeavour to save you from all
these multiplied mischiefs and disgraces ?   Would the
little, silly, canvass prattle of obeying instructions, and
having no opinions but yours, and such idle senseless
tales, which amuse the vacant ears of unthinking men,
have saved you from " the pelting of that pitiless
storm," to which the loose improvidence, the cowardly
rashness, of those who dare not look danger in the
face, so as to provide against it in time, and therefore
throw themselves headlong into the midst of it, have
exposed this degraded nation, beaten down and prostrate on the earth, unsheltered, unarmed, unresisting ?
Was I an Irishman on that day, that I boldly with-
stood our pride ? or on the day that I hung down my
head, and wept in shame and silence over the humiliation of Great Britain ?   I became unpopular in England for the one, and in Ireland for the other.   What
then ?   What obligation lay on me to be popular ?   I
was bound to serve both kingdoms.   To be pleased
with my service was their affair, not mine.

I was an Irishman in the Irish business, just as
much as I was an American when, on the same principles, I wished you to concede to America at a time

when she prayed concession at our feet.   Just as much
was I an American when I wished Parliament to offer
terms in victory, and not to wait the well-chosen hour
of defeat, for making good by weakness and by supplication a claim of prerogative, pre-eminence, and
authority.

Instead of requiring it from me, as a point of duty,
to kindle with your passions, had you all been as cool
as I was, you would have been saved from disgraces
and distresses that are unutterable.   Do you remember
our commission?   We sent out a solemn embassy
across the Atlantic Ocean, to lay the Crown, the Peerage,
the Commons of Great Britain, at the feet of the
American Congress.   That our disgrace might want
no sort of brightening and burnishing, observe who
they were that composed this famous embassy!   My
Lord Carlisle is among the first ranks of our nobility.
He is the identical man who, but two years before, had
been put forward at the opening of a session in the
House of Lords as the mover of a haughty and rigorous
address against America.   He was put in the front of
the embassy of submission.   Mr. Eden was taken from
the office of Lord Suffolk, to whom he was then Under
Secretary of State; from the office of that Lord Suffolk
who, but a few weeks before, in his place in Parliament
did not deign to inquire where a congress of vagrants
was to be found.   This Lord Suffolk sent Mr. Eden to
find these vagrants, without knowing where this king's
generals were to be found, who were joined in the

same commission of supplicating those whom they were sent to subdue. They enter the capital of America only to abandon it; and these assertors and representatives of the dignity of England, at the tail of a flying army, let fly their Parthian shafts of memorials and remonstrances at random behind them. Their promises and their offers, their flatteries and their menaces, were all despised; and we were saved from the disgrace of their formal reception, only because the congress scorned to receive them; whilst the state-house of independent Philadelphia opened her doors to the public entry of the ambassador of France. From war and blood we went to submission; and from sub-mission plunged back again to war and blood—to desolate and be desolated, without measure, hope, or end. I am a Royalist; I blushed for this degradation of the Crown. I am a Whig; I blushed for the dis-honour of Parliament. I am a true Englishman; I felt to the quick for the disgrace of England. I am a man; I felt for the melancholy reverse of human affairs in the fall of the first power in the world.

To read what was approaching in Ireland, in the black and bloody characters of the American war, was a painful, but it was a necessary part of my public duty. For, gentlemen, it is not your fond desires or mine that can alter the nature of things; by contend-ing against which, what have we got, or shall ever get, but defeat and shame? I did not obey your instruc-tions: No. I conformed to the instructions of truth

and nature, and maintained your interest, against your
opinions, with a constancy that became me.   A representative worthy of you ought to be a person of
stability.   I am to look, indeed, to your opinions; but
to such opinions as you and I *must* have five years
hence.   I was not to look to the flash of the day.   I
knew that you chose me, in my place, along with
others, to be a pillar of the State, and not a weather-
cock on the top of the edifice, exalted for my levity
and versatility, and of no use but to indicate the
shiftings of every fashionable gale.   Would to God
the value of my sentiments on Ireland and on America
had been at this day a subject of doubt and discussion!
No matter what my sufferings had been, so that this
kingdom had kept the authority I wished it to maintain, by a grave foresight, and by an equitable temperance in the use of its power.

The next article of charge on my public conduct, and that which I find rather the most prevalent of all is Lord Beauchamp's Bill.   I mean
his Bill of last session, for reforming the law-
process concerning imprisonment.   It is said, to
aggravate the offence, that I treated the petition
of this city with contempt even in presenting it to
the House, and expressed myself in terms of marked
disrespect.   Had this latter part of the charge been
true, no merits on the side of the question which I
took could possibly excuse me.   But I am incapable
of treating this city with disrespect.   Very fortunately

at this minute (if my bad eyesight does not deceive
me) the worthy [1] gentleman deputed on this business
stands directly before me.   To him I appeal whether
I did not, though it militated with my oldest and my
most recent public opinions, deliver the petition with
a strong and more than usual recommendation to the
consideration of the House on account of the character
and consequence of those who signed it.   I believe
the worthy gentleman will tell you that the very day
I received it I applied to the Solicitor—now the
Attorney-General—to give it an immediate consideration, and he most obligingly and instantly consented
to employ a great deal of his very valuable time to
write an explanation of the Bill.   I attended the committee with all possible care and diligence, in order
that every objection of yours might meet with a solu-
tion, or produce an alteration.   I entreated your
learned recorder (always ready in business in which
you take a concern) to attend.   But what will you
say to those who blame me for supporting Lord
Beauchamp's Bill, as a disrespectful treatment of your
petition, when you hear that out of respect to you I
myself was the cause of the loss of that very Bill ?
For the noble lord who brought it in, and who, I must
say, has much merit for this and some other measures,
at my request consented to put it off for a week, which
the Speaker's illness lengthened to a fortnight ; and
then the frantic tumult about Popery drove that and

[1] Mr. Williams.

every rational business from the House.   So that if I
chose to make a defence of myself on the little principles of a culprit pleading in his exculpation, I might
not only secure my acquittal, but make merit with the
opposers of the Bill.   But I shall do no such thing.
The truth is that I did occasion the loss of the Bill,
and by a delay caused by my respect to you.   But
such an event was never in my contemplation.   And
I am so far from taking credit for the defeat of that
measure, that I cannot sufficiently lament my misfortune if but one man, who ought to be at large, has
passed a year in prison by my means.   I am a debtor
to the debtors.   I confess judgment.   I owe what, if
ever it be in my power, I shall most certainly pay,—
ample atonement and usurious amends to liberty and
humanity for my unhappy lapse.   For, gentlemen,
Lord Beauchamp's Bill was a law of justice and policy
as far as it went—I say as far as it went, for its fault
was its being in the remedial part miserably defective.

There are two capital faults in our law with relation to civil debts.   One is that every man is presumed solvent—a presumption, in innumerable cases,
directly against truth.   Therefore, the debtor is ordered,
on a supposition of ability and fraud, to be coerced his
liberty until he makes payment.   By this means, in
all cases of civil insolvency, without a pardon from his
creditor, he is to be imprisoned for life—and thus
a miserable mistaken invention of artificial science
operates to change a civil into a criminal judgment, and

to scourge misfortune or indiscretion with a punishment which the law does not inflict on the greatest crimes.

The next fault is, that the inflicting of that punishment is not on the opinion of an equal and public judge; but is referred to the arbitrary discretion of a private, nay interested, and irritated, individual. He who formally is, and substantially ought to be, the judge, is in reality no more than ministerial, a mere executive instrument of a private man, who is at once judge and party. Every idea of judicial order is subverted by this procedure. If the insolvency be no crime, why is it punished with arbitrary imprisonment? If it be a crime, why is it delivered into private hands to pardon without discretion, or to punish without mercy and without measure?

To these faults—gross and cruel facts in our law—the excellent principle of Lord Beauchamp's Bill applied some sort of remedy. I know that credit must be preserved; but equity must be preserved too; and it is impossible that anything should be necessary to commerce, which is inconsistent with justice. The principle of credit was not weakened by that Bill. God forbid! The enforcement of that credit was only put into the same public judicial hands on which we depend for our lives, and all that makes life dear to us. But, indeed, this business was taken up too warmly both here and elsewhere. The Bill was extremely mistaken. It was supposed to enact what

it never enacted, and complaints were made of clauses
in it as novelties, which existed before the noble lord
that brought in the Bill was born.   There was a
fallacy that ran through the whole of the objections.   The gentlemen who opposed the Bill always
argued as if the option lay between that Bill and the
ancient law.   But this is a grand mistake.   For, practically, the option is between, not that Bill and the old
law, but between that Bill and those occasional laws,
called acts of grace.   For the operation of the old law
is so savage, and so inconvenient to society, that for a
long time past, once in every Parliament, and lately
twice, the legislature has been obliged to make a
general arbitrary jail-delivery, and at once to set open,
by its sovereign authority, all the prisons in England.

Gentlemen, I never relished acts of grace ; nor ever
submitted to them but from despair of better.   They
are a dishonourable invention, by which, not from
humanity, not from policy, but merely because we have
not room enough to hold these victims of the absurdity of our laws, we turn loose upon the public
three or four thousand naked wretches, corrupted by
habits, debased by the ignominy of a prison.   If the
creditor had a right to those carcases as a natural
security for his property, I am sure we have no right
to deprive him of that security.   But if the few pounds
of flesh were not necessary to his security, we had not
a right to detain the unfortunate debtor without any
benefit at all to the person who confined him.   Take

it as you will, we commit injustice.   Now Lord Beauchamp's Bill intended to do deliberately and with great
caution and circumspection, upon each several case,
and with all attention to the just claimant, what acts
of grace do in a much greater measure, and with very
little care, caution, or deliberation.

I suspect that here too, if we contrive to oppose
this Bill, we shall be found in a struggle against the
nature of things.   For as we grow enlightened, the
public will not bear, for any length of time, to pay for
the maintenance of whole armies of prisoners, nor—at
their own expense—submit to keep jails as a sort of
garrisons, merely to fortify the absurd principle of
making men judges in their own cause.   For credit
has little or no concern in this cruelty.   I speak in a
commercial assembly.   You know that credit is given,
because capital *must* be employed ; that men calculate
the chances of insolvency ; and they either withhold
the credit, or make the debtor pay the risk in the
price.   The counting-house has no alliance with the
jail.   Holland understands trade as well as we, and
she has done much more than this obnoxious Bill
intended to do.   There was not, when Mr. Howard
visited Holland, more than one prisoner for debt in the
great city of Rotterdam.   Although Lord Beauchamp's
Act (which was previous to this Bill, and intended to
feel the way for it) has already preserved liberty to
thousands, and though it is not three years since the
last Act of grace passed, yet, by Mr. Howard's last

account, there were near three thousand again in jail.
I cannot name this gentleman without remarking that
his labours and writings have done much to open the
eyes and hearts of mankind.   He has visited all
Europe ;—not to survey the sumptuousness of palaces,
or the stateliness of temples ; not to make accurate
measurements of the remains of ancient grandeur, nor
to form a scale of the curiosity of modern art ; not to
collect medals, or collate manuscripts, but to dive into
the depths of dungeons; to plunge into the infection of
hospitals ; to survey the mansions of sorrow and pain ;
to take the gauge and dimensions of misery, depression,
and contempt ; to remember the forgotten, to attend to
the neglected, to visit the forsaken ; and to compare
and collate the distresses of all men in all countries.
His plan is original ; and it is as full of genius as it is
of humanity.   It was a voyage of discovery ; a circum-
navigation of charity.   Already the benefit of his
labour is felt more or less in every country.   I hope
he will anticipate his final reward by seeing all its
effects fully realised in his own.   He will receive—not
by detail, but in gross—the reward of those who visit
the prisoner ; and he has so forestalled and monopolised
this branch of charity that there will be, I trust, little
room to merit by such acts of benevolence hereafter.

Nothing now remains to trouble you with but the
fourth charge against me—the business of the Roman
Catholics.   It is a business closely connected with the
rest.   They are all on one and the same principle.

My little scheme of conduct, such as it is, is all
arranged. I could do nothing but what I have done
on this subject without confounding the whole train
of my ideas, and disturbing the whole order of my life.
Gentlemen, I ought to apologise to you for seeming to
think anything at all necessary to be said upon this
matter. The calumny is fitter to be scrawled with the
midnight chalk of incendiaries, with " No popery " on
walls and doors of devoted houses, than to be mentioned in any civilised company. I had heard that
the spirit of discontent on that subject was very prevalent here. With pleasure I find that I have been
grossly misinformed. If it exists at all in this city,
the laws have crushed its exertions, and our morals
have shamed its appearance in daylight. I have pursued this spirit wherever I could trace it, but it still
fled from me. It was a ghost which all had heard of,
but none had seen. None would acknowledge that
he thought the public proceeding with regard to our
Catholic dissenters to be blameable, but several were
sorry it had made an ill impression upon others, and
that my interest was hurt by my share in the business.
I find with satisfaction and pride that not above four
or five in this city (and I dare say these misled by
some gross misrepresentation) have signed that symbol
of delusion and bond of sedition—that libel on the
national religion and English character—the Protestant Association. It is therefore, gentlemen, not by
way of cure but of prevention, and lest the arts of

wicked men may prevail over the integrity of any one amongst us, that I think it necessary to open to you the merits of this transaction pretty much at large, and I beg your patience upon it; for, although the reasonings that have been used to depreciate the act are of little force, and though the authority of the men concerned in this ill design is not very imposing, yet the audaciousness of these conspirators against the national honour, and the extensive wickedness of their attempts, have raised persons of little importance to a degree of evil eminence, and imparted a sort of sinister dignity to proceedings that had their origin in only the meanest and blindest malice.

In explaining to you the proceedings of Parliament which have been complained of, I will state to you,— first, the thing that was done;—next, the person who did it;—and lastly, the grounds and reasons upon which the legislature proceeded in this deliberate act of public justice and public prudence.

Gentlemen, the condition of our nature is such, that we buy our blessings at a price. The Reformation—one of the greatest periods of human improvement—was a time of trouble and confusion. The vast structure of superstition and tyranny, which had been for ages in rearing, and which was combined with the interest of the great and of the many, which was moulded into the laws, the manners, and civil institutions of nations, and blended with the frame and policy of states, could not be brought to the ground without

a fearful struggle; nor could it fall without a violent
concussion of itself and all about it.   When this great
revolution was attempted in a more regular mode by
Government, it was opposed by plots and seditions of
the people; when by popular efforts, it was repressed
as rebellion by the hand of power; and bloody executions (often bloodily returned) marked the whole of its
progress through all its stages.   The affairs of religion,
which are no longer heard of in the tumult of our
present contentions, made a principal ingredient in the
wars and politics of that time; the enthusiasm of
religion threw a gloom over the politics; and political
interests poisoned and perverted the spirit of religion
upon all sides.   The Protestant religion in that violent
struggle, infected, as the Popish had been before, by
worldly interests and worldly passions, became a perse-
cutor in its turn, sometimes of the new sects, which
carried their own principles farther than it was convenient to the original reformers, and always of the
body from whom they parted: and this persecuting
spirit arose, not only from the bitterness of retaliation,
but from the merciless policy of fear.

It was long before the spirit of true piety and true
wisdom, involved in the principles of the Reformation,
could be depurated from the dregs and feculence of
the contention with which it was carried through.
However, until this be done, the Reformation is not
complete; and those who think themselves good Protestants from their animosity to others, are in that

respect no Protestants at all. It was at first thought
necessary, perhaps, to oppose to Popery another
Popery to get the better of it. Whatever was the
cause, laws were made in many countries, and in this
kingdom in particular, against Papists, which are as
bloody as any of those which had been enacted by the
popish princes and states ; and where those laws were
not bloody, in my opinion they were worse ; as they
were slow, cruel outrages on our nature, and kept men
alive only to insult in their persons every one of the
rights and feelings of humanity. I pass those statutes,
because I would spare your pious ears the repetition
of such shocking things ; and I come to that particular
law, the repeal of which has produced so many unnatural and unexpected consequences.

A statute was fabricated in the year 1699, by which
the saying mass (a Church-service in the Latin tongue,
not exactly the same as our liturgy, but very near it,
and containing no offence whatsoever against the laws,
or against good morals) was forged into a crime, pun-
ishable with perpetual imprisonment. The teaching
school—a useful and virtuous occupation—even the
teaching in a private family—was in every Catholic
subjected to the same unproportioned punishment.
Your industry, and the bread of your children, was
taxed for a pecuniary reward to stimulate avarice to
do what nature refused, to inform and prosecute on
this law. Every Roman Catholic was, under the same
Act, to forfeit his estate to his nearest Protestant rela-

tion, until, through a profession of what he did not believe, he redeemed by his hypocrisy what the law had transferred to the kinsman as the recompense of his profligacy.   When thus turned out of doors from his paternal estate, he was disabled from acquiring any other by any industry, donation, or charity; but was rendered a foreigner in his native land, only because he retained the religion, along with the property, handed down to him from those who had been the old inhabitants of that land before him.

Does any one who hears me approve this scheme of things, or think there is common justice, common sense, or common honesty in any part of it? If any does, let him say it, and I am ready to discuss the point with temper and candour.   But instead of approving, I perceive a virtuous indignation beginning to rise in your minds on the mere cold stating of the statute.

But what will you feel when you know from history how this statute passed, and what were the motives, and what the mode of making it? A party in this nation, enemies to the system of the Revolution, were in opposition to the government of King William. They knew that our glorious deliverer was an enemy to all persecution.   They knew that he came to free us from slavery and popery, out of a country where a third of the people are contented Catholics under a Protestant government.   He came with a part of his army composed of those very Catholics, to overset the

power of a popish prince. Such is the effect of a
tolerating spirit : and so much is liberty served in every
way, and by all persons, by a manly adherence to its
own principles. Whilst freedom is true to itself, everything becomes subject to it; and its very adversaries
are an instrument in its hands.

The party I speak of (like some amongst us who
would disparage the best friends of their country) resolved to make the king either violate his principles
of toleration, or incur the odium of protecting Papists.
They therefore brought in this Bill, and made it purposely wicked and absurd, that it might be rejected.
The then court-party, discovering their game, turned
the tables on them, and returned their Bill to them
stuffed with still greater absurdities, that its loss might
lie upon its original authors. They, finding their own
ball thrown back to them, kicked it back again to their
adversaries. And thus this Act, loaded with the double
injustice of two parties, neither of whom intended to
pass what they hoped the other would be persuaded
to reject, went through the legislature, contrary to the
real wish of all parts of it, and of all the parties that
composed it. In this manner these insolent and profligate factions, as if they were playing with balls and
counters, made a sport of the fortunes and liberties
of their fellow-creatures. Other acts of persecution
have been acts of malice. This was a subversion of
justice from wantonness and petulance. Look into the
history of Bishop Burnet. He is a witness without
exception.

The effects of the Act have been as mischievous as its origin was ludicrous and shameful. From that time every person of that communion, lay and ecclesiastic, has been obliged to fly from the face of day. The clergy, concealed in garrets in private houses, or obliged to take a shelter (hardly safe to themselves, but infinitely dangerous to their country) under the privileges of foreign ministers, officiated as their servants, and under their protection. The whole body of the Catholics, condemned to beggary and to ignorance in their native land, have been obliged to learn the principle of letters, at the hazard of all their other principles, from the charity of your enemies. They have been taxed to their ruin at the pleasure of necessitous and profligate relations, and according to the measure of their necessity and profligacy. Examples of this are many and affecting. Some of them are known by a friend who stands near me in this hall, It is but six or seven years since a clergyman of the name of Malony, a man of morals, neither guilty nor accused of anything noxious to the State, was condemned to perpetual imprisonment for exercising the functions of his religion ; and after lying in jail two or three years, was relieved by the mercy of Government from perpetual imprisonment, on condition of perpetual banishment. A brother of the Earl of Shrewsbury, a Talbot,—a name respectable in this country, whilst its glory is any part of its concern— was hauled to the bar of the Old Bailey, among

common felons, and only escaped the same doom,
either by some error in the process, or that the wretch
who brought him there could not correctly describe
his person,—I now forget which.   In short, the persecution would never have relented for a moment, if
the judges, superseding (though with an ambiguous
example) the strict rule of their artificial duty by the
higher obligation of their conscience, did not constantly
throw every difficulty in the way of such informers.
But so ineffectual is the power of legal evasion against
legal iniquity, that it was but the other day that a lady
of condition, beyond the middle of life, was on the
point of being stripped of her whole fortune by a near
relation, to whom she had been a friend and bene-
factor; and she must have been totally ruined, without
a power of redress or mitigation from the courts of
law, had not the legislature itself rushed in, and by a
special Act of Parliament rescued her from the injustice
of its own statutes.   One of the Acts authorising such
things was that which we in part repealed, knowing
what our duty was, and doing that duty as men of
honour and virtue, as good Protestants, and as good
citizens.   Let him stand forth that disapproves what
we have done.

Gentlemen, bad laws are the worst sort of tyranny.
In such a country as this they are of all bad things
the worst,—worse by far than any where else ; and they
derive a particular malignity even from the wisdom
and soundness of the rest of our institutions.   For

very obvious reasons you cannot trust the Crown with
a dispensing power over any of your laws.   However,
a government, be it as bad as it may, will, in the exercise of a discretionary power, discriminate times and
persons, and will not ordinarily pursue any man when
its own safety is not concerned.   A mercenary informer
knows no distinction.   Under such a system, the obnoxious people are slaves, not only to the Government,
but they live at the mercy of every individual ; they
are at once the slaves of the whole community, and of
every part of it ; and the worst and most unmerciful
men are those on whose goodness they most depend.

In this situation men not only shrink from the
frowns of a stern magistrate ; but they are obliged to
fly from their very species.   The seeds of destruction
are sown in civil intercourse, in social habitudes.   The
blood of wholesome kindred is infected.   Their tables
and beds are surrounded with snares.   All the means
given by Providence to make life safe and comfortable
are perverted into instruments of terror and torment.
This species of universal subserviency, that makes the
very servant who waits behind your chair the arbiter
of your life and fortune, has such a tendency to degrade
and abase mankind, and to deprive them of that assured
and liberal state of mind which alone can make us
what we ought to be, that I vow to God I would
sooner bring myself to put a man to immediate death
for opinions I disliked, and so to get rid of the man
and his opinions at once, than to fret him with a

feverish being, tainted with the jail-distemper of a contagious servitude, to keep him above ground—an animated mass of putrefaction, corrupted himself, and corrupting all about him.

The Act repealed was of this direct tendency; and it was made in the manner which I have related to you. I will now tell you by whom the Bill of repeal was brought into Parliament. I find it has been industriously given out in this city (from kindness to me, unquestionably) that I was the mover or the seconder. The fact is, I did not once open my lips on the subject during the whole progress of the Bill. I do not say this as disclaiming my share in that measure. Very far from it. I inform you of this fact, lest I should seem to arrogate to myself the merits which belong to others. To have been the man chosen out to redeem our fellow-citizens from slavery; to purify our laws from absurdity and injustice; and to cleanse our religion from the blot and stain of persecution, would be an honour and happiness to which my wishes would undoubtedly aspire; but to which nothing but my wishes could have possibly entitled me. That great work was in hands in every respect far better qualified than mine. The mover of the Bill was Sir George Savile.

When an act of great and signal humanity was to be done, and done with all the weight and authority that belonged to it, the world could cast its eyes upon none but him. I hope that few things which have a tend-

ency to bless or to adorn life have wholly escaped my
observation in my passage through it. I have sought the
acquaintance of that gentleman, and have seen him in
all situations. He is a true genius; with an understanding vigorous and acute and refined, and distinguishing even to excess; and illuminated with a most
unbounded, peculiar, and original cast of imagination.
With these he possesses many external and instrumental advantages; and he makes use of them all.
His fortune is among the largest—a fortune which,
wholly unencumbered, as it is, with one single charge
from luxury, vanity, or excess, sinks under the benevolence of its dispenser. This private benevolence,
expanding itself into patriotism, renders his whole
being the estate of the public, in which he has not
reserved a *peculium* for himself of profit, diversion, or
relaxation. During the session, the first in, and the
last out of the House of Commons, he passes from the
senate to the camp; and seldom seeing the seat of his
ancestors, he is always in the senate to serve his
country, or in the field to defend it. But in all well-
wrought compositions, some particulars stand out more
eminently than the rest; and the things which will
carry his name to posterity are his two Bills; I mean
that for a limitation of the claims of the Crown upon
landed estates; and this for the relief of the Roman
Catholics. By the former, he has emancipated property;
by the latter he has quieted conscience; and by both
he has taught that grand lesson to Government and

subject,—no longer to regard each other as adverse
parties.

Such was the mover of the Act that is complained
of by men who are not quite so good as he is—an Act,
most assuredly not brought in by him from any partiality to the sect which is the object of it.   For among
his faults I really cannot help reckoning a greater
degree of prejudice against that people than becomes
so wise a man.   I know that he inclines to a sort of
disgust, mixed with a considerable degree of asperity,
to the system; and he has few, or rather no habits
with any of its professors.   What he has done was on
quite other motives.   The motives were these, which
he declared in his excellent speech on his motion for
the Bill; namely, his extreme zeal to the Protestant
religion, which he thought utterly disgraced by the
Act of 1699; and his rooted hatred to all kind of
oppression, under any colour, or upon any pretence
whatsoever.

The seconder was worthy of the mover and of the
motion.   I was not the seconder; it was Mr. Dunning,
Recorder of this city.   I shall say the less of him
because his near relation to you makes you more
particularly acquainted with his merits.   But I should
appear little acquainted with them, or little sensible of
them, if I could utter his name on this occasion without expressing my esteem for his character.   I am not
afraid of offending a most learned body, and most
jealous of its reputation for that learning, when I say

he is the first of his profession.   It is a point settled
by those who settle everything else; and I must add
(what I am enabled to say from my own long and
close observation) that there is not a man, of any profession, or in any situation, of a more erect and independent spirit; of a more proud honour; a more
manly mind; a more firm and determined integrity.
Assure yourselves that the names of two such men
will bear a great load of prejudice in the other scale
before they can be entirely outweighed.

With this mover and this seconder agreed the *whole*
House of Commons, the *whole* House of Lords, the
whole bench of bishops, the king, the Ministry, the
Opposition, all the distinguished clergy of the Establishment, all the eminent lights (for they were consulted) of the dissenting churches.   This according
voice of national wisdom ought to be listened to with
reverence.   To say that all these descriptions of
Englishmen unanimously concurred in a scheme for
introducing the Catholic religion, or that none of them
understood the nature and effects of what they were
doing so well as a few obscure clubs of people, whose
names you never heard of, is shamelessly absurd.
Surely it is paying a miserable compliment to the
religion we profess, to suggest that everything eminent
in the kingdom is indifferent, or even adverse to that
religion, and that its security is wholly abandoned to
the zeal of those who have nothing but their zeal to
distinguish them.   In weighing this unanimous con-

currence of whatever the nation has to boast of, I hope
you will recollect that all these concurring parties do by
no means love one another enough to agree in any point,
which was not both evidently and importantly right.

To prove this; to prove that the measure was both
clearly and materially proper, I will next lay before
you (as I promised) the political grounds and reasons
for the repeal of that penal statute; and the motives
to its repeal at that particular time.

Gentlemen, America—— When the English nation
seemed to be dangerously, if not irrecoverably divided;
when one, and that the most growing branch, was torn
from the parent stock, and engrafted on the power of
France, a great terror fell upon this kingdom. On a
sudden we awakened from our dreams of conquest, and
saw ourselves threatened with an immediate invasion,
which we were at that time very ill prepared to resist.
You remember the cloud that gloomed over us all. In
that hour of our dismay, from the bottom of the hiding-
places into which the indiscriminate rigour of our
statutes had driven them, came out the body of the
Roman Catholics. They appeared before the steps of
a tottering throne with one of the most sober,
measured, steady, and dutiful addresses that was ever
presented to the Crown. It was no holiday ceremony;
no anniversary compliment of parade and show. It
was signed by almost every gentleman of that persuasion of note or property in England. At such a crisis,
nothing but a decided resolution to stand or fall with

their country could have dictated such an address; the direct tendency of which was to cut off all retreat, and to render them peculiarly obnoxious to an invader of their own communion. The address showed what I long languished to see—that all the subjects of England had cast off all foreign views and connections, and that every man looked for his relief from every grievance at the hands only of his own natural government.

It was necessary, on our part, that the natural government should show itself worthy of that name. It was necessary, at the crisis I speak of, that the supreme power of the State should meet the conciliatory dispositions of the subject. To delay protection would be to reject allegiance. And why should it be rejected, or even coldly and suspiciously received? If any independent Catholic state should choose to take part with this kingdom in a war with France and Spain, that bigot (if such a bigot could be found) would be heard with little respect; who could dream of objecting his religion to an ally, whom the nation would not only receive with its freest thanks, but purchase with the last remains of its exhausted treasure. To such an ally we should not dare to whisper a single syllable of those base and invidious topics, upon which some unhappy men would persuade the State to reject the duty and allegiance of its own members. Is it then because foreigners are in a condition to set our malice at defiance, that with *them* we are willing to contract engagements of friendship, and to keep them

with fidelity and honour; but that, because we conceive some descriptions of our countrymen are not
powerful enough to punish our malignity, we will
not permit them to support our common interest?
Is it on that ground that our anger is to be kindled
by their offered kindness? Is it on that ground
that they are to be subjected to penalties, because
they are willing, by actual merit, to purge themselves from imputed crimes? Lest, by an adherence
to the cause of their country, they should acquire a
title to fair and equitable treatment, are we resolved
to furnish them with causes of eternal enmity; and
rather supply them with just and founded motives to
disaffection, than not to have that disaffection in existence to justify an oppression which, not from policy
but disposition, we have predetermined to exercise?

What shadow of reason could be assigned why, at
a time when the most Protestant part of this Protestant
empire found for its advantage to unite with the two
principal popish states, to unite itself in the closest
bonds with France and Spain for our destruction, that
we should refuse to unite with our own Catholic
countrymen for our own preservation? Ought we,
like madmen, to tear off the plasters that the lenient
hand of prudence had spread over the wounds and
gashes which in our delirium of ambition we had given
to our own body? No person ever reprobated the
American war more than I did, and do, and ever shall.
But I never will consent that we should lay additional

voluntary penalties upon ourselves for a fault which carries but too much of its own punishment in its own nature.   For one, I was delighted with the proposal of internal peace.   I accepted the blessing with thankfulness and transport; I was truly happy to find *one* good effect of our civil distractions—that they had put an end to all religious strife and heartburning in our own bowels.   What must be the sentiments of a man who would wish to perpetuate domestic hostility, when the causes of dispute are at an end; and who, crying out for peace with one part of the nation on the most humiliating terms, should deny it to those who offer friendship without any terms at all?

But if I was unable to reconcile such a denial to the contracted principles of local duty, what answer could I give to the broad claims of general humanity? I confess to you freely that the sufferings and distresses of the people of America in this cruel war have at times affected me more deeply than I can express.   I felt every Gazette of triumph as a blow upon my heart, which has an hundred times sunk and fainted within me at all the mischiefs brought upon those who bear the whole brunt of war in the heart of their country.   Yet the Americans are utter strangers to me—a nation among whom I am not sure that I have a single acquaintance.   Was I to suffer my mind to be so unaccountably warped; was I to keep such iniquitous weights and measures of temper and of reason as to sympathise with those who are in

open rebellion against an authority which I respect, at
war with a country which by every title ought to be,
and is most dear to me ; and yet to have no feeling
at all for the hardships and indignities suffered by
men who, by their very vicinity, are bound up in a
nearer relation to us ; who contribute their share, and
more than their share, to the common prosperity ; who
perform the common offices of social life, and who obey
the laws to the full as well as I do ?   Gentlemen, the
danger to the State being out of the question (of which,
let me tell you, statesmen themselves are apt to have
but too exquisite a sense) I could assign no one reason
of justice, policy, or feeling, for not concurring most
cordially, as most cordially I did concur, in softening
some part of that shameful servitude under which
several of my worthy fellow-citizens were groaning.

Important effects followed this act of wisdom.
They appeared at home and abroad, to the great benefit of this kingdom ; and, let me hope, to the advantage
of mankind at large.   It betokened union among ourselves.   It showed soundness, even on the part of the
persecuted, which generally is the weak side of every
community.   But its most essential operation was not
in England.   The act was immediately, though very
imperfectly, copied in Ireland ; and this imperfect
transcript of an imperfect act, this first faint sketch of
toleration, which did little more than disclose a principle and mark out a disposition, completed in a most
wonderful manner the re-union to the State of all the

Catholics of that country. It made us what we ought always to have been,—one family, one body, one heart and soul, against the family-combination, and all other combinations of our enemies. We have indeed obligations to that people, who received such small benefits with so much gratitude; and for which gratitude and attachment to us I am afraid they have suffered not a little in other places.

I dare say you have all heard of the privileges indulged to the Irish Catholics residing in Spain. You have likewise heard with what circumstances of severity they have been lately expelled from the seaports of that kingdom; driven into the inland cities; and there detained as a sort of prisoners of State. I have good reason to believe that it was the zeal to our Government and our cause (somewhat indiscreetly expressed in one of the addresses of the Catholics of Ireland) which has thus drawn down on their heads the indignation of the court of Madrid; to the inexpressible loss of several individuals, and in future, perhaps, to the great detriment of the whole of their body. Now that our people should be persecuted in Spain for their attachment to this country, and persecuted in this country for their supposed enmity to us, is such a jarring reconciliation of contradictory distresses,—is a thing at once so dreadful and ridiculous, that no malice short of diabolical would wish to continue any human creatures in such a situation. But honest men will not forget either their merit or their sufferings. There

are men (and many, I trust, there are) who, out of love
to their country and their kind, would torture their
invention to find excuses for the mistakes of their
brethren; and who, to stifle dissension, would construe
even doubtful appearances with the utmost favour:
such men will never persuade themselves to be in-
genious and refined in discovering disaffection and
treason in the manifest, palpable signs of suffering
loyalty.   Persecution is so unnatural to them, that they
gladly snatch the very first opportunity of laying aside
all the tricks and devices of penal politics; and of
returning home, after all their irksome and vexatious
wanderings, to our natural family mansion, to the
grand social principle that unites all men, in all descriptions, under the shadow of an equal and impartial
justice.

Men of another sort—I mean the bigoted enemies
to liberty—may perhaps in their politics make no account of the good or ill affection of the Catholics of
England, who are but a handful of people (enough to
torment but not enough to fear)—perhaps not so many,
of both sexes and of all ages, as fifty thousand.   But,
gentlemen, it is possible you may not know that the
people of that persuasion in Ireland amount at least
to sixteen or seventeen hundred thousand souls.   I
do not at all exaggerate the number.   A *nation* to be
persecuted !   Whilst we were masters of the sea, embodied with America, and in alliance with half the
powers of the Continent, we might perhaps, in that

remote corner of Europe, afford to tyrannise with impunity. But there is a revolution in our affairs which makes it prudent to be just. In our late awkward contest with Ireland about trade, had religion been thrown in, to ferment and embitter the mass of discontents, the consequences might have been truly dreadful. But very happily, that cause of quarrel was previously quieted by the wisdom of the Acts I am commending.

Even in England, where I admit the danger from the discontent of that persuasion to be less than in Ireland; yet even here, had we listened to the counsels of fanaticism and folly, we might have wounded ourselves very deeply, and wounded ourselves in a very tender part. You are apprised that the Catholics of England consist mostly of our best manufacturers. Had the Legislature chosen, instead of returning their declarations of duty with correspondent goodwill, to drive them to despair, there is a country at their very door to which they would be invited—a country in all respects as good as ours, and with the finest cities in the world ready built to receive them. And thus the bigotry of a free country, and in an enlightened age, would have re-peopled the cities of Flanders, which, in the darkness of two hundred years ago, had been desolated by the superstition of a cruel tyrant. Our manufacturers were the growth of the persecutions in the Low Countries. What a spectacle would it be to Europe, to see us at this time of day, balancing the

M

account of tyranny with those very countries, and by our persecutions driving back trade and manufacture, as a sort of vagabonds, to their original settlement! But I trust we shall be saved this last of disgraces.

So far as to the effect of the Act on the interests of this nation.   With regard to the interests of mankind at large, I am sure the benefit was very considerable.   Long before this Act, indeed, the spirit of toleration began to gain ground in Europe.   In Holland, the third part of the people are Catholics ; they live at ease, and are a sound part of the State.   In many parts of Germany, Protestants and Papists partake the same cities, the same councils, and even the same churches.   The unbounded liberality of the King of Prussia's conduct on this occasion is known to all the world, and it is of a piece with the other grand maxims of his reign.   The magnanimity of the imperial court, breaking through the narrow principles of its predecessors, has indulged its Protestant subjects, not only with property, with worship, with liberal education, but with honours and trusts, both civil and military. A worthy Protestant gentleman of this country now fills, and fills with credit, a high office in the Austrian Netherlands.   Even the Lutheran obstinacy of Sweden has thawed at length, and opened a toleration to all religions.   I know myself that in France the Protestants begin to be at rest.   The army—which in that country is everything—is open to them ; and some of the military rewards and decorations which the laws deny are supplied by others, to make the service acceptable and honourable.   The first minister of finance in that country is a Protestant.   Two years' war without a tax is among the first-fruits of their liberality.   Tarnished as the glory of this nation is, and as far as it has waded into the shades of an eclipse, some beams of its former illumination still play upon its surface; and what is done in England is still looked to as argument and as example.   It is certainly true that no law of this country ever met with such universal applause abroad, or was so likely to produce the perfection of that tolerating spirit which, as I observed, has been long gaining ground in Europe; for abroad it was universally thought that we had done what, I am sorry to say, we had not—they thought we had granted a full toleration.   That opinion was, however, so far from hurting the Protestant cause, that I declare, with the most serious solemnity, my firm belief that no one thing done for these fifty years past was so likely to prove deeply beneficial to our religion at large as Sir George Savile's Act.   In its effects it was "an Act for tolerating and protecting Protestantism throughout Europe:" and I hope that those who were taking steps for the quiet and settlement of our Protestant brethren in other countries will even yet rather consider the steady equity of the greater and better part of the people of Great Britain, than the vanity and violence of a few.

I perceive, gentlemen, by the manner of all about me, that you look with horror on the wicked clamour

which has been raised on this subject; and that instead of an apology for what was done, you rather
demand from me an account, why the execution of
the scheme of toleration was not made more answer-
able to the large and liberal grounds on which it was
taken up?   The question is natural and proper; and
I remember that a great and learned magistrate,[1]
distinguished for his strong and systematic understanding, and who at that time was a member of the
House of Commons, made the same objection to the
proceeding.   The statutes, as they now stand, are,
without doubt, perfectly absurd.   But I beg leave to
explain the cause of this gross imperfection in the
tolerating plan as well and as shortly as I am able.
It was universally thought that the session ought not
to pass over without doing *something* in this business.
To revise the whole body of the penal statutes was
conceived to be an object too big for the time.   The
penal statute, therefore, which was chosen for repeal
(chosen to show our disposition to conciliate, not to
perfect a toleration), was this act of ludicrous cruelty,
of which I have just given you the history.   It is an
Act which, though not by a great deal so fierce and
bloody as some of the rest, was infinitely more ready
in the execution.   It was the Act which gave the
greatest encouragement to those pests of society,
mercenary informers, and interested disturbers of
household peace; and it was observed with truth,

[1] The Chancellor.

that the prosecutions, either carried to conviction or compounded for many years, had been all commenced upon that Act. It was said, that whilst we were deliberating on a more perfect scheme, the spirit of the age would never come up to the execution of the statutes which remained ; especially as more steps, and a co-operation of more minds and powers, were required towards a mischievous use of them, than for the execution of the Act to be repealed : that it was better to unravel this texture from below than from above, beginning with the latest, which, in general practice, is the severest evil. It was alleged that this slow proceeding would be attended with the advantage of a progressive experience ; and that the people would grow reconciled to toleration, when they should find by the effects, that justice was not so irreconcilable an enemy to convenience as they had imagined.

These, gentlemen, were the reasons why we left this good work in the rude, unfinished state in which good works are commonly left, through the tame circumspection with which a timid prudence so frequently enervates beneficence. In doing good, we are generally cold, and languid, and sluggish ; and of all things afraid of being too much in the right. But the works of malice and injustice are quite in another style. They are finished with a bold masterly hand ; touched as they are with the spirit of those vehement passions that call forth all our energies, whenever we oppress and persecute.

Thus this matter was left for the time, with a full determination in Parliament not to suffer other and worse statutes to remain for the purpose of counteracting the benefits proposed by the repeal of one penal law ; for nobody then dreamed of defending what was done as a benefit, on the ground of its being no benefit at all.   We were not then ripe for so mean a subterfuge.

I do not wish to go over the horrid scene that was afterwards acted.   Would to God it could be expunged for ever from the annals of this country ! But since it must subsist for our shame, let it subsist for our instruction.   In the year 1780 there were found in this nation men deluded enough (for I give the whole to their delusion), on pretences of zeal and piety, without any sort of provocation whatsoever, real or pretended, to make a desperate attempt, which would have consumed all the glory and power of this country in the flames of London ; and buried all law, order, and religion, under the ruins of the metropolis of the Protestant world.   Whether all this mischief done, or in the direct train of doing, was in their original scheme, I cannot say—I hope it was not—but this would have been the unavoidable consequence of their proceedings, had not the flames they had lighted up in their fury been extinguished in their blood.

All the time that this horrid scene was acting, or avenging, as well as for some time before, and ever since, the wicked instigators of this unhappy multitude, guilty with every aggravation of all their crimes, and screened in a cowardly darkness from their punishment, continued without interruption, pity, or remorse, to blow up the blind rage of the populace, with a continued blast of pestilential libels, which infected and poisoned the very air we breathed in.

The main drift of all the libels and all the riots was to force Parliament (to persuade us was hopeless) into an act of national perfidy, which has no example. For, gentlemen, it is proper you should all know what infamy we escaped by refusing that repeal, for a refusal of which, it seems, I, among others, stand somewhere or other accused.   When we took away, on the motives which I had the honour of stating to you, a few of the innumerable penalties upon an oppressed and injured people; the relief was not absolute, but given on a stipulation and compact between them and us; for we bound down the Roman Catholics with the most solemn oaths, to bear true allegiance to this Government; to abjure all sort of temporal power in any other; and to renounce, under the same solemn obligations, the doctrines of systematic perfidy, with which they stood (I conceive very unjustly) charged.   Now our modest petitioners came up to us, most humbly praying nothing more than that we should break our faith without any one cause whatsoever of forfeiture assigned; and when the subjects of this kingdom had, on their part, fully performed their engagement, we should refuse, on our part,

the benefit we had stipulated on the performance of
those very conditious that were prescribed by our own
authority, and taken on the sanction of our public
faith, that is to say—when we had inveigled them
with fair promises within our door, we were to shut it
on them; and, adding mockery to outrage, to tell
them, "Now we have got you fast—your consciences
are bound to a power resolved on your destruction.
We have made you swear that your religion obliges
you to keep your faith: fools as you are! we will now
let you see that our religion enjoins us to keep no
faith with you." They who would advisedly call upon
us to do such things must certainly have thought us
not only a convention of treacherous tyrants, but a
gang of the lowest and dirtiest wretches that ever
disgraced humanity. Had we done this, we should
have indeed proved that there were *some* in the world
whom no faith could bind; and we should have *convicted* ourselves of that odious principle of which Papists
stood *accused* by those very savages who wished us, on
that accusation, to deliver them over to their fury.

In this audacious tumult, when our very name and
character as gentlemen was to be cancelled for ever,
along with the faith and honour of the nation, I, who
had exerted myself very little on the quiet passing of
the Bill, thought it necessary then to come forward.
I was not alone: but though some distinguished
members on all sides, and particularly on ours, added
much to their high reputation by the part they took

on that day (a part which will be remembered as long
as honour, spirit, and eloquence have estimation in the
world), I may and will value myself so far, that, yielding in abilities to many, I yielded in zeal to none.
With warmth and with vigour, and animated with a
just and natural indignation, I called forth every
faculty that I possessed, and I directed it in every
way in which I could possibly employ it, I laboured
night and day. I laboured in Parliament: I laboured
out of Parliament. If, therefore, the resolution of the
House of Commons, refusing to commit this act of
unmatched turpitude, be a crime, I am guilty among
the foremost. But, indeed, whatever the faults of that
House may have been, no one member was found
hardy enough to propose so infamous a thing; and on
full debate we passed the resolution against the petitions with as much unanimity as we had formerly
passed the law of which these petitions demanded the
repeal.

There was a circumstance (justice will not suffer
me to pass it over) which, if anything could enforce
the reasons I have given, would fully justify the act
of relief, and render a repeal, or anything like a
repeal, unnatural, impossible. It was the behaviour
of the persecuted Roman Catholics under the acts of
violence and brutal insolence which they suffered. I
suppose there are not in London less than four or five
thousand of that persuasion from my country, who do
a great deal of the most laborious works in the metro-

polis; and they chiefly inhabit those quarters which
were the principal theatre of the fury of the bigoted
multitude. They are known to be men of strong
arms and quick feelings, and more remarkable for a
determined resolution than clear ideas, or much foresight. But though provoked by everything that can
stir the blood of men, their houses and chapels in
flames, and with the most atrocious profanations of
everything which they hold sacred before their eyes,
not a hand was moved to retaliate, or even to defend.
Had a conflict once begun, the rage of their persecutors would have redoubled. Thus fury increasing by
the reverberation of outrages, house being fired for
house, and church for chapel, I am convinced—that no
power under heaven could have prevented a general
conflagration; and at this day London would have
been a tale. But I am well informed—and the thing
speaks it—that their clergy exerted their whole influence to keep their people in such a state of forbear-
ance and quiet as, when I look back, fills me with
astonishment; but not with astonishment only. Their
merits on that occasion ought not to be forgotten—nor
will they when Englishmen come to recollect themselves. I am sure it were far more proper to have
called them forth, and given them the thanks of both
Houses of Parliament, than to have suffered those
worthy clergymen and excellent citizens to be hunted
into holes and corners, whilst we are making low-
minded inquisitions into the number of their people;

as if a tolerating principle was never to prevail, unless we were very sure that only a few could possibly take advantage of it. But indeed we are not yet well recovered of our fright. Our reason, I trust, will return with our security ; and this unfortunate temper will pass over like a cloud.

Gentlemen, I have now laid before you a few of the reasons for taking away the penalties of the Act of 1699, and for refusing to establish them on the riotous requisition of 1780. Because I would not suffer anything which may be for your satisfaction to escape, permit me just to touch on the objections urged against our Act and our resolves, and intended as a justification of the violence offered to both Houses. " Parliament," they assert, " was too hasty, and they ought, in so essential and alarming a change, to have proceeded with a far greater degree of deliberation." The direct contrary. Parliament was too slow. They took fourscore years to deliberate on the repeal of an Act which ought not to have survived a second session. When at length, after a procrastination of near a century, the business was taken up, it proceeded in the most public manner, by the ordinary stages, and as slowly as a law so evidently right as to be resisted by none would naturally advance. Had it been read three times in one day, we should have shown only a becoming readiness to recognise, by protection, the undoubted dutiful behaviour of those whom we had but too long punished for offences of presumption or

conjecture.   But for what end was that Bill to linger
beyond the usual period of an unopposed measure?
Was it to be delayed until a rabble in Edinburgh
should dictate to the Church of England what measure
of persecution was fitting for her safety?   Was it to
be adjourned until a fanatical force could be collected
in London, sufficient to frighten us out of all our ideas
of policy and justice?   Were we to wait for the profound lectures on the reason of State, ecclesiastical and
political, which the Protestant Association have since
condescended to read to us?   Or were we seven
hundred peers and commoners the only persons
ignorant of the ribald invectives which occupy the
place of argument in those remonstrances, which every
man of common observation has heard a thousand
times over, and a thousand times over had despised?
All men had before heard what they have to say; and
all men at this day know what they dare to do;
and I trust, all honest men are equally influenced by
the one, and by the other.

But they tell us, that those our fellow-citizens,
whose chains we have a little relaxed, are enemies to
liberty and our free constitution.   Not enemies I presume to their *own* liberty.   And as to the constitution,
until we give them some share in it, I do not know
on what pretence we can examine into their opinions
about a business in which they have no interest or
concern.   But, after all, are we equally sure that they
are adverse to our constitution, as that our statutes

are hostile and destructive to them? For my part I have reason to believe their opinions and inclinations in that respect are various, exactly like those of other men; and if they lean more to the Crown than I, and than many of you think *we* ought, we must remember tha' he who aims at another's life is not to be surprised if he flies into any sanctuary that will receive him. The tenderness of the executive power is the natural asylum of those upon whom the laws have declared war; and to complain that men are inclined to favour the means of their own safety is so absurd, that one forgets the injustice in the ridicule.

I must fairly tell you that, so far as my principles are concerned (principles that I hope will only depart with my last breath) I have no idea of a liberty unconnected with honesty and justice. Nor do I believe that any good constitutions of government or of freedom can find it necessary for their security to doom any part of the people to a permanent slavery. Such a constitution of freedom, if such can be, is in effect no more than another name for the tyranny of the strongest faction; and factions in republics have been, and are full as capable as monarchs, of the most cruel oppression and injustice. It is but too true that the love, and even the very idea of genuine liberty, is extremely rare. It is but too true that there are many whose whole scheme of freedom is made up of pride, perverseness, and insolence. They feel themselves in a state of thraldom, they imagine that their

souls are cooped and cabined in unless they have some
man, or some body of men, dependent on their mercy.
This desire of having some one below them descends
to those who are the very lowest of all—and a Protestant cobbler, debased by his poverty, but exalted by
his share of the ruling Church, feels a pride in knowing
it is by his generosity alone that the peer whose foot-
man's instep he measures is able to keep his chaplain
from a jail.   This disposition is the true source of the
passion which many men in very humble life have
taken to the American war.   *Our* subjects in America ;
our colonies ;   *our* dependants.   This lust of party-
power is the liberty they hunger and thirst for ; and
this siren song of ambition has charmed ears that
one would have thought were never organised to that
sort of music.

This way of *proscribing the citizens by denominations
and general descriptions*, dignified by the name of
reason of State, and security for constitutions and
commonwealths, is nothing better at bottom than the
miserable invention of an ungenerous ambition which
would fain hold the sacred trust of power without any
of the virtues or any of the energies that give a title
to it—a receipt of policy made up of a detestable compound of malice, cowardice, and sloth.   They would
govern men against their will, but in that government
they would be discharged from the exercise of vigilance, providence, and fortitude ;   and therefore, that
they may sleep on their watch, they consent to take

some one division of the society into partnership of
the tyranny over the rest. But let Government, in
what form it may be, comprehend the whole in its
justice, and restrain the suspicious by its vigilance;
let it keep watch and ward; let it discover by its
sagacity and punish by his firmness, all delinquency
against its power, whenever delinquency exists in the
overt acts; and then it will be as safe as ever God
and nature intended it should be. Crimes are the
acts of individuals and not of denominations; and
therefore arbitrarily to class men under general descriptions, in order to proscribe and punish them in the
lump for a presumed delinquency, of which perhaps
but a part, perhaps none at all, are guilty, is indeed a
compendious method, and saves a world of trouble
about proof; but such a method, instead of being law,
is an act of unnatural rebellion against the legal
dominion of reason and justice; and this vice in any
constitution that entertains it at one time or other will
certainly bring on its ruin.

We are told that this is not a religious persecution, and its abettors are loud in disclaiming all
severities on account of conscience. Very fine indeed !
Then let it be so, they are not persecutors, they are
only tyrants. With all my heart. I am perfectly
indifferent concerning the pretexts upon which we
torment one another, or whether it be for the constitution of the Church of England, or for the constitution
of the State of England, that people choose to make

their fellow-creatures wretched. When we were sent
into a place of authority, you that sent us had yourselves but one commission to give. You could give
us none to wrong or oppress, or even to suffer any kind
of oppression or wrong, on any grounds whatsoever—
not on political, as in the affairs of America; not on
commercial, as in those of Ireland; not in civil, as in
the laws for debt; not in religious, as in the statutes
against Protestant or Catholic dissenters. The diversified but connected fabric of universal justice is well
cramped and bolted together in all its parts, and, depend
upon it, I never have employed, and I never shall
employ, any engine of power which may come into my
hands, to wrench it asunder. All shall stand, if I can
help it, and all shall stand connected. After all, to
complete this work, much remains to be done; much
in the east, much in the west. But, great as the work
is, if our will be ready, our powers are not deficient.

Since you have suffered me to trouble you so much
on this subject, permit me, gentlemen, to detain you a
little longer. I am indeed most solicitous to give you
perfect satisfaction. I find there are some of a better
and softer nature than the persons with whom I have
supposed myself in debate, who neither think ill of the
Act of relief, nor by any means desire the repeal; yet
who, not accusing but lamenting what was done, on
account of the consequences, have frequently expressed
their wish that the late Act had never been made.
Some of this description, and persons of worth I have

met with in this city.   They conceive that the prejudices, whatever they might be, of a large part of the
people ought not to have been shocked; that their
opinions ought to have been previously taken, and
much attended to; and that thereby the late horrid
scenes might have been prevented.

I confess my notions are widely different, and I
never was less sorry for any action of my life.   I like
the Bill the better, on account of the events of all
kinds that followed it.   It relieved the real sufferers,
it strengthened the State, and, by the disorders that
ensued, we had clear evidence that there lurked a
temper somewhere which ought not to be fostered by
the laws.   No ill consequences whatever could be
attributed to the Act itself.   We knew beforehand, or
we were poorly instructed, that toleration is odious to
the intolerant; freedom to oppressors; property to
robbers; and all kinds and degrees of prosperity to
the envious.   We knew that all these kinds of men
would gladly gratify their evil dispositions under the
sanction of law and religion if they could: if they
could not, yet, to make way to their objects, they would
do their utmost to subvert all religion and all law.
This we certainly knew.   But knowing this, is there
any reason because thieves break in and steal, and
thus bring detriment to you, and draw ruin on themselves, that I am to be sorry that you are in possession of shops and of warehouses, and of wholesome
laws to protect them?   Are you to build no houses

because desperate men may pull them down upon their own heads ?   Or, if a malignant wretch will cut his own throat because he sees you give alms to the necessitous and deserving, shall his destruction be attributed to your charity and not to his own deplorable madness ?   If we repent of our good actions, what, I pray you, is left for our faults and follies ?   It is not the beneficence of the laws, it is the unnatural temper which beneficence can fret and sour, that is to be lamented.   It is this temper which, by all rational means, ought to be sweetened and corrected.   If froward men should refuse this cure, can they vitiate anything but themselves ?   Does evil so react upon good as not only to retard its motion, but to change its nature ?   If it can so operate, then good men will always be in the power of the bad : and virtue, by a dreadful reverse of order, must lie under perpetual subjection and bondage to vice.

As to the opinion of the people, which some think in such cases is to be implicitly obeyed, nearly two years' tranquillity which followed the Act, and its instant imitation in Ireland, proved abundantly that the late horrible spirit was, in a great measure, the effect of insidious art, and perverse industry, and gross misrepresentation.   But suppose that the dislike had been much more deliberate and much more general than I am persuaded it was, when we know that the opinions of even the greatest multitudes are the standard of rectitude, I shall think myself obliged to make those

opinions the masters of my conscience.   But if it may
be doubted whether Omnipotence itself is competent
to alter the essential constitution of right and wrong,
sure I am that such *things* as they and I are possessed
of no such power.   No man carries farther than I do
the policy of making government pleasing to the
people.   But the widest range of this politic com-
plaisance is confined within the limits of justice.   I
would not only consult the interest of the people, but
I would cheerfully gratify their humours.   We are all
a sort of children that must be soothed and managed.
I think I am not austere or formal in my nature.   I
would bear, I would even myself play my part in, any
innocent buffooneries, to divert them.   But I never
will act the tyrant for their amusement.   If they will
mix malice in their sports, I shall never consent to
throw them any living, sentient creature whatsoever—
no, not so much as a kitling—to torment.

   " But if I profess all this impolitic stubbornness, I
may chance never to be elected into Parliament."   It
is certainly not pleasing to be put out of the public
service.   But I wish to be a member of Parliament to
have my share of doing good and resisting evil.   It
would therefore be absurd to renounce my objects, in
order to obtain my seat.   I deceive myself indeed
most grossly, if I had not much rather pass the re-
mainder of my life hidden in the recesses of the deepest
obscurity, feeding my mind even with the visions and
imaginations of such things, than to be placed on the

most splendid throne of the universe, tantalised with
a denial of the practice of all which can make the
greatest situation any other than the greatest curse.
Gentlemen, I have had my day. I can never sufficiently express my gratitude to you for having set me
in a place wherein I could lend the slightest help to
great and laudable designs. If I have had my share
in any measure giving quiet to private property and
private conscience; if by my vote I have aided in
securing to families the best possession, peace; if I
have joined in reconciling kings to their subjects, and
subjects to their prince; if I have assisted to loosen
the foreign holdings of the citizen, and taught him to
look for his protection to the laws of his country, and
for his comfort to the goodwill of his countrymen;—if
I have thus taken my part with the best of men in
the best of their actions, I can shut the book; I might
wish to read a page or two more, but this is enough
for my measure,—I have not lived in vain.

And now, gentlemen, on this serious day, when I
come, as it were, to make up my account with you,
let me take to myself some degree of honest pride on
the nature of the charges that are against me. I do
not here stand before you accused of venality, or of
neglect of duty. It is not said that, in the long
period of my service, I have in a single instance
sacrificed the slightest of your interests to my ambition, or to my fortune. It is not alleged that, to
gratify any anger or revenge of my own or of my

party, I have had a share in wronging or oppressing any description of men, or any one man in any description. No! the charges against me are all of one kind—that I have pushed the principles of general justice and benevolence too far ; farther than a cautious policy would warrant; and farther than the opinions of many would go along with me. In every accident which may happen through life—in pain, in sorrow, in depression and distress—I will call to mind this accusation, and be comforted.

Gentlemen, I submit the whole to your judgment. Mr. Mayor, I thank you for the trouble you have taken on this occasion ; in your state of health it is particularly obliging. If this company should think it advisable for me to withdraw, I shall respectfully retire ; if you think otherwise, I shall go directly to the Council House and to the Change, and, without a moment's delay, begin my canvass.

VI

A LETTER to A PEER OF IRELAND on the PENAL
LAWS AGAINST IRISH CATHOLICS, previous to the
late repeal of a part thereof in the Session of the
Irish Parliament, held A.D. 1782.

CHARLES STREET, LONDON, *Feb.* 21, 1782.

MY LORD,

I AM obliged to your lordship for your communication
of the heads of Mr. Gardiner's Bill. I had received it
in an earlier stage of its progress from Mr. Braughall,
and I am still in that gentleman's debt, as I have not
made him the proper return for the favour he has done
me. Business, to which I was more immediately called,
and in which my sentiments had the weight of one
vote, occupied me every moment since I received his
letter. This first morning which I can call my own,
I give with great cheerfulness to the subject on which
your lordship has done me the honour of desiring my
opinion. I have read the heads of the Bill with the
amendments. Your lordship is too well acquainted
with men and with affairs to imagine that any true

judgment can be formed on the value of a great measure of policy from the perusal of a piece of paper. At present I am much in the dark with regard to the state of the country which the intended law is to be applied to.[1] It is not easy for me to determine whether or no it was wise (for the sake of expunging the black letter of laws, which, menacing as they were in the language, were every day fading into disuse) solemnly to reaffirm the principles, and to re-enact the provisions of a code of statutes, by which you are totally excluded from the PRIVILEGES OF THE COMMONWEALTH from the highest to the lowest, from the most material of the civil professions, from the army, and even from education, where alone education is to be had.

Whether this scheme of indulgence, grounded at once on contempt and jealousy, has a tendency gradually to produce something better and more liberal, I cannot tell, for want of having the actual map of the country. If this should be the case, it was right in you to accept it, such as it is. But if this should be one of the experiments which have sometimes been made before the temper of the nation was ripe for a real reformation, I think it may possibly have ill effects by disposing the penal matter in a more systematic order, and thereby fixing a permanent bar against

[1] The sketch of the Bill sent to Mr. Burke, along with the repeal of some Acts, reaffirmed many others in the penal code. It was altered afterwards, and the clauses reaffirming the incapacities left out, but they all still exist, and are in full force.

any relief that is truly substantial. The whole merit
or demerit of the measure depends upon the .plans and
dispositions of those by whom the Act was made concurring with the general temper of the Protestants of
Ireland, and their aptitude to admit in time of some
part of that equality, without which you never can be
FELLOW-CITIZENS. Of all this I am wholly ignorant.
All my correspondence with men of public importance
in Ireland has for some time totally ceased. On the
first Bill for the relief of the ROMAN CATHOLICS of
Ireland I was, without any call of mine, consulted
both on your side of the water and on this. On the
present occasion I have not heard a word from any
man in office, and know as little of the intentions of
the British Government as I know of the temper of
the Irish Parliament. I do not find that any opposition was made by the principal persons of the minority
in the House of Commons, or that any is apprehended
from them in the House of Lords. The whole of the
difficulty seems to lie with the principal men in
Government, under whose protection this Bill is
supposed to be brought in. This violent opposition
and cordial support, coming from one and the same
quarter, appears to me something mysterious, and
hinders me from being able to make any clear judgment of the merit of the present measure, as compared
with the actual state of the country and the general
views of Government, without which one can say
nothing that may not be very erroneous.

To look at the Bill in the abstract, it is neither more nor.less than a renewed act of UNIVERSAL, UNMITI-GATED, INDISPENSABLE, EXCEPTIONLESS DISQUALIFI-CATION.

One would imagine that a Bill, inflicting such a multitude of incapacities, had followed on the heels of a conquest made by a very fierce enemy, under the impression of recent animosity and resentment. No man on reading that Bill could imagine he was reading an Act of amnesty and indulgence, following a recital of the good behaviour of those who are the objects of it : which recital stood at the head of the Bill, as it was first introduced ; but I suppose for its incongruity with the body of the piece, was afterwards omitted.— This I say on memory. It, however, still recites the oath, and that Catholics ought to be considered as good and loyal subjects to his Majesty, his Crown and Government. Then follows a universal exclusion of those GOOD and LOYAL subjects from every (even the lowest) office of trust and profit ; from any vote at an election ; from any privilege in a town corporate ; from being even a freeman of such a corporation ; from serving on grand juries ; from a vote at a vestry ; from having a gun in his house ; from being a barrister, attorney, or solicitor, etc. etc. etc.

This has surely much more the air of a table of proscription than an act of grace. What must we suppose the laws concerning those *good* subjects to have been, of which this is a relaxation ? I know

well that there is a cant language current, about the
difference between an exclusion from employments
even to the most rigorous extent, and an exclusion
from the natural benefits arising from a man's own
industry. I allow that under some circumstances the
difference is very material in point of justice, and that
there are considerations which may render it advisable
for a wise government to keep the leading parts of
every branch of civil and military administration in
hands of the best trust; but a total exclusion from the
commonwealth is a very different thing. When a
government subsists (as governments formerly did) on
an estate of its own, with but few and inconsiderable
revenues drawn from the subject, then the few officers
which existed in such establishments were naturally
at the disposal of that government, which paid the
salaries out of its own coffers; there an exclusive preference could hardly merit the name of proscription.
Almost the whole produce of a man's industry at that
time remained in his own purse to maintain his family.
But times alter, and the *whole* estate of government is
from private contribution. When a very great portion
of the labour of individuals goes to the State, and is
by the State again refunded to individuals through the
medium of offices, and in this circuitous progress from
the private to the public, and from the public again to
the private fund, the families from whom the revenue
is taken are indemnified, and an equitable balance between the Government and the subject is established.

But if a great body of the people, who contribute to this State lottery, are excluded from all the prizes, the stopping the circulation with regard to them may be a most cruel hardship, amounting in effect to being double and treble taxed; and it will be felt as such to the very quick by all the families high and low of those hundreds of thousands who are denied their chance in the returned fruits of their own industry. This is the thing meant by those who look upon the public revenue only as a spoil; and will naturally wish to have as few as possible concerned in the division of the booty. If a State should be so unhappy as to think it cannot subsist without such a barbarous proscription, the persons so proscribed ought to be indemnified by the remission of a large part of their taxes, by an immunity from the offices of public burden, and by an exemption from being pressed into any military or naval service.

Common sense and common justice dictate this at least, as some sort of compensation to a people for their slavery. How many families are incapable of existing if the little offices of the revenue and little military commissions are denied them! To deny them at home, and to make the happiness of acquiring some of them somewhere else, felony, or high treason, is a piece of cruelty, in which, till very lately, I did not suppose this age capable of persisting. Formerly a similarity of religion made a sort of country for a man in some quarter or other. A refugee for religion was a pro-

tected character.   Now, the reception is cold indeed;
and, therefore, as the asylum abroad is destroyed, the
hardship at home is doubled.   This hardship is the
more intolerable because the professions are shut up.
The Church is so of course.   Much is to be said on
that subject in regard to them and to the Protestant
dissenters.   But that is a chapter by itself.   I am
sure I wish well to that Church, and think its
ministers among the very best citizens of your country.
However, such as it is, a great walk in life is forbidden
ground to seventeen hundred thousand of the inhabitants of Ireland.   Why are they excluded from the
law ?   Do not they expend money in their suits ?
Why may not they indemnify themselves by profiting
in the persons of some for the losses incurred by others?
Why may not they have persons of confidence, whom
they may, if they please, employ in the agency of their
affairs ?   The exclusion from the law, from grand
juries, from sheriffships and under-sheriffships, as
well as from freedom in any corporation, may subject
them to dreadful hardships, as it may exclude them
wholly from all that is beneficial, and expose them to
all that is mischievous in a trial by jury.   This was
manifestly within my own observation, for I was three
times in Ireland from the year 1760 to the year 1767,
where I had sufficient means of information concerning
the inhuman proceedings (among which were many
cruel murders, besides an infinity of outrages and
oppressions, unknown before in a civilised age) which

prevailed during that period in consequence of a pretended conspiracy among *Roman Catholics* against the king's Government. I could dilate upon the mischief that may happen from those which have happened upon this head of disqualification if it were at all necessary.

The head of exclusion from votes for members of Parliament is closely connected with the former. When you cast your eye on the statute-book, you will see that no *Catholic*, even in the ferocious Acts of Queen Anne, was disabled from voting on account of his religion. The only conditions required for that privilege were the oaths of allegiance and abjuration— both oaths relative to a civil concern. Parliament has since added another oath of the same kind, and yet a House of Commons adding to the securities of government in proportion as its danger is confessedly lessened, and professing both confidence and indulgence in effect, takes away the privilege left by an Act full of jealousy and professing persecution.

The taking away of a vote is the taking away the shield which the subject has, not only against the oppression of power, but that worst of all oppressions, the persecution of private society and private manners. No candidate for parliamentary influence is obliged to the least attention towards them, either in cities or counties. On the contrary, if they should become obnoxious to any bigoted or malignant people amongst whom they live, it will become the interest of those

who court popular favour to use the numberless means
which always reside in magistracy and influence to
oppress them.   The proceedings in a certain county in
Munster during the unfortunate period I have mentioned, read a strong lecture on the cruelty of depriving
men of that shield, on account of their speculative
opinions.   The Protestants of Ireland feel well and
naturally on the hardship of being bound by laws, in
the enacting of which they do not directly or indirectly
vote.   The bounds of these matters are nice, and hard
to be settled in theory, and perhaps they have been
pushed too far.   But how they can avoid the necessary
application of the principles they use in their disputes
with others to their disputes with their fellow-citizens,
I know not.

It is true, the words of this Act do not create a
disability ; but they clearly and evidently suppose it.
There are few *Catholic* freeholders to take the benefit
of the privilege, if they were permitted to partake it :
but the manner in which this very right in freeholders
at large is defended, is not on the idea that the freeholders do really and truly represent the people ; but
that all people being capable of obtaining freeholds, all
those who by their industry and sobriety merit this
privilege, have the means of arriving at votes.   It is
the same with the corporations.

The laws against foreign education are clearly the
very worst part of the old code.   Besides your laity,
you have the succession of about 4000 clergymen to

provide for. These, having no lucrative objects in prospect, are taken very much out of the lower orders of the people. At home they have no means whatsoever provided for their attaining a clerical education, or indeed any education at all. When I was in Paris, about seven years ago, I looked at everything, and lived with every kind of people, as well as my time admitted. I saw there the Irish college of the Lombard, which seemed to me a very good place of education, under excellent orders and regulations, and under the government of a very prudent and learned man (the late Dr. KELLY). This college was possessed of an annual fixed revenue of more than a thousand pounds a year; the greatest part of which had arisen from the legacies and benefactions of persons educated in that college, and who had obtained promotions in France, from the emolument of which promotions they made this grateful return. One in particular I remember, to the amount of ten thousand livres, annually, as it is recorded on the donor's monument in their chapel.

It has been the custom of poor persons in Ireland to pick up such knowledge of the Latin tongue as, under the general discouragements, and occasional pursuits of magistracy, they were able to acquire; and receiving orders at home, were sent abroad to obtain a clerical education. By officiating in petty chaplainships, and performing, now and then, certainly offices of religion for small gratuities, they received the means of maintaining themselves, until they were able to

complete their education. Through such difficulties
and discouragements, many of them arrived at a very
considerable proficiency, so as to be marked and
distinguished abroad. These persons afterwards, by
being sunk in the most abject poverty, despised and
ill-treated by the high orders among Protestants, and
not much better esteemed or treated, even by the few
persons of fortune of their own persuasion, and
contracting the habits and ways of thinking of the
poor and uneducated, among whom they were obliged
to live, in a few retained little or no traces of the
talents and acquirements, which distinguished them in
the early periods of their lives. Can we, with justice,
cut them off from the use of places of education,
founded, for the greater part, from the economy of
poverty and exile, without providing something that is
equivalent at home ?

Whilst this restraint of foreign and domestic
education was part of a horrible and impious system
of servitude, the members were well fitted to the body.
To render men patient under a deprivation of all the
rights of human nature, everything which could give
them a knowledge or feeling of those rights was
rationally forbidden. To render humanity fit to be
insulted, it was fit that it should be degraded. But
when we profess to restore men to the capacity for
property, it is equally irrational and unjust to deny
them the power of improving their minds as well as
their fortunes. Indeed, I have ever thought that the

prohibition of the means of improving our rational nature to be the worst species of tyranny that the insolence and perverseness of mankind ever dared to exercise. This goes to all men, in all situations, to whom education can be denied.

Your lordship mentions a proposal which came from my friend the provost, whose benevolence and enlarged spirit I am perfectly convinced of—which is, the proposal of erecting a few sizerships in the college for the education (I suppose) of Roman Catholic clergymen.[1] He certainly meant it well, but coming from such a man as he is, it is a strong instance of the danger of suffering any description of men to fall into entire contempt. The charities intended for them are not perceived to be fresh insults, and the true nature of their wants and necessities being unknown, remedies wholly unsuitable to the nature of their complaint are provided for them. It is to feed a sick Gentoo with beef broth, and to foment his wounds with brandy. If the other parts of the University were open to them as well on the foundation as otherwise, the offering of sizerships would be a proportioned part of a *general* kindness. But when everything *liberal* is withheld, and only that which is *servile* is permitted, it is easy to conceive upon what footing they must be in such a place.

Mr. Hutchinson must well know the regard and

---

[1] It appears that Mr. Hutchinson meant this only as one of the means for their relief in point of education.

O

honour I have for him, and he cannot think my dissenting from him in this particular arises from a disregard of his opinion—it only shows that I think he has lived in Ireland. To have any respect for the character and person of a Popish priest there——oh ! 'tis an uphill work indeed. But until we come to respect what stands in a respectable light with others, we are very deficient in the temper which qualifies us to make any laws and regulations about them. It even disqualifies us from being charitable to them with any effect or judgment.

When we are to provide for the education of any body of men, we ought seriously to consider the particular functions they are to perform in life. A Roman Catholic clergyman is the minister of a very ritual religion, and by his profession subject to many restraints. His life is a life full of strict observances, and his duties are of a laborious nature towards himself, and of the highest possible trust towards others. The duty of confession alone is sufficient to set in the strongest light the necessity of his having an appropriated mode of education. The theological opinions and peculiar rights of one religion never can be properly taught in universities founded for the purposes and on the principles of another, which in many points are directly opposite. If a Roman Catholic clergyman, intended for celibacy and the function of confession, is not strictly bred in a seminary where these things are respected, inculcated, and enforced as sacred, and not made the subject of derision and obloquy, he will be ill fitted for the former, and the latter will be indeed in his hands a terrible instrument.

There is a great resemblance between the whole frame and constitution of the Greek and Latin churches. The secular clergy in the former, by being married, living under little restraint, and having no particular education suited to their function, are universally fallen into such contempt that they are never permitted to aspire to the dignities of their own church. It is not held respectful to call them *papas*, their true and ancient appellation, but those who wish to address them with civility always call them *hieromonachi*. In consequence of this disrespect, which, I venture to say, in such a church must be the consequence of a secular life, a very great degeneracy from reputable Christian manners has taken place throughout almost the whole of that great member of the Christian Church.

It was so with the Latin church before the restraint on marriage. Even that restraint gave rise to the greatest disorders before the Council of Trent, which, together with the emulation raised and the good examples given by the reformed churches, wherever they were in view of each other, has brought on that happy amendment which we see in the Latin communion, both at home and abroad.

The Council of Trent has wisely introduced the discipline of seminaries, by which priests are not

trusted for a clerical institution even to the severe
discipline of their colleges; but, after they pass
through them, are frequently, if not for the greater
part, obliged to pass through peculiar methods having
their particular ritual function in view. It is in a
great measure to this and to similar methods used in
foreign education, that the Roman Catholic clergy of
Ireland, miserably provided for, living among low and
ill-regulated people, without any discipline of sufficient
force to secure good manners, have been prevented
from becoming an intolerable nuisance to the country,
instead of being, as I conceive they generally are, a
very great service to it.

The ministers of Protestant churches require a
different mode of education, more liberal and more
fit for the ordinary intercourse of life. That religion
having little hold on the minds of people by external
ceremonies and extraordinary observances, or separate
habits of living, the clergy make up the deficiency by
cultivating their minds with all kinds of ornamental
learning, which the liberal provision made in England
and Ireland for the parochial clergy (to say nothing of
the ample church preferments, with little or no duties
annexed), and the comparative lightness of parochial
duties, enables the greater part of them in some considerable degree to accomplish.

This learning, which I believe to be pretty general,
together with a higher situation, and more chastened
by the opinion of mankind, forms a sufficient security

for the morals of the established clergy, and for their
sustaining their clerical character with dignity.   It is
not necessary to observe that all these things are, however, collateral to their function, and that except in
preaching, which may be and is supplied, and often
best supplied, out of printed books, little else is necessary for a Protestant minister than to be able to read
the English language,—I mean for the exercise of his
function, not to the qualification of his admission to it.
But a Popish parson in Ireland may do very well
without any considerable classical erudition, or any
proficiency in pure or mixed mathematics, or any
knowledge of civil history.   Even if the Catholic
clergy should possess those acquisitions, as at first
many of them do, they soon lose them in the painful
course of professional and parochial duties; but they
must have all the knowledge, and, what is to them
more important than the knowledge, the discipline
necessary to those duties.   All modes of education,
conducted by those whose minds are cast in another
mould, as I may say, and whose original ways of
thinking are formed upon the reverse pattern, must be
to them not only useless but mischievous.   Just as I
should suppose the education in a Popish ecclesiastical
seminary would be ill fitted for a Protestant clergyman.
To educate a Catholic priest in a Protestant seminary
would be much worse.   The Protestant educated
amongst Catholics has only something to reject: what
he keeps may be useful.   But a Catholic parish priest

learns little for his peculiar purpose and duty in a Protestant college.

All this, my lord, I know very well will pass for nothing with those who wish that the popish clergy should be illiterate, and in a situation to produce contempt and detestation. Their minds are wholly taken up with party squabbles, and I have neither leisure nor inclination to apply any part of what I have to say to those who never think of religion, or of the commonwealth, in any other light than as they tend to the prevalence of some faction in either. I speak on a supposition that there is a disposition *to take the State in the condition in which it is found*, and to improve it *in that state* to the best advantage. Hitherto the plan for the government of Ireland has been to sacrifice the civil prosperity of the nation to its religious improvement. But if people in power there are at length come to entertain other ideas, they will consider the good order, decorum, virtue, and morality of every description of men among them as of infinitely greater importance than the struggle (for it is nothing better) to change those descriptions by means which put to hazard objects which, in my poor opinion, are of more importance to religion and to the State than all the polemical matter which has been agitated among men from the beginning of the world to this hour.

On this idea, an education fitted *to each order and division of men, such as they are found*, will be thought an affair rather to be encouraged than discountenanced; and until institutions at home, suitable to the occasions and necessities of the people, are established, and which are armed, as they are abroad, with authority to coerce the young men to be formed in them, by a strict and severe discipline,—the means they have at present of a cheap and effectual education in other countries should not continue to be prohibited by penalties and modes of inquisition, not fit to be mentioned to ears that are organised to the chaste sounds of equity and justice.

Before I had written thus far, I heard of a scheme of giving to the Castle the patronage of the presiding members of the Catholic clergy. At first I could scarcely credit it; for I believe it is the first time that the presentation to other people's alms has been desired in any country. If the State provides a suitable maintenance and temporality for the governing members of the Irish Roman Catholic Church, and for the clergy under them, I should think the project, however improper in other respects, to be by no means unjust. But to deprive a poor people, who maintain a second set of clergy out of the miserable remains of what is left after taxing and tithing,—to deprive them of the disposition of their own charities among their own communion,—would, in my opinion, be an intolerable hardship. Never were the members of one religious sect fit to appoint the pastors to another. Those who have no regard for their welfare, reputa-

tion, or internal quiet, will not appoint such as are
proper.   The seraglio of Constantinople is as equitable
as we are, whether Catholics or Protestants; and where
their own sect is concerned, full as religious.   But the
sport which they make of the miserable dignities of
the Greek Church,—the little factions of the harem to
which they make them subservient, the continual sale
to which they expose and re-expose the same dignity,
and by which they squeeze all the inferior orders of
the clergy,—is (for I have had particular means of
being acquainted with it) nearly equal to all the other
oppressions together, exercised by Mussulmen over the
unhappy members of the Oriental Church.   It is a
great deal to suppose that even the present Castle
would nominate bishops for the Roman Church of
Ireland, with a religious regard for its welfare.   Perhaps they cannot, perhaps they dare not do it.

But suppose them to be well inclined, as I know
that I am, to do the Catholics all kind of justice,
I declare I would not, if it were in my power, take
that patronage on myself.   I know I ought not to do
it.   I belong to another community, and it would be
intolerable usurpation for me to affect such authority,
where I conferred no benefit, or even if I did confer
(as in some degree the seraglio does) temporal advantages.   But, allowing that the *present* Castle finds itself
fit to administer the government of a Church which
they solemnly forswear, and forswear with very hard
words and many evil epithets, and that as often as

they qualify themselves for the power which is to give this very patronage, or to give anything else that they desire,—yet they cannot ensure themselves that a man like the late Lord Chesterfield will not succeed to them. This man, while he was duping the credulity of Papists with fine words in private, and commending their good behaviour during a rebellion in Great Britain (as it well deserved to be commended and rewarded), was capable of urging penal laws against them in a speech from the throne, and of stimulating with provocatives the wearied and half-exhausted bigotry of the then Parliament of Ireland. They set to work, but they were at a loss what to do; for they had already almost gone through every contrivance which could *waste the vigour* of their country; but after much struggle they produced a child of their old age, the shocking and unnatural act about marriages, which tended to finish the scheme for making the people not only two distinct parties for ever, but keeping them as two distinct species in the same land. Mr. Gardiner's humanity was shocked at it, as one of the worst parts of that truly barbarous system, if one could well settle the preference, where almost all the parts were outrages on the rights of humanity and the laws of nature.

Suppose an atheist, playing the part of a bigot, should be in power again in that country, do you believe that he would faithfully and religiously administer the trust of appointing pastors to a Church, which, wanting every other support, stands in tenfold

need of ministers who will be dear to the people committed to their charge, and who will exercise a really
paternal authority amongst them ?   But if the superior
power was always in a disposition to dispense con-
scientiously, and like an upright trustee and guardian
of these rights which he holds for those with whom he
is at variance, has he the capacity and means of doing
it ?   How can the Lord-Lieutenant form the least
judgment of their merits, so as to discern which of the
Popish priests is fit to be made a bishop ?   It cannot
be : the idea is ridiculous.   He will hand them over
to lords-lieutenants of counties, justices of the peace,
and other persons, who, for the purpose of vexing and
turning to derision this miserable people, will pick out
the worst and most obnoxious they can find amongst
the clergy to set over the rest.   Whoever is complained
against by his brother will be considered as persecuted ;
whoever is censured by his superior will be looked
upon as oppressed ; whoever is careless in his opinions
and loose in his morals will be called a liberal man,
and will be supposed to have incurred hatred, because
he was not a bigot.   Informers, tale-bearers, perverse
and obstinate men, flatterers, who turn their back upon
their flock, and court the Protestant gentlemen of the
country, will be the objects of preferment.   And then
I run no risk in foretelling that whatever order, quiet,
and morality you have in the country, will be lost.
A Popish clergy who are not restrained by the most
austere subordination will become a nuisance, a real

public grievance of the heaviest kind, in any country that entertains them; and instead of the great benefit which Ireland does, and has long derived from them, if they are educated without any idea of discipline and obedience, and then put under bishops who do not owe their station to their good opinion, and whom they cannot respect, that nation will see disorders of which, bad as things are, it has yet no idea. I do not say this as thinking the leading men in Ireland would exercise this trust worse than others. Not at all. No man, no set of men living are fit to administer the affairs, or regulate the interior economy of a Church to which they are enemies.

As to government, if I might recommend a prudent caution to them, it would be to innovate as little as possible upon speculation in establishments from which, as they stand, they experience no material inconvenience to the repose of the country,—*quieta non movere.* I could say a great deal more, but I am tired, and am afraid your lordship is tired too. I have not sat to this letter a single quarter of an hour without interruption. It has grown long, and probably contains many repetitions from my total want of leisure to digest and consolidate my thoughts; and as to my expressions, I could wish to be able perhaps to measure them more exactly. But my intentions are fair, and I certainly mean to offend nobody.

.   .   .   .

Thinking over this matter more maturely, I see no

reason for altering my opinion in any part. The
Act as far as it goes, is good undoubtedly. It amounts,
I think, very nearly to a *toleration* with respect to
religious ceremonies, but it puts a new bolt on civil
rights, and rivets it to the old one in such a manner
that neither, I fear, will be easily loosened. What I
could have wished would be to see the civil advantages
take the lead ; the other of a religious toleration, I conceive, would follow (in a manner) of course. From what
I have observed, it is pride, arrogance, and a spirit of
domination, and not a bigoted spirit of religion, that
has caused and kept up those oppressive statutes. I
am sure I have known those who have oppressed
Papists in their civil rights exceedingly indulgent to
them in their religious ceremonies, and who really
wished them to continue Catholics, in order to furnish
pretences for oppression. These persons never saw a
man (by converting) escape out of their power, but
with grudging and regret. I have known men to
whom I am not uncharitable in saying (though they
are dead) that they would have become Papists in
order to oppress Protestants, if, being Protestants, it
was not in their power to oppress Papists. It is injustice, and not a mistaken conscience, that has been the
principle of persecution, at least as far as it has fallen
under my observation. However, as I began, so I end.
I do not know the map of the country. Mr. Gardiner
who conducts this great and difficult work, and those
who support him, are better judges of the business

than I can pretend to be, who have not set my foot in Ireland these sixteen years.   I have been given to understand that I am not considered as a friend to that country, and I know that pains have been taken to lessen the credit that I might have had there.

.   .   .   .   .   .

I am so convinced of the weakness of interfering in any business without the opinion of the people in whose business I interefere, that I do not know how to acquit myself of what I have now done.—I have the honour to be, with high regard and esteem, my Lord, your Lordship's most obedient and humble servant, etc.,   EDMUND BURKE.

VII.

A LETTER to Sir H. Langrishe, Bart., M.P., on the
Subject of the Roman Catholics of Ireland,
AND THE PROPRIETY OF ADMITTING THEM TO THE
ELECTIVE FRANCHISE, CONSISTENTLY WITH THE
PRINCIPLES OF THE CONSTITUTION AS ESTABLISHED
AT THE REVOLUTION, 1792.

My dear Sir,

Your remembrance of me with sentiments of so much
kindness has given me the most sincere satisfaction.
It perfectly agrees with the friendly and hospitable
reception which my son and I received from you some
time since, when, after an absence of twenty-two years,
I had the happiness of embracing you among my few
surviving friends.

I really imagined that I should not again interest
myself in any public business. I had, to the best of
my moderate faculties, paid my club to the society
which I was born in some way or other to serve; and
I thought I had a right to put on my night-gown and
slippers, and wish a cheerful evening to the good com-

pany I must leave behind.   But if our resolutions of
vigour and exertion are so often broken or procrastin-
ated in the execution, I think we may be excused if
we are not very punctual in fulfilling our engagements
to indolence and inactivity.   I have indeed no power
of action, and am almost a cripple, even with regard
to thinking; but you descend with force into the
stagnant pool, and you cause such a fermentation as
to cure at least one impotent creature of his lameness,
though it cannot enable him either to run or to
wrestle.

You see by the paper [1] I take that I am likely to
be long, with malice prepense.   You have brought
under my view a subject always difficult, at present
critical.   It has filled my thoughts, which I wish to
lay open to you with the clearness and simplicity
which your friendship demands from me.   I thank
you for the communication of your ideas.   I should be
still more pleased if they had been more your own.
What you hint I believe to be the case,—that if you
had not deferred to the judgment of others, our
opinions would not differ more materially at this day
than they did when we used to confer on the same
subject so many years ago.   If I still persevere in
my old opinions, it is no small comfort to me that
it is not with regard to doctrines properly yours that I
discover my indocility.

The case upon which your letter of the 10th of

---

[1] The letter is written on folio sheets.

December turns is hardly before me with precision
enough to enable me to form any very certain judgment upon it.   It seems to be some plan of further
indulgence proposed for the Catholics of Ireland.
You observe that your "general principles are not
changed, but that *times and circumstances are altered*."
I perfectly agree with you that times and circumstances, considered with reference to the public, ought
very much to govern our conduct, though I am
far from slighting, when applied with discretion to
those circumstances, general principles and maxims
of policy.   I cannot help observing, however, that
you have said rather less upon the inapplicability of
your own old principles to the *circumstances* that are
likely to influence your conduct against these principles, than of the *general* maxims of State, which I
can very readily believe not to have great weight
with you personally.

In my present state of imperfect information, you
will pardon the errors into which I may easily fall.
The principles you lay down are, "that the Roman
Catholics should enjoy everything *under* the State,
but should not be *the State itself*."   And you add,
" that when you exclude them from being *a part of
the State*, you rather conform to the spirit of the age
than to any abstract doctrine;" but you consider the
constitution as already established — that our State
is Protestant.   " It was declared so at the Revolution.
It was so provided in the Acts for settling the succes-

sion of the Crown—the king's coronation oath was enjoined, in order to keep it so. The king, as first magistrate of the State, is obliged to take the oath of abjuration,[1] and to subscribe the declaration; and, by laws subsequent, every other magistrate and member of the State, legislative and executive, are bound under the same obligation."

As to the plan to which these maxims are applied, I cannot speak, as I told you, positively about it, because neither from your letter nor from any information I have been able to collect, do I find anything settled, either on the part of the Roman Catholics themselves or on that of any persons who may wish to conduct their affairs in Parliament. But if I have leave to conjecture, something is in agitation towards admitting them, under *certain qualifications*, to have *some share* in the election of members of Parliament. This, I understand, is the scheme of those who are entitled to come within your description of persons of consideration, property, and character; and firmly attached to the king and constitution, as by " law established, with a grateful sense of your former concessions, and a patient reliance on the benignity of Parliament for the further mitigation of the laws that still affect them." As to the low, thoughtless, wild and profligate, who have joined themselves with those of other professions but of the same character, you are

---

[1] A small error of fact as to the abjuration oath; but of no importance in the argument.

P

not to imagine that, for a moment, I can suppose them
to be met with anything else than the manly and
enlightened energy of a firm government, supported
by the united efforts of all virtuous men, if ever their
proceedings should become so considerable as to demand
its notice.   I really think that such associations should
be crushed in their very commencement.

Setting, therefore, this case out of the question, it
becomes an object of very serious consideration whether,
because wicked men of *various* descriptions are engaged
in seditious courses, the rational, sober, and valuable
part of *one* description should not be indulged in their
sober and rational expectations?   You who have looked
deeply into the spirit of the Popery laws, must be perfectly sensible that a great part of the present mischief
which we abhor in common (if it at all exists) has
arisen from them.   Their declared object was to reduce
the Catholics of Ireland to a miserable populace, without property, without estimation, without education.
The professed object was to deprive the few men who,
in spite of those laws, might hold or retain any property amongst them, of all sort of influence or authority
over the rest.   They divided the nation into two distinct bodies, without common interest, sympathy, or
connection.   One of these bodies was to possess *all*
the franchises, *all* the property, *all* the education; the
other was to be composed of drawers of water and
cutters of turf for them.   Are we to be astonished
when, by the efforts of so much violence in conquest,

and so much policy in regulation, continued without
intermission for near a hundred years, we had reduced
them to a mob; that whenever they came to act at all,
many of them would act exactly like a mob, without
temper, measure, or foresight ?   Surely it might be
just now a matter of temperate discussion whether
you ought not to apply a remedy to the real cause of
the evil.   If the disorder you speak of be real and
considerable, you ought to raise an aristocratic interest,
that is, an interest of property and education, amongst
them, and to strengthen, by every prudent means, the
authority and influence of men of that description.
It will deserve your best thoughts to examine whether
this can be done without giving such persons the
means of demonstrating to the rest, that something
more is to be got by their temperate conduct than
can be expected from the wild and senseless projects
of those who do not belong to their body, who have
no interest in their well-being, and only wish to make
them the dupes of their turbulent ambition.

If the absurd persons you mention find no way of
providing for liberty but by overturning this happy
constitution and introducing a frantic democracy, let
us take care how we prevent better people from any
rational expectations of partaking in the benefits of
that constitution *as it stands*.   The maxims you establish cut the matter short.   They have no sort of connection with the good or the ill behaviour of the
persons who seek relief, or with the proper or improper

means by which they seek it.   They form a perpetual
bar to all pleas and to all expectations.

You begin by asserting that " the Catholics ought
to enjoy all things *under* the State, but that they
ought not to *be the State.*"   A position which, I believe,
in the latter part of it, and in the latitude there expressed, no man of common sense has ever thought
proper to dispute; because the contrary implies that
the State ought to be in them *exclusively.*   But before
you have finished the line, you express yourself as if
the other member of your proposition—namely, that
" they ought not to be *a part* of the State,"—were
necessarily included in the first; whereas I conceive
it to be as different as a part is from the whole—that
is, just as different as possible.   I know, indeed, that
it is common with those who talk very differently
from you—that is, with heat and animosity—to confound those things, and to argue the admission of the
Catholics into any—however minute and subordinate
—parts of the State, as a surrender into their hands
of the whole government of the kingdom.   To them
I have nothing at all to say.

Wishing to proceed with a deliberative spirit and
temper in so very serious a question, I shall attempt
to analyse, as well as I can, the principles you lay
down, in order to fit them for the grasp of an understanding so little comprehensive as mine.   " State,"
" Protestant," " Revolution."   These are terms which,
if not well explained, may lead us into many errors.

In the word *State,* I conceive there is much ambiguity. The State is sometimes used to signify *the whole commonwealth,* comprehending all its orders, with the several privileges belonging to each.   Sometimes it signifies only *the higher and ruling part* of the commonwealth, which we commonly call *the Government.*   In the first sense, to be under the State, but not the State itself, *nor any part of it,* that is, to be nothing at all in the commonwealth, is a situation perfectly intelligible; but to those who fill that situation, not very pleasant, when it is understood.   It is a state of *civil servitude* by the very force of the definition.   *Servorum non est respublica* is a very old and a very true maxim. This servitude, which makes men *subject* to a State without being *citizens,* may be more or less tolerable from many circumstances; but these circumstances, more or less favourable, do not alter the nature of the thing.   The mildness by which absolute masters exercise their dominion leaves them masters still.   We may talk a little presently of the manner in which the majority of the people of Ireland (the Catholics) are affected by this situation, which at present undoubtedly is theirs; and which you are of opinion ought so to continue for ever.

In the other sense of the word *State,* by which is understood the *Supreme Government* only, I must observe this upon the question—that to exclude whole classses of men entirely from this *part* of government, cannot be considered as *absolute slavery.*   It only implies a lower and degraded state of citizenship; such is (with more or less strictness) the condition of all countries in which a hereditary nobility possess the exclusive rule. This may be no bad mode of government, provided that the personal authority of individual nobles be kept in due bounds; that their cabals and factions are guarded against with a severe vigilance; and that the people (who have no share in granting their own money) are subjected to but light impositions, and are otherwise treated with attention, and with indulgence to their humours and prejudices.

The Republic of Venice is one of those which strictly confines all the great functions and offices, such as are truly *State* functions and *State* offices, to those who, by hereditary right or admission, are noble Venetians. But there are many offices, and some of them not mean nor unprofitable (that of Chancellor is one), which are reserved for the *Cittadini*. Of these all citizens of Venice are capable. The inhabitants of the *Terra firma*, who are mere subjects of conquest, that is, as you express it, under the State, but "not a part of it," are not, however, subjects in so very rigorous a sense as not to be capable of numberless subordinate employments. It is, indeed, one of the advantages attending the narrow bottom of their aristocracy (narrow as compared with their acquired dominions, otherwise broad enough), that an exclusion from such employments cannot possibly be made amongst their subjects. There are, besides, advantages in States so constituted by which those who are considered as of an inferior race are indemnified for their exclusion from the government and from nobler employments.   In all these countries, either by express law, or by usage more operative, the noble casts are almost universally in their turn excluded from commerce, manufacture, farming of land, and in general from all lucrative civil professions.   The nobles have the monopoly of honour ; the plebeians a monopoly of all the means of acquiring wealth.   Thus some sort of a balance is formed among conditions ; a sort of compensation is furnished to those who, in a *limited sense*, are excluded from the government of the State.

Between the extreme of *a total exclusion*, to which your maxim goes, and *an universal unmodified capacity*, to which the fanatics pretend, there are many different degrees and stages, and a great variety of temperaments, upon which prudence may give full scope to its exertions.   For you know that the decisions of prudence (contrary to the system of the insane reasoners) differ from those of judicature ; and that almost all the former are determined on the more or the less, the earlier or the later, and on a balance of advantage and inconvenience, of good and evil.

In all considerations which turn upon the question of vesting or continuing the State solely and exclusively in some one description of citizens, prudent legislators will consider how far the *general form and principles of their commonwealth render it fit to be cast into an*

oligarchical shape, or to remain always in it.   We know
that the Government of Ireland (the same as the British)
is not in its constitution *wholly* aristocratical; and as
it is not such in its form, so neither is it in its spirit.
If it had been inveterately aristocratical, exclusions
might be more patiently submitted to.   The lot of one
plebeian would be the lot of all; and an habitual
reverence and admiration of certain families might
make the people content to see government wholly in
hands to whom it seemed naturally to belong.   But
our constitution has *a plebeian member*, which forms an
essential integrant part of it.   A plebeian oligarchy is
a monster; and no people not absolutely domestic or
predial slaves will long endure it.   The Protestants of
Ireland are not *alone* sufficiently the people to form a
democracy; and they are *too numerous* to answer the
ends and purposes of *an aristocracy*.   Admiration, that
first source of obedience, can be only the claim or the
imposture of a few.   I hold it to be absolutely impossible for two millions of plebeians, composing, certainly,
a very clear and decided majority in that class, to become so far in love with six or seven hundred thousand
of their fellow-citizens (to all outward appearance
plebeians like themselves, and many of them tradesmen, servants, and otherwise inferior to some of them)
as to see with satisfaction, or even with patience, an
exclusive power vested in them, by which *constitutionally* they become the absolute masters, and by the
manners derived from their circumstances, must be

capable of exercising upon them, daily and hourly, an insulting and vexatious superiority. Neither are the majority of the Irish indemnified (as in some aristocracies) for this state of humiliating vassalage (often inverting the nature of things and relations) by having the lower walks of industry wholly abandoned to them. They are rivalled, to say the least of the matter, in every laborious and lucrative course of life ; while every franchise, every honour, every trust, every place down to the very lowest and least confidential (besides whole professions), is reserved for the master cast.

Our constitution is not made for great, general, and proscriptive exclusions ; sooner or later it will destroy them, or they will destroy the constitution. In our constitution there has always been a difference between *a franchise* and *an office*, and between the capacity for the one and for the other. Franchises were supposed to belong to the *subject*, as *a subject*, and not *as a member of the governing part of the State*. The policy of government has considered them as things very different ; for whilst Parliament excluded by the Test Acts (and for a while these Test Acts were not a dead letter, as now they are in England) Protestant dissenters from all civil and military employments, they *never touched their right of voting for members of Parliament or sitting in either House,*—a point I state, not as approving or condemning, with regard to them, the measure of exclusion from employments, but to prove that the distinction has been admitted in legislature, as, in truth, it is founded in reason.

I will not here examine whether the principles of the British [the Irish] constitution be wsie or not. I must assume that they are, and that those who partake the franchises which make it partake of a benefit. They who are excluded from votes (under proper qualifications inherent in the constitution that gives them) are excluded, not from the *State,* but from the *British constitution.* They cannot by any possibility, whilst they hear its praises continually rung in their ears, and are present at the declaration which is so generally and so bravely made by those who possess the privilege—that the best blood in their veins ought to be shed to preserve their share in it; they, the disfranchised part, cannot, I say, think themselves in a *happy* state, to be utterly excluded from all its direct and all its consequential advantages. The popular part of the constitution must be to them by far the most odious part of it. To them it is not *an actual,* and, if possible, still less a *virtual* representation. It is indeed the direct contrary. It is power unlimited placed in the hands of *an adverse* description, *because it is an adverse description.* And if they who compose the privileged body have not an interest, they must but too frequently have motives of pride, passion, petulance, peevish jealousy, or tyrannic suspicion, to urge them to treat the excluded people with contempt and rigour.

This is not a mere theory, though, whilst men are

men, it is a theory that cannot be false.   I do not
desire to revive all the particulars in my memory—I
wish them to sleep for ever; but it is impossible I
should wholly forget what happened in some parts of
Ireland, with very few and short intermissions, from
the year 1761 to the year 1766, both inclusive.   In
a country of miserable police, passing from the extremes of laxity to the extremes of rigour,—among a
neglected, and therefore disorderly, populace,—if any
disturbance or sedition from any grievance, real or
imaginary, happened to arise, it was presently perverted from its true nature, often criminal enough in
itself to draw upon it a severe appropriate punishment;
it was metamorphosed into a conspiracy against the
State, and prosecuted as such.   Amongst the Catholics,
as being by far the most numerous and the most
wretched, all sorts of offenders against the laws must
commonly be found.   The punishment of low people
for the offences usual among low people would warrant
no inference against any descriptions of religion or of
politics.   Men of consideration from their age, their
profession, or their character,—men of proprietary
landed estates, substantial renters, opulent merchants,
physicians, and titular bishops,—could not easily be
suspected of riot in open day, or of nocturnal assemblies for the purpose of pulling down hedges, making
breaches in park walls, firing barns, maiming cattle,
and outrages of a similar nature, which characterise
the disorders of an oppressed or a licentious populace.

But when the evidence given on the trial for such misdemeanours qualified them as overt acts of high treason, and when witnesses were found (such witnesses as they were) to depose to the taking of oaths of allegiance by the rioters to the king of France, to their being paid by his money, and embodied and exercised under his officers, to overturn the State for the purposes of that potentate,—in that case the rioters might (if the witness was believed) be supposed only the troops and persons more reputable, the leaders and commanders in such a rebellion. All classes in the obnoxious description who could not be suspected in the lower crime of riot, might be involved in the odium, in the suspicion, and sometimes in the punishment of a higher and far more criminal species of offence. These proceedings did not arise from any one of the Popery laws since repealed, but from this circumstance—that when it answered the purposes of an election party, or a malevolent person of influence to forge such plots, the people had no protection. The people of that description have no hold on the gentlemen who aspire to be popular representatives. The candidates neither love, nor respect, nor fear them individually or collectively. I do not think this evil (an evil amongst a thousand others) at this day entirely over; for I conceive I have lately seen some indication of a disposition perfectly similar to the old one; that is, a disposition to carry the imputation of crimes from persons to descriptions, and wholly to

alter the character and quality of the offences themselves.

This universal exclusion seems to me a serious evil,
because many collateral oppressions besides what I
have just now stated have arisen from it. In things
of this nature, it would not be either easy or proper to
quote chapter and verse; but I have great reason to
believe, particularly since the Octennial Act, that several
have refused at all to let their lands to Roman Catholics,
because it would so far disable them from promoting
such interests in counties as they were inclined to
favour. They who consider also the state of all sorts
of tradesmen, shopkeepers, and particularly publicans
in towns, must soon discern the disadvantages under
which those labour who have no votes. It cannot be
otherwise, whilst the spirit of elections and the ten-
dencies of human nature continue as they are. If
property be artificially separated from franchise, the
franchise must in some way or other, and in some
proportion, naturally attract property to it. Many are
the collateral disadvantages amongst a *privileged* people,
which must attend on those who have *no* privileges.

Among the rich each individual, with or without a
franchise, is of importance; the poor and the middling
are no otherwise so than as they obtain some collective
capacity, and can be aggregated to some corps. If
legal ways are not found, illegal will be resorted to;
and seditious clubs and confederacies, such as no man
living holds in greater horror than I do, will grow and

flourish in spite, I am afraid, of anything which can be done to prevent the evil. Lawful enjoyment is the surest method to prevent unlawful gratification. Where there is property there will be less theft; where there is marriage there will always be less fornication.

I have said enough of the question of state, *as it affects the people merely as such.* But it is complicated with a political question relative to religion, to which it is very necessary I should say something; because the term *Protestant* which you apply is too general for the conclusions which one of your accurate understanding would wish to draw from it, and because a great deal of argument will depend on the use that is made of that term.

It is *not* a fundamental part of the settlement at the Revolution that the State should be Protestant without *any qualification of the term.* With a qualification it is unquestionably true : not in all its latitude. With the qualification, it was true before the Revolution. Our predecessors in legislation were not so irrational (not to say impious) as to form an operose ecclesiastical establishment, and even to render the State itself in some degree subservient to it, when their religion (if such it might be called) was nothing but a mere *negation* of some other—without any positive idea either of doctrine, discipline, worship, or morals in the scheme which they professed themselves, and which they imposed upon others even under penalties and incapacities—No! No! This never could have been done even by reasonable atheists. They who think religion of no importance to the State have abandoned it to the conscience or caprice of the individual; they make no provision for it whatsoever, but leave every club to make or not a voluntary contribution towards its support, according to their fancies. This would be consistent. The other always appeared to me to be a monster of contradiction and absurdity. It was for that reason that, some years ago, I strenuously opposed the clergy who petitioned, to the number of about three hundred, to be freed from the subscription to the thirty-nine articles without proposing to substitute any other in their place. There never has been a religion of the State (the few years of the Parliament only excepted) but that of *the Episcopal Church of England,*—the Episcopal Church of England, before the Reformation connected with the See of Rome, since then disconnected and protesting against some of her doctrines, and against the whole of her authority as binding in our National Church. Nor did the fundamental laws of this kingdom (in Ireland it has been the same) ever know at any period any other Church *as an object of establishment;* or, in that light, any other Protestant religion. Nay, our Protestant *toleration* itself, at the Revolution and until within a few years, required a signature of thirty-six, and a part of the thirty-seventh, out of the thirty-nine articles. So little idea had they at the Revolution of *establishing* Protestantism indefinitely, that they did not indefinitely *tolerate* it under

that name.   I do not mean to praise that strictness
where nothing more than merely religious toleration is
concerned.   Toleration, being a part of moral and
political prudence, ought to be tender and large.   A
tolerant Government ought not to be too scrupulous in
its investigations, but may bear without blame not only
very ill-grounded doctrines, but even many things that
are positively vices, where they are *adulta et prævalida.*
The good of the commonwealth is the rule which rides
over the rest, and to this every other must completely
submit.

The Church of Scotland knows as little of Protestantism *undefined* as the Churches of England and Ireland do.   She has by the Articles of Union secured to
herself the perpetual establishment of *the Confession of
Faith,* and the *Presbyterian* Church government.   In
England, even during the troubled interregnum, it was
not thought fit to establish a *negative* religion ; but the
Parliament settled the *Presbyterian* as the Church
discipline ; the *Directory* as the rule of public *worship;*
and the *Westminster Catechism* as the institute of *faith.*
This is to show that at no time was the Protestant
religion, *undefined,* established here or anywhere else,
as I believe.   I am sure that when the three religions
were established in Germany, they were expressly
characterised and declared to be the *Evangelic,* the
Reformed, and the *Catholic,* each of which has its Confession of Faith and its settled discipline ; so that you
always may know the best and the worst of them, to

enable you to make the most of what is good, and to correct or to qualify, or to guard against, whatever may seem evil or dangerous.

As to the coronation oath, to which you allude, as opposite to admitting a Roman Catholic to the use of any franchise whatsoever, I cannot think that the king would be perjured if he gave his assent to any regulation which Parliament might think fit to make with regard to that affair.   The king is bound by law, as clearly specified in several Acts of Parliament, to be in communion with the Church of England.   It is a part of the tenure by which he holds his crown; and though no provision was made till the Revolution, which could be called positive and valid in law, to ascertain this great principle, I have always considered it as in fact fundamental that the King of England should be of the Christian religion, according to the national legal church for the time being.   I conceive it was so before the Reformation.   Since the Reformation it became doubly necessary, because the king is the head of that Church,—in some sort an ecclesiastical person ; and it would be incongruous and absurd to have the head of the Church of one faith, and the members of another. The king may *inherit* the crown as a *Protestant*, but he cannot *hold it*, according to law, without being a Protestant *of the Church of England*.

Before we take it for granted that the king is bound by his coronation oath not to admit any of his Catholic subjects to the rights and liberties which ought to belong to them as Englishmen (not as religionists), or to settle the conditions or proportions of such admission by an Act of Parliament, I wish you to place before your eyes that oath itself, as it is settled in the Act of William and Mary.

" Will you to the utmost of your power maintain—
   1   2   3
" The laws of God, the true profession of the gospel—
                4
'' and the Protestant reformed religion *as it is estab-*
                        5
" *lished by law*.   And will you preserve unto *bishops*
" and clergy, and the churches committed to *their*
" charge, all such rights and privileges as by law do,
" or shall appertain to them, or any of them.—All this
" I promise to do."

Here are the coronation engagements of the king. In them I do not find one word to preclude His Majesty from consenting to any arrangement which Parliament may make with regard to the civil privileges of any part of his subjects.

It may not be amiss, on account of the light which it will throw on this discussion, to look a little more narrowly into the matter of that oath, in order to discover how far it has hitherto operated, or how far in future it ought to operate, as a bar to any proceedings of the Crown and Parliament in favour of those against whom it may be supposed that the king has engaged to support the Protestant Church of England in the two kingdoms in which it is established by law. First, the king swears he will maintain to the utmost of his power " the laws of God." I suppose it means the natural moral laws. Secondly, he swears to maintain " the true profession of the gospel." By which, I suppose, is understood *affirmatively* the Christian religion." Thirdly, that he will maintain " the Protestant reformed religion." This leaves me no power of supposition or conjecture, for that Protestant reformed religion is defined and described by the subsequent words, " established by law," and in this instance, to define it beyond all possibility of doubt, he " swears to maintain the bishops and clergy, and the churches committed to their charge," in their rights present and future.

The oath as effectually prevents the king from doing anything to the prejudice of the Church in favour of sectaries, Jews, Mahometans, or plain avowed infidels, as if he should do the same thing in favour of the Catholics. You will see that it is the same Protestant Church, so described, that the king is to maintain and communicate with, according to the Act of Settlement of the 12th and 13th of William III. This Act of the 5th of Anne, made in prospect of the Union, is entitled, " An Act for securing the Church of England as by law established." It meant to guard the Church implicitly against any other mode of Protestant religion which might creep in by means of the

Union. It proves beyond all doubt that the Legislature did not mean to guard the Church on one part only, and to leave it defenceless and exposed upon every other. This Church, in that Act, is declared to be "fundamental and essential" for ever, in the constitution of the United Kingdom, so far as England is concerned; and I suppose as the law stands, even since the Independence, it is so in Ireland.

All this shows that the religion which the king is bound to maintain has a positive part in it as well as a negative; and that the positive part of it (in which we are in perfect agreement with the Catholics and with the Church of Scotland) is infinitely the most valuable and essential. Such an agreement we had with Protestant dissenters in England of those descriptions; who came under the Toleration Act of King William and Queen Mary,—an Act coeval with the Revolution, and which ought, on the principles of the gentlemen who oppose the relief to the Catholics, to have been held sacred and unalterable. Whether we agree with the present Protestant dissenters in the points at the Revolution held essential and fundamental among Christians, or in any other fundamental, at present it is impossible for us to know, because, at their own very earnest desire, we have repealed the Toleration Act of William and Mary, and discharged them from the signature required by that Act; and because, for the far greater part, they publicly declare against all manner of confessions of faith, even the *consensus*.

For reasons forcible enough at all times, but at this time particularly forcible with me, I dwell a little the longer upon this matter, and take the more pains, to put us both in mind that it was not settled at the Revolution, that the State should be Protestant, in the latitude of the term, but in a defined and limited sense only, and that, in that sense only, the king is sworn to maintain it.   To suppose that the king has sworn with his utmost power to maintain what it is wholly out of his power to discover, or which, if he could discover, he might discover to consist of things directly contradictory to each other, some of them perhaps impious, blasphemous, and seditious upon principle, would be not only a gross, but a most mischievous absurdity.   If mere dissent from the Church of Rome be a merit, he that dissents the most perfectly is the most meritorious.   In many points we hold strongly with that Church.   He that dissents throughout with that Church will dissent with the Church of England, and then it will be a part of his merit that he dissents with ourselves—a whimsical species of merit for any set of men to establish.   We quarrel to extremity with those who, we know, agree with us in many things, but we are to be so malicious even in the principle of our friendships, that we are to cherish in our bosom those who accord with us in nothing, because whilst they despise ourselves, they abhor, even more than we do, those with whom we have some disagreement.   A man is certainly the most

perfect Protestant, who protests against the whole
Christian religion.   Whether a person's having no
Christian religion be a title to favour, in exclusion to
the largest description of Christians who hold all the
doctrines of Christianity, though holding along with
them some errors and some superfluities, is rather
more than any man who has not become recreant and
apostate from his baptism, will, I believe, choose to
affirm.   The countenance given from a spirit of controversy to that negative religion may, by degrees,
encourage light and unthinking people to a total
indifference to everything positive in matters of
doctrine ; and, in the end, of practice too.   If continued
it would play the game of that sort of active, proselyt-
ising, and persecuting atheism, which is the disgrace
and calamity of our time, and which we see to be as
capable of subverting a government as any mode can
be of misguided zeal for better things.

Now let us fairly see what course has been taken
relative to those against whom, in part at least, the
king has sworn to maintain a Church, *positive in its
doctrine and its discipline*.   The first thing done, even
when the oath was fresh in the mouth of the sovereigns,
was to give a toleration to Protestant dissenters, *whose
doctrines they ascertained*.   As to the mere civil
privileges which the dissenters held as subjects before
the Revolution, these were not touched at all.   The
laws have fully permitted in a qualification for all offices
to such dissenters *an occasional conformity*—a thing I

believe singular, where tests are admitted.   The Act
called the Test Act itself is, with regard to them, grown
to be hardly anything more than a dead letter.   Whenever the dissenters cease by their conduct to give any
alarm to the Government in Church and State, I think
it very probable that even this matter, rather disgust-
ful than inconvenient to them, may be removed, or at
least so modified as to distinguish the qualification to
those offices which really *guide the State* from those
which are *merely instrumental*, or that some other and
better tests may be put in their place.

So far as to England.   In Ireland you have outrun
us.   Without waiting for an English example, you
have totally, and without any modification whatsoever,
repealed the test as to Protestant dissenters.   Not
having the Repealing Act by me, I ought not to say
positively that there is no exception in it, but if it be
what I suppose it is, you know very well that a Jew
in religion, or a Mahometan, or even *a public, declared
atheist* and blasphemer, is perfectly qualified to be
Lord-Lieutenant, a Lord Justice, or even keeper of the
king's conscience; and by virtue of his office (if with
you it be as it is with us) administrator to a great part
of the ecclesiastical patronage of the Crown.

Now let us deal a little fairly.   We must admit
that Protestant dissent was one of the quarters from
which danger was apprehended at the Revolution, and
against which a part of the coronation oath was
peculiarly directed.   By this unqualified repeal you

certainly did not mean to deny that it was the duty of
the Crown to preserve the Church against Protestant
dissenters; or taking this to be the true sense of the
two Revolution Acts of King William, and of the previous and subsequent Union Acts of Queen Anne, you
did not declare by this most unqualified repeal, by which
you broke down all the barriers not invented, indeed,
but carefully preserved at the Revolution,—you did
not then and by that proceeding declare that you had
advised the king to perjury towards God, and perfidy
towards the Church. No! far, very far from it; you
never would have done it if you did not think it could
be done with perfect repose to the royal conscience,
and perfect safety to the national established religion.
You did this upon a full consideration of the circumstances of your country. Now, if circumstances required it, why should it be contrary to the king's oath
—his Parliament judging on those circumstances—to
restore to his Catholic people in such measure, and
with such modification as the public wisdom shall
think proper to add, *some part* in these franchises
which they formerly had held without any limitation
at all, and which, upon no sort of urgent reason at the
time they were deprived of? If such means can with
any probability be shown from circumstances rather to
add strength to our mixed ecclesiastical and secular
constitution than to weaken it, surely they are means
infinitely to be preferred to penalties, incapacities, and
proscriptions continued from generation to generation.

They are perfectly consistent with the other parts of
the coronation oath in which the king swears to maintain " the laws of God and the true profession of the
gospel, and to govern the people according to the
statutes in Parliament agreed upon, and the laws and
customs of the realm." In consenting to such a
statute, the Crown would act at least as agreeably to
the laws of God, and to the true profession of the
gospel, and to the laws and customs of the kingdom,
as George I. did when he passed the statute which
took from the body of the people everything which to
that hour, and even after the monstrous Acts of the
2d and 8th of Anne (the objects of our common
hatred), they still enjoyed inviolate.

It is hard to distinguish, with the least degree of
accuracy, what laws are fundamental, and what not.
However, there is a distinction between them authorised by the writers on jurisprudence, and recognised in
some of our statutes. I admit the Acts of King
William and Queen Anne to be fundamental, but they
are not the only fundamental laws. The law called
Magna Charta, by which it is provided that " no man
shall be disseised of his liberties and free customs but
by the judgment of his peers or the laws of the land"
(meaning clearly for some proved crime tried and
adjudged), I take to be a *fundamental law*. Now,
although this Magna Charta, or some of the Statutes
establishing it, provide that that law shall be perpetual,
and all Statutes contrary to it shall be void, yet I

cannot go so far as to deny the authority of statutes made in defiance of Magna Charta and all its principles. This, however, I will say, that it is a very venerable law made by very wise and learned men, and that the Legislature, in their attempt to perpetuate it, even against the authority of future Parliaments, have shown their judgment that it is *fundamental* on the same grounds and in the same manner as the Act of the 5th of Anne has considered and declared the establishment of the Church of England to be fundamental. Magna Charta, which secured these franchises to the subjects, regarded the rights of freeholders in counties to be as much a fundamental part of the constitution as the establishment of the Church of England was thought either at that time or in the Act of King William or in Act of Queen Anne.

The churchmen who led in that transaction certainly took care of the material interest of which they were the natural guardians. It is the first article of Magna Charta " that the Church of England shall be free," etc. etc. But at that period churchmen, and barons, and knights took care of the franchises and free customs of the people too. Those franchises are part of the constitution itself, and inseparable from it. It would be a very strange thing if there should not only exist anomalies in our laws—a thing not easy to prevent—but that the fundamental parts of the constitution should be perpetually and irreconcilably at variance with each other. I cannot persuade myself that the lovers of our Church are not as able to find effectual ways of reconciling its safety with the franchises of the people, as the ecclesiastics of the thirteenth century were able to do. I cannot conceive how anything worse can be said of the Protestant religion of the Church of England than this, that wherever it is judged proper to give it a legal establishment, it becomes necessary to deprive the body of the people, if they adhere to their old opinions, of " their liberties and of all their free customs," and to reduce them to a state of *civil* servitude.

There is no man on earth, I believe, more willing than I am to lay it down as a fundamental of the con- stitution that the Church of England should be united and even identified with it ; but, allowing this, I cannot allow that all *laws of regulation,* made from time to time in support of that fundamental law, are, of course, equally fundamental and equally unchangeable. This would be to confound all the branches of legislation and of juris- prudence. The *Crown* and the personal safety of the monarch are *fundamentals* in our constitution ; yet, I hope that no man regrets that the rabble of statutes got together during the reign of Henry VIII. by which treasons are multiplied with so prolific an energy have been all repealed in a body, although they were all, or most of them, made in support of things truly funda- mental in our constitution. So were several of the Acts by which the Crown exercised its supremacy, such as the Act of Elizabeth for making the *High Com-*

mission Courts and the like, as well as things made
treason in the time of Charles II. None of this
species of *secondary and subsidiary laws* have been
held fundamental. They have yielded to circumstances, particularly where they were thought, even in
their consequences or obliquely, to affect other fundamentals. How much more certainly ought they to
give way, when, as in our case, they affect, not here
and there in some particular point or in their consequence, but universally, collectively, and directly the
fundamental franchises of a people equal to the whole
inhabitants of several respectable kingdoms and states;
equal to the subjects of the Kings of Sardinia or of
Denmark; equal to those of the United Netherlands,
and more than are to be found in all the states of
Switzerland. This way of proscribing men by whole
nations, as it were, from all the benefits of the constitution to which they were born, I never can believe to
be politic or expedient, much less necessary for the
existence of any State or Church in the world. Whenever I shall be convinced—which will be late and
reluctantly—that the safety of the Church is utterly inconsistent with all the civil rights whatsoever of the
far larger part of the inhabitants of our country, I
shall be extremely sorry for it, because I shall think
the church to be truly in danger. It is putting things
into the position of an ugly alternative, into which I
hope in God they never will be put.

I have said most of what occurs to me on the topics

you touch upon relative to the religion of the king and
his coronation oath.   I shall conclude the observations
which I wished to submit to you on this point by
assuring you that I think you the most remote that
can be conceived from the metaphysicians of our times,
who are the most foolish of men, and who, dealing in
universals and essences, see no difference between more
and less, and who of course would think that the reason
of the law which obliged the king to be a communicant
of the Church of England would be as valid to exclude
a Catholic from being an exciseman, or to deprive a
man who has five hundred a year under that description from voting on a par with a factitious Protestant
dissenting freeholder of forty shillings.

Recollect, my dear friend, that it was a fundamental
principle in the French monarchy, whilst it stood, that
the State should be Catholic, yet the edict of Nantz
gave, not a full ecclesiastical, but a complete civil
establishment, with places of which only they were
capable, to the Calvinists of France ; and there were
very few employments indeed of which they were not
capable.   The world praised the Cardinal de Richelieu,
who took the first opportunity to strip them of their
fortified places and cautionary towns.   The same world
held, and does hold in execration (so far as that business is concerned), the memory of Louis XIV. for the
total repeal of that favourable edict, though the talk of
" fundamental laws, established religion, religion of the
prince, safety to the State," etc. etc. was then as largely

held, and with as bitter a revival of the animosities of
the civil confusions during the struggles between the
parties as now they can be in Ireland.

Perhaps there are persons who think that the same
reasons do not hold when the religious relation of the
sovereign and subject is changed, but they who have
their shop full of false weights and measures, and who
imagine that the adding or taking away the name of
Protestant or Papist, Guelph or Ghibelline, alters all
the principles of equity, policy, and prudence, leave us
no common data upon which we can reason.   I therefore pass by all this, which on you will make no
impression, to come to what seems to be a serious consideration in your mind : I mean the dread you express
of "reviewing for the purpose of altering the *principles of the Revolution*." This is an interesting topic,
on which I will, as fully as your leisure and mine
permits, lay before you the ideas I have formed.

First, I cannot possibly confound in my mind all
the things which were done at the Revolution with the
principles of the Revolution.   As in most great changes,
many things were done from the necessities of the time,
well or ill understood, from passion or from vengeance,
which were not only not perfectly agreeable to its
principles, but in the most direct contradiction to them.
I shall not think that the *deprivation of some millions of
people of all the rights of citizens, and all interest in the
constitution in and to which they were born,* was a thing
conformable to the *declared principles* of the Revolu-

tion. This I am sure is true relatively to England
(where the operation of these *anti-principles* comparatively were of little extent) ; and some of our late laws,
in repealing Acts made immediately after the Revolution, admit that some things then done were not done
in the true spirit of the Revolution. But the Revolution operated differently in England and Ireland in
many and these essential particulars. Supposing the
principles to have been altogether the same in both
kingdoms, by the application of those principles to very
different objects, the whole spirit of the system was
changed, not to say reversed. In England it was the
struggle of the *great body* of the people for the establishment of their liberties against the efforts of a very
small faction who would have oppressed them. In
Ireland it was the establishment of the power of the
smaller number at the expense of the civil liberties and
properties of the far greater part, and at the expense of
the political liberties of the whole. It was, to say the
truth, not a revolution but a conquest, which is not to
say a great deal in its favour. To insist on everything
done in Ireland at the Revolution would be to insist
on the severe and jealous policy of a conqueror in the
crude settlement of his new acquisition as a *permanent*
rule for its future government. This no power in no
country that ever I heard of has done or professed to
do, except in Ireland, where it is done, and possibly by
some people will be professed. Time has, by degrees,
in all other places and periods, blended and coalited

the conquered with the conquerors. So, after some time, and after one of the most rigid conquests that we read of in history, the Normans softened into the English. I wish you to turn your recollection to the fine speech of Cerealis to the Gauls, made to dissuade them from revolt. Speaking of the Romans,—" *Nos quamvis toties lacessiti, jure victoriæ id solum vobis addidimus, quo pacem tueremur : nam neque quies gentium sine armis; neque arma sine stipendiis; neque stipendia sine tributis, haberi queant. Cætera in communi sita sunt : ipsi plerumque nostris exercitibus presidetis : ipsi has aliasque provincias regitas : nil seperatum clausumve*—Proinde pacem et urbem, quam *victores victique eodem jure obtinemus*, amate, colite." You will consider whether the arguments used by that Roman to these Gauls would apply to the case in Ireland ; and whether you could use so plausible a preamble to any severe warning you might think it proper to hold out to those who should resort to sedition, instead of supplication, to obtain any object that they may pursue with the governing power.

For a much longer period than that which had sufficed to blend the Romans with the nation to which of all others they were the most adverse, the Protestants settled in Ireland consider themselves in no other light than that of a sort of a colonial garrison to keep the natives in subjection to the other state of Great Britain. The whole spirit of the Revolution in Ireland was that of not the mildest conqueror. In truth, the spirit of those proceedings did not commence at that era, nor was religion of any kind their primary object. What was done was not in the spirit of a contest between two religious factions, but between two adverse nations. The statutes of Kilkenny show that the spirit of the popery laws, and some even of their actual provisions, as applied between Englishry and Irishry, had existed in that harassed country before the words Protestant and Papist were heard of in the world. If we read Baron Finglass, Spenser, and Sir John Davis, we cannot miss the true genius and policy of the English Government there before the Revolution, as well as during the whole reign of Queen Elizabeth. Sir John Davis boasts of the benefits received by the natives by extending to them the English law, and turning the whole kingdom into shire ground. But the appearance of things alone was changed. The original scheme was never deviated from for a single hour. Unheard-of confiscations were made in the northern parts, upon grounds of plots and conspiracies, never proved upon their supposed authors. The war of chicane succeeded to the war of arms and of hostile statutes ; and a regular series of operations was carried on, particularly from Chichester's time, in the ordinary courts of justice, and by special commissions and inquisitions; first, under pretence of tenures, and then of titles in the Crown, for the purpose of the total extirpation of the interest of the natives in their own soil—until this species of

R

subtle ravage, being carried to the last excess of
oppression and insolence under Lord Strafford, it
kindled the flames of that rebellion which broke out
in 1641. By the issue of that war, by the turn
which the Earl of Clarendon gave to things at the
Restoration, and by the total reduction of the kingdom
of Ireland in 1691, the ruin of the native Irish, and,
in a great measure too, of the first races of the English,
was completely accomplished. The new English interest was settled with as solid a stability as anything
in human affairs can look for. All the penal laws of
that unparalleled code of oppression, which were made
after the last event, were manifestly the effects of
national hatred and scorn towards a conquered people,
whom the victors delighted to trample upon, and were
not at all afraid to provoke. They were not the effect
of their fears, but of their security. They who carried
on this system looked to the irresistible force of Great
Britain for their support in their acts of power. They
were quite certain that no complaints of the natives
would be heard on this side of the water with any
other sentiments than those of contempt and indignation. Their cries served only to augment their
torture. Machines which could answer their purposes
so well must be of an excellent contrivance. Indeed, in England, the double name of the complain-
ant, Irish and Papists (it would be hard to say which
singly was the most odious), shut up the hearts of
every one against them. Whilst that temper pre-

vailed in all its force to a time within our memory, every measure was pleasing and popular, just in proportion as it tended to harass and ruin a set of people who were looked upon as enemies to God and man ; and, indeed, as a race of bigoted savages who were a disgrace to human nature itself.

However, as the English in Ireland began to be domiciliated, they began also to recollect that they had a country. The *English interest*, at first by faint and almost insensible degrees, but at length openly and avowedly, became an *independent Irish interest ;* full as independent as it could ever have been if it had continued in the persons of the native Irish, and it was maintained with more skill and more consistency than probably it would have been in theirs. With their views the *Anglo-Irish* changed their maxims ; it was necessary to demonstrate to the whole people that there was something at least of a common interest combined with the independency, which was to become the object of common exertions. The mildness of Government produced the first relaxation towards the Irish ; the necessities and, in part too, the temper that predominated at this great change, produced the second and the most important of these relaxations. English Government and Irish Legislature felt jointly the propriety of this measure. The Irish Parliament and nation became independent.

The true Revolution to you—that which most intrinsically and substantially resembled the English

Revolution of 1688—was the Irish Revolution of 1782.
The Irish Parliament of 1782 bore little resemblance
to that which sat in that kingdom after the period
of the first of these Revolutions. It bore a much
nearer resemblance to that which sat under King
James. The change of the Parliament in 1782 from
the character of the Parliament which, as a token of
its indignation, had burned all the journals indiscrimi-
nately of the former Parliament in the Council Chamber,
was very visible. The address of King William's Parliament—the Parliament which assembled after the
Revolution—amongst other causes of complaint (many
of them sufficiently just), complains of the repeal by
their predecessors of Poyning's law; no absolute idol
with the Parliament of 1782.

Great Britain, finding the Anglo-Irish highly animated with a spirit which had indeed shown itself
before, though with little energy and many interrup-
tions, and therefore suffered a multitude of uniform
precedents to be established against it, acted, in my
opinion, with the greatest temperance and wisdom.
She saw that the disposition of the *leading part* of the
nation would not permit them to act any longer the
part of a *garrison*. She saw that true policy did not
require that they ever should have appeared in that
character, or, if it had done so formerly, the reasons
had now ceased to operate. She saw that the Irish
of her race were resolved to build their constitution
and their politics upon another bottom. With those

things under her view, she instantly complied with the
whole of your demands, without any reservation whatsoever.   She surrendered that boundless superiority
for the preservation of which, and the acquisition, she
had supported the English colonies in Ireland for so
long a time, and so vast an expense (according to the
standard of those ages) of her blood and treasure.

When we bring before us the matter which history
affords for our selection, it is not improper to examine
the spirit of the several precedents which are candidates for our choice.   Might it not be as well for your
statesmen on the other side of the water to take an
example from this latter, and surely more conciliatory
Revolution, as a pattern for your conduct towards your
own fellow-citizens, than from that of 1688, when a
paramount sovereignty over both you and them was
more loftily claimed, and more sternly exerted, than
at any former or at any subsequent period.   Great
Britain, in 1782, rose above the vulgar ideas of policy,
the ordinary jealousies of State, and all the sentiments
of national pride and national ambition.   If she had
been more disposed than, I thank God for it, she was
to listen to the suggestions of passion than to the dictates of prudence, she might have urged the principles,
the maxims, the policy, the practice of the Revolution,
against the demands of the leading description in
Ireland, with full as much plausibility, and full as
good a grace, as any amongst them can possibly do

against the supplications of so vast and extensive a description of their own people.

A good deal, too, if the spirit of domination and exclusion had prevailed in England, might have been excepted against some of the means then employed in Ireland whilst her claims were in agitation. They were, at least, as much out of ordinary course as those which are now objected against admitting your people to any of the benefits of an English constitution. Most certainly, neither with you nor here was any one ignorant of what was at that time said, written, and done. But on all sides we separated the means from the end, and we separated the cause of the moderate and rational from the ill-intentioned and seditious, which, on such occasions, are so frequently apt to march together. At that time, on your part, you were not afraid to review what was done at the Revolution of 1688, and what had been continued during the subsequent flourishing period of the British Empire. The change then made was a great and fundamental alteration. In the execution it was an operose business on both sides of the water. It required the repeal of several laws, the modification of many, and a new course to be given to an infinite number of legislative, judicial, and official practices and usages in both kingdoms. This did not frighten any of us. You are now asked to give, in some moderate measure, to your fellow-citizens what Great Britain gave to you without any measure at all. Yet, notwithstanding all the difficulties at the time and the apprehensions which some very well-meaning people entertained, through the admirable temper in which this revolution (or restoration in the nature of a revolution) was conducted in both kingdoms, it has hitherto produced no inconvenience to either, and, I trust, with the continuance of the same temper, that it never will. I think that this small, inconsiderable change (relative to an exclusive statute not made at the Revolution) for restoring the people to the benefits from which the green soreness of a civil war had not excluded them, will be productive of no sort of mischief whatsoever. Compare what was done in 1782 with what is wished in 1792; consider the spirit of what has been done at the several periods of reformation, and weigh maturely whether it be exactly true that conciliatory concessions are of good policy only in discussions between nations, but that among descriptions in the same nation they must always be irrational and dangerous. What have you suffered in your peace, your prosperity, or, in what ought ever to be dear to a nation, your glory, by the last act by which you took the property of that people under the protection of the *laws*? What reasons have you to dread the consequences of admitting the people possessing that property to some share in the protection of the *constitution*?

I do not mean to trouble you with anything to remove the objections—I will not call them arguments —against this measure, taken from a ferocious hatred

to all that numerous description of Christians. It
would be to pay a poor compliment to your understanding or your heart. Neither *your* religion nor
your politics consists " in odd perverse antipathies."
You are not resolved to persevere in proscribing from
the constitution so many millions of your countrymen,
because, in contradiction to experience and to common
sense, you think proper to imagine that their principles
are subversive of common human society. To that I
shall only say, that whosoever has a temper which can
be gratified by indulging himself in these good-natured
fancies, ought to do a great deal more. For an exclusion from the privileges of British subjects is not a
cure for so terrible a distemper of the human mind as
they are pleased to suppose in their countrymen. I
rather conceive a participation in those privileges to be
itself a remedy for some mental disorders.

As little shall I detain you with matters that can
as little obtain admission into a mind like yours ; such
as the fear, or pretence of fear, that, in spite of your
own power, and the trifling power of Great Britain,
you may be conquered by the Pope ; or that this commodious bugbear (who is of infinitely more use to
those who pretend to fear, than to those who love him)
will absolve His Majesty's subjects from their allegiance, and send over the Cardinal of York to rule you
as his viceroy ; or that, by the plenitude of his power,
he will take that fierce tyrant, the King of the French,
out of his jail, and arm that nation (which on all occa-

sions treats His Holiness so very politely) with his
bulls and pardons, to invade poor old Ireland, to
reduce you to Popery and slavery, and to force the
free-born, naked feet of your people into the wooden
shoes of that arbitrary monarch. I do not believe that
discourses of this kind are held, or that anything like
them will be held, by any who walk about without a
keeper. Yet I confess that, on occasions of this
nature, I am the most afraid of the weakest reasonings,
because they discover the strongest passions. These
things will never be brought out in definite propositions. They would not prevent pity towards any persons ; they would only cause it for those who were
capable of talking in such a strain. But I know, and
am sure, that such ideas as no man will distinctly produce to another, or hardly venture to bring in any
plain shape to his own mind—he will utter in obscure,
ill-explained doubts, jealousies, surmises, fears, and
apprehensions ; and that, in such a fog, they will
appear to have a good deal of size, and will make an
impression, when, if they were clearly brought forth
and defined, they would meet with nothing but scorn
and derision.

There is another way of taking an objection to this
concession, which I admit to be something more
plausible, and worthy of a more attentive examination.
It is, that this numerous class of people is mutinous,
disorderly, prone to sedition, and easy to be wrought
upon by the insidious arts of wicked and designing

men ; that, conscious of this, the sober, rational, and
wealthy part of that body, who are totally of another
character, do by no means desire any participation for
themselves, or for any one else of their description, in
the franchises of the British constitution.

I have great doubt of the exactness of any part of
this observation.   But let us admit that the body of
the Catholics are prone to sedition (of which, as I have
said, I entertain much doubt), is it possible that any
fair observer, or fair reasoner, can think of confining
this description to them only ?   I believe it to be
possible for men to be mutinous and seditious who
feel no grievance ; but I believe no man will assert
seriously that, when people are of a turbulent spirit,
the best way to keep them in order is to furnish them
with something substantial to complain of.

You separate very properly the sober, rational, and
substantial part of their description from the rest.
You give, as you ought to do, weight only to the
former.   What I have always thought of the matter
is this—that the most poor, illiterate, and uninformed
creatures upon earth are judges of a *practical* oppression.   It is a matter of feeling ; and as such persons
generally have felt most of it, and are not of an over-
lively sensibility, they are the best judges of it.   But
for the *real cause*, or the *appropriate remedy*, they
ought never to be called into council about the one or
the other.   They ought to be totally shut out ; because
their reason is weak ; because, when once roused, their

passions are ungoverned; because they want information; because the smallness of the property, which
individually they possess, renders them less attentive
to the consequence of the measures they adopt in
affairs of moment.   When I find a great cry amongst
the people who speculate little, I think myself called
seriously to examine into it, and to separate the real
cause from the ill effects of the passion it may excite;
and the bad use which artful men may make of an
irritation of the popular mind.   Here we must be
aided by persons of a contrary character; we must
not listen to the desperate or the furious; but it is
therefore necessary for us to distinguish who are the
really indigent, and the *really* intemperate.   As to the
persons who desire this part in the constitution, I have
no reason to imagine that they are men who have
nothing to lose and much to look for in public confusion.   The popular meeting, from which apprehensions have been entertained, has assembled.   I have
accidentally had conversation with two friends of mine,
who know something of the gentleman who was put
into the chair upon that occasion; one of them has
had money transactions with him; the other, from
curiosity, has been to see his concerns; they both tell
me he is a man of some property; but you must be
the best judge of this, who by your office are likely to
know his transactions.   Many of the others are
certainly persons of fortune; and all, or most, fathers
of families, men in respectable ways of life, and some

of them far from contemptible, either for their information, or for the abilities which they have shown in the
discussion of their interests.   What such men think it
for their advantage to acquire, ought not, *prima facie*,
to be considered as rash or heady, or incompatible with
the public safety or welfare.

I admit that men of the best fortunes and reputa-
tions, and of the best talents and education too, may,
by accident, show themselves furious and intemperate
in their desires.   This is a great misfortune when it
happens; for the first presumptions are undoubtedly
in their favour.   We have two standards of judging
in this case of the sanity and sobriety of any proceedings—of unequal certainty indeed, but neither of
them to be neglected : the first is by the value of the
object sought, the next is by the means through which
it is pursued.

The object pursued by the Catholics is, I understand, and have all along reasoned as if it were so, in
some degree or measures to be again admitted to the
franchises of the constitution.   Men are considered as
under some derangement of their intellects when they
see good and evil in a different light from other men ;
when they choose nauseous and unwholesome food, and
reject such as to the rest of the world seems pleasant,
and is' known to be nutritive.   I have always considered the British constitution, not to be a thing in
itself so vicious, as that none but men of deranged
understanding, and turbulent tempers could desire a

share in it; on the contrary, I should think very indifferently of the understanding and temper of any body
of men who did not wish to partake of this great and
acknowledged benefit. I cannot think quite so favourably either of the sense or temper of those—if any
such there are—who would voluntarily persuade their
brethren that the object is not fit for them, or they
for the object. Whatever may be my thoughts concerning them, I am quite sure that they who hold such
language must forfeit all credit with the rest. This is
infallible—if they conceive any opinion of their judgment, they cannot possibly think them their friends.
There is, indeed, one supposition which would reconcile
the conduct of such gentlemen to sound reason, and to
the purest affection towards their fellow-sufferers; it is
that they act under the impression of a well-grounded
fear for the general interest. If they should be told,
and should believe the story that they dare attempt
to make their condition better, they will infallibly
make it worse—that if they aim at obtaining liberty,
they will have their slavery doubled — that their
endeavour to put themselves upon anything which
approaches towards an equitable footing with their
fellow-subjects will be considered as an indication of a
seditious and rebellious disposition — such a view of
things ought perfectly to restore the gentlemen who
so anxiously dissuade their countrymen from wishing
a participation with the privileged part of the people
to the good opinion of their fellows. But what is to

them a very full justification, is not quite so honourable to that power from whose maxims and temper
so good a ground of rational terror is furnished.   I
think arguments of this kind will never be used by
the friends of a Government which I greatly respect ;
or by any of the leaders of an Opposition whom I
have the honour to know, and the sense to admire.
I remember Polybius tells us, that during his cap-
tivity in Italy as a Peloponnesian hostage, he solicited
old Cato to intercede with the senate for his release,
and that of his countrymen ; this old politician told
him that he had better continue in his present condition, however irksome, than apply again to that
formidable authority for their relief ; that he ought to
imitate the wisdom of his countryman Ulysses, who,
when he was once out of the den of the Cyclops,
had too much sense to venture again into the same
cavern.   But I conceive too high an opinion of the
Irish Legislature to think that they are to their fellow-
citizens what the grand oppressors of mankind were
to a people whom the fortune of war had subjected
to their power.   For though Cato could use such a
parallel with regard to his senate, I should really
think it nothing short of impious to compare an
Irish Parliament to a den of Cyclops.   I hope the
people, both here and with you, will always apply to
the House of Commons with becoming modesty; but at
the same time with minds unembarrassed with any
sort of terror.

As to the means which the Catholics employ to obtain this object, so worthy of sober and rational minds, I do admit that such means may be used in the pursuit of it, as may make it proper for the Legislature, in this case, to defer their compliance until the demandants are brought to a proper sense of their duty. A concession in which the governing power of our country loses its dignity is dearly bought, even by him who obtains his object. All the people have a deep interest in the dignity of Parliament. But as the refusal of franchises which are drawn out of the first vital stamina of the British constitution, is a very serious thing, we ought to be very sure that the manner and spirit of the application is offensive and dangerous indeed, before we ultimately reject all applications of this nature. The mode of application, I hear, is by petition. It is the manner in which all the sovereign powers in the world are approached ; and I never heard (except in the case of James II.) that any prince considered this manner of supplication to be contrary to the humility of a subject, or to the respect due to the person or authority of the sovereign. This rule and a correspondent practice are observed from the Grand Seignior down to the most petty Prince or Republic in Europe.

You have sent me several papers, some in print, some in manuscript. I think I had seen all of them, except the formula of association. I confess they appear to me to contain matter mischievous and cap-

able of giving alarm, if the spirit in which they are
written should be found to make any considerable
progress.   But I am at a loss to know how to apply
them as objections to the case now before us.   When
I find that the *general committee,* which acts for the
Roman Catholics in Dublin, prefers the association proposed in the written draft you have sent me, to a respectful application in Parliament, I shall think the
persons who sign such a paper to be unworthy of any
privilege which may be thought fit to be granted ; and
that such men ought, by *name,* to be excepted from
any benefit under the constitution to which they offer
this violence.   But I do not find that this form of a
seditious league has been signed by any person whatsoever, either on the part of the supposed projectors, or
on the part of those whom it is calculated to seduce.
I do not find on inquiry that such a thing was mentioned, or even remotely alluded to, in the general
meeting of the Catholics, from which so much violence
was apprehended.   I have considered the other publications signed by individuals on the part of certain
societies—I may mistake, for I have not the honour
of knowing them personally, but I take Mr. Butler and
Mr. Tandy not to be Catholics, but members of the
Established Church.   Not *one* that I recollect of these
publications which you and I equally dislike appears
to be written by persons of that persuasion.   Now, if,
whilst a man is doubtfully soliciting a favour from
Parliament, any person should choose, in an improper

manner, to show his inclination towards the cause depending; and if that *must* destroy the cause of the petitioner, then not only the petitioner, but the Legislature itself is in the power of any weak friend or artful enemy that the supplicant or that the Parliament may have. A man must be judged by his own actions only. Certain Protestant dissenters make seditious propositions to the Catholics, which it does not appear that they have yet accepted. It would be strange that the tempter should escape all punishment, and that he who, under circumstances full of seduction and full of provocation, has resisted the temptation, should incur the penalty. You know that with regard to the dissenters, who are *stated* to be the chief movers in this vile scheme of altering the principles of election to a right of voting by the head, you are not able (if you ought even to wish such a thing) to deprive them of any part of the franchises and privileges which they hold on a footing of perfect equality with yourselves. *They* may do what they please with constitutional impunity; but the others cannot even listen with civility to an invitation from them to an ill-judged scheme of liberty, without forfeiting for ever all hopes of any of those liberties which we admit to be sober and rational.

It is known, I believe, that the greater, as well as the sounder part of our excluded countrymen have not adopted the wild ideas and wilder engagements which have been held out to them; but have rather chosen to

S

hope small and safe concessions from the legal power, than boundless objects from trouble and confusion. This mode of action seems to me to mark men of sobriety, and to distinguish them from those who are intemperate from circumstance or from nature. But why do they not instantly disclaim and disavow those who make such advances to them? In this, too, in my opinion, they show themselves no less sober and circumspect. In the present moment, nothing short of insanity could induce them to take such a step. Pray consider the circumstances. Disclaim, says somebody, all union with the dissenters. Right —but when this your injunction is obeyed, shall I obtain the object which I solicit from *you?* Oh, no, nothing at all like it! But, in punishing us by an exclusion from the constitution through the great gate, for having been invited to enter into it by a postern, will you punish by deprivation of their privileges, or mulct in any other way, those who have tempted us? Far from it—we mean to preserve all *their* liberties and immunities, as *our* life-blood. We mean to cultivate *them* as brethren, whom we love and respect— with *you* we have no fellowship. We can bear with patience their enmity to ourselves; but their friendship with you we will not endure. But mark it well! All our quarrels with *them* are always to be revenged upon you. Formerly it is notorious that we should have resented with the highest indignation your presuming to show any ill-will to them. You must not suffer

them now to show any good-will to you.   Know—
and take it once for all—that it is, and ever has been,
and ever will be, a fundamental maxim in our politics,
that you are not to have any part, or shadow, or name
of interest whatever in our State ; that we look upon
you as under an irreversible outlawry from our constitution—as perpetual and unalliable aliens.

Such, my dear sir, is the plain nature of the argument drawn from the revolution maxims, enforced by
a supposed disposition in the Catholics to unite with
the dissenters.   Such it is, though it were clothed in
never such bland and civil forms, and wrapped up, as
a poet says, in a thousand "artful folds of sacred
lawn."   For my own part, I do not know in what
manner to shape such arguments so as to obtain admission for them into a rational understanding.   Everything of this kind is to be reduced, at last, to threats
of power.   I cannot say *væ victis*, and then throw the
sword into the scale.   I have no sword ; and if I had,
in this case most certainly I would not use it as a
make-weight in political reasoning.

Observe, on these principles, the difference between
the procedure of the Parliament and the dissenters
towards the people in question.   One employs courtship, the other force.   The dissenters offer bribes, the
Parliament nothing but the *front negative* of a stern
and forbidding authority.   A man may be very wrong
in his ideas of what is good for him.   But no man
affronts me, nor can therefore justify my affronting

him, by offering to make me as happy as himself, according to his own ideas of happiness. This the dissenters do to the Catholics. You are on the different extremes. The dissenters offer, with regard to constitutional rights and civil advantages of all sorts, *everything*; you refuse *everything*. With them there is boundless, though not very assured hope; with you, a very sure and very unqualified despair. The terms of alliance from the dissenters offer a representation of the commons, chosen out of the people by the head. This is absurdly and dangerously large in my opinion; and that scheme of election is known to have been, at all times, perfectly odious to me. But I cannot think it right of course to punish the Irish Roman Catholics by a universal exclusion, because others, whom you would not punish at all, propose a universal admission. I cannot dissemble to myself that in this very kingdom many persons who are not in the situation of the Irish Catholics, but who, on the contrary, enjoy the full benefit of the constitution as it stands, and some of whom, from the effect of their fortunes, enjoy it in a large measure, had some years ago associated to procure great and undefined changes (they considered them as reforms) in the popular part of the constitution. Our friend, the late Mr. Flood (no slight man), proposed in his place, and in my hearing, a representation not much less extensive than this for England; in which every house was to be inhabited by a voter—*in addition* to all the actual votes by other titles (some of the corporate) which we know do not require a house or a shed.   Can I forget that a person of the very highest rank, of very large fortune, and of the first class of ability, brought a Bill into the House of Lords, in the headquarters of aristocracy, containing identically the same project, for the supposed adoption of which by a club or two, it is thought right to extinguish all hopes in the Roman Catholics of Ireland ?   I cannot say it was very eagerly embraced or very warmly pursued. But the Lords neither did disavow the Bill, nor treat it with any disregard, nor express any sort of disapprobation of its nobler author, who has never lost, with king or people, the least degree of the respect and consideration which so justly belong to him.

I am not at all enamoured, as I have told you, with this plan of representation ; as little do I relish any bandings or associations for procuring it.   But if the question was to be put to you and me—*universal* popular representation, or *none at all for us and ours* —we should find ourselves in a very awkward position. I do not like this kind of dilemmas, especially when they are practical.

Then, since our oldest fundamental laws follow, or rather couple, freehold with franchise ; since no principle of the Revolution shakes these liberties ; since the oldest of one of the best monuments of the constitution demands for the Irish the privilege which they supplicate ; since the principles of the Revolution coincide with the declarations of the Great Charter ;

since the practice of the Revolution, in this point, did not contradict its principles; since, from that event, twenty-five years had elapsed, before a domineering party, on a party principle, had ventured to disfranchise, without any proof whatsoever of abuse, the greater part of the community; since the king's coronation oath does not stand in his way to the performance of his duty to all his subjects; since you have given to all other dissenters these privileges without limit, which are hitherto withheld, without any limitation whatsoever, from the Catholics; since no nation in the world has ever been known to exclude so great a body of men (not born slaves) from the civil State, and all the benefits of its constitution; the whole question comes before Parliament as a matter for its prudence. I do not put the thing on a question of right. That discretion which in judicature is well said by Lord Coke to be a crooked cord, in legislature is a golden rule. Supplicants ought not to appear too much in the character of litigants. If the subject thinks so highly and reverently of the sovereign authority as not to claim anything of right, so that it may seem to be independent of the power and free choice of its government; and if the sovereign, on his part, considers the advantages of the subjects as their right, and all their reasonable wishes as so many claims; in the fortunate conjunction of these mutual dispositions are laid the foundations of a happy and prosperous commonwealth. For my own

part, desiring of all things that the authority of the
Legislature under which I was born, and which I
cherish, not only with a dutiful awe, but with a
partial and cordial affection, to be maintained in the
utmost possible respect, I never will suffer myself to
suppose, that, at bottom, their discretion will be found
to be at variance with their justice.

The whole being at discretion, I beg leave just to
suggest some matters for your consideration—Whether
the Government, in Church or State, is likely to be
more secure by continuing causes of grounded discontent, to a very great number (say two millions) of the
subjects? or whether the constitution, combined and
balanced as it is, will be rendered more solid by
depriving so large a part of the people of all concern,
or interest, or share, in its representation, actual or
virtual? I here mean to lay an emphasis on the
word *virtual*. Virtual representation is that in which
there is a communion of interests, and a sympathy in
feelings and desires between those who act in the
name of any description of people, and the people in
whose name they act, though the trustees are not
actually chosen by them. This is virtual representation. Such a representation I think to be, in many
cases, even better than the actual. It possesses most
of its advantages, and is free from many of its inconveniences; it corrects the irregularities in the literal
representation when the shifting current of human
affairs, or the acting of public interests in different

ways, carry it obliquely from its first line of direction.
The people may err in their choice; but common
interest and common sentiment are rarely mistaken.
But this sort of virtual representation cannot have a
long or sure existence, if it has not a substratum in
the actual.　The member must have some relation to
the constituent.　As things stand, the Catholic, as a
Catholic, and belonging to a description, has no *virtual*
relation to the representative, but the *contrary*.　There
is a relation in mutual obligation.　Gratitude may not
always have a very lasting power; but the frequent
recurrence of an application for favours will revive
and refresh it, and will necessarily produce some
degree of mutual attention.　It will produce at least
acquaintance.　The several descriptions of people will
not be kept so much apart as they now are, as if they
were not only separate nations, but separate species.
The stigma and reproach, the hideous mask will be
taken off, and men will see each other as they are.
Sure I am, that there have been thousands in Ireland,
who have never conversed with a Roman Catholic in
their whole lives, unless they happened to talk to
their gardener's workmen, or to ask their way, when
they had lost it, in their sports; or, at best, who had
known them only as footmen, or other domestics, of
the second and third order : and so averse were they,
some time ago, to have them near their persons, that
they would not employ even those who could never
find their way beyond the stable.　I well remember a

great, and in many respects a good man, who adver-
tised for a blacksmith ; but at the same time added,
he must be a Protestant. It is impossible that such a
state of things, though natural goodness in many
persons will undoubtedly make exceptions, must not
produce alienation on the one side, and pride and
insolence on the other.

Reduced to a question of discretion, and that discretion exercised solely upon what will appear best for
the conservation of the State on its present basis, I
should recommend it to your serious thoughts, whether
the narrowing of the foundation is always the best way
to secure the building ? The body of disfranchised
men will not be perfectly satisfied to remain always in
that state. If they are not satisfied, you have two
millions of subjects in your bosom full of uneasiness ;
not that they cannot overturn the Act of Settlement,
and put themselves and you under an arbitrary master ; or that they are not premitted to spawn a hydra
of wild republics, on principles of a pretended natural
equality in man ; but because you will not suffer them
to enjoy the ancient, fundamental, tried advantages of
a British constitution ; that you will not permit them
to profit of the protection of a common father, or the
freedom of common citizens ; and that the only reason
which can be assigned for this disfranchisement has a
tendency more deeply to ulcerate their minds than the
act of exclusion itself. What the consequence of such
feelings must be, it is for you to look to. To warn is
not to menace.

I am far from asserting that men will not excite disturbances without just cause. I know that such an assertion is not true. But neither is it true that disturbances have never just complaints for their origin. I am sure that it is hardly prudent to furnish them with such causes of complaint .as every man who thinks the British constitution a benefit may think at least colourable and plausible.

Several are in dread of the manœuvres of certain persons among the dissenters, who turn this ill-humour to their own ill purposes. You know better than I can how much these proceedings of certain among the dissenters are to be feared. You are to weigh, with the temper which is natural to you, whether it may be for the safety of our establishment, that the Catholics should be ultimately persuaded that they have no hope to enter into the constitution but through the dissenters.

Think, whether this be the way to prevent or dissolve factious combinations against the Church or the State. Reflect seriously on the possible consequences of keeping in the heart of your country a bank of discontent, every hour accumulating, upon which every description of seditious men may draw at pleasure. They whose principles of faction will dispose them to the establishment of an arbitrary monarchy, will find a nation of men who have no sort of interest in freedom; but who will have an interest in that equality of justice or favour with which a wise despot must view all his subjects who do not attack the foundations of his power. Love of liberty itself may, in such men, become the means of establishing an arbitrary domination. On the other hand, they who wish for a democratic republic, will find a set of men who have no choice between civil servitude, and the entire ruin of a mixed constitution.

Suppose the people of Ireland divided into three parts; of these (I speak within compass) two are Catholic. Of the remaining third one-half is composed of dissenters. There is no natural union between those descriptions. It may be produced. If the two parts Catholic be driven into a close confederacy with half the third part of Protestants, with a view to a change in the constitution in Church or State, or both, and you rest the whole of their security on a handful of gentlemen, clergy, and their dependants; compute the strength *you have in Ireland* to oppose to grounded discontent, to capricious innovation, to blind popular fury, and to ambitious turbulent intrigue.

You mention that the minds of some gentlemen are a good deal heated, and that it is often said that, rather than submit to such persons having a share in their franchises, they would throw up their independence and precipitate a union with Great Britain. I have heard a discussion concerning such a union amongst all sorts of men ever since I remember anything. For my own part, I have never been able to bring my mind to anything clear and decisive upon

the subject. There cannot be a more arduous question.
As far as I can form an opinion, it would not be for
the mutual advantage of the two kingdoms. Persons,
however, more able than I am, think otherwise. But,
whatever the merits of this union may be, to make it
a *menace,* it must be shown to be an *evil ;* and an evil
more particularly to those who are threatened with it
than to those who hold it out as a terror. I really do
not see how this threat of a union can operate, or
that the Catholics are more likely to be losers by that
measure than the Churchmen.

The humours of the people, and of politicians too,
are so variable in themselves, and are so much under
the occasional influence of some leading men, that it is
impossible to know what turn the public mind here
would take on such an event. There is but one thing
certain concerning it. Great divisions and vehement
passions would precede this union, both on the measure
itself and on its terms ; and particularly, this very
question of a share in the representation for the
Catholics, from whence the project of a union originated, would form a principal part in the discussion ;
and in the temper in which some gentlemen seem
inclined to throw themselves, by a sort of high indig-
nant passion, into the scheme, those points would not
be deliberated with all possible calmness.

From my best observation I should greatly doubt
whether, in the end, these gentlemen would obtain
their object, so as to make the exclusion of two

millions of their countrymen a fundamental article in
the union.   The demand would be of a nature quite
unprecedented.   You might obtain the union; and yet
a gentleman who, under the new union establishment,
would aspire to the honour of representing his country,
might possibly be as much obliged, as he may fear to
be, under the old separate establishment, to the un-
supportable mortification of asking his neighbours, who
have a different opinion concerning the elements in the
sacrament for their votes.

I believe, nay, I am sure, that the people of
Great Britain, with or without a union, might be depended upon, in cases of any real danger, to aid the
Government of Ireland with the same cordiality as
they would support their own, against any wicked
attempts to shake the security of the happy constitution in Church and State.   But before Great Britain
engages in any quarrel, the *cause of the dispute* would
certainly be a part of her consideration.   If confusions
should arise in that kingdom from too steady an attachment to a proscriptive monopolising system, and from
the resolution of regarding the franchise, and in it the
security of the subject as belonging rather to religious
opinions than to civil qualification and civil conduct, I
doubt whether you might quite certainly reckon on
obtaining an aid of force from hence for the support of
that system.   We might extend your distractions to
this country by taking part in them.   England will be
indisposed, I suspect, to send an army for the conquest

of Ireland. What was done in 1782 is a decisive proof of her sentiments of justice and moderation. She will not be fond of making another American war in Ireland. The principles of such a war would but too much resemble the former one. The well-disposed and the ill-disposed in England would (for different reasons perhaps) be equally averse to such an enterprise. The confiscations, the public auctions, the private grants, the plantations, the transplantations, which formerly animated so many adventurers, even among sober citizens, to such Irish expeditions, and which possibly might have animated some of them to the American, can have no existence in the case that we suppose.

Let us form a supposition (no foolish or ungrounded supposition) that in an age when men are infinitely more disposed to heat themselves with political than religious controversies, the former should entirely prevail, as we see that in some places they have prevailed, over the latter; and that the Catholics of Ireland, from the courtship paid them on the one hand, and the high tone of refusal on the other, should, in order to enter into all the rights of subjects, all become Protestant dissenters, and as the others do, take all your oaths. They would all obtain their civil objects; and the change, for any thing I know to the contrary (in the dark as I am about the Protestant dissenting tenets), might be of use to the health of their souls. But, what security our constitution in Church or State could derive from that event I cannot possibly discern. Depend upon it, it is as true as nature is true, that if you force them out of the religion of habit, education, or opinion, it is not to yours they will ever go. Shaken in their minds, they will go to that where the dogmas are fewest; where they are the most uncertain; where they lead them the least to a consideration of what they have abandoned. They will go to that uniformly democratic system to whose first movements they owed their emancipation. I recommend you seriously to turn this in your mind. Believe that it requires your best and maturest thoughts. Take what course you please—union or no union; whether the people remain Catholics or become Protestant dissenters, sure it is, that the present state of monopoly *cannot* continue.

If England were animated, as I think she is not, with her former spirit of domination, and with the strong theological hatred which she once cherished for that description of her fellow-Christians and fellow-subjects, I am yet convinced, that after the fullest success in a ruinous struggle, you would be obliged to abandon that monopoly. We were obliged to do this, even when everything promised success in the American business. If you should make this experiment at last, under the pressure of any necessity, you never can do it well. But if, instead of falling into a passion, the leading gentlemen of the country themselves should undertake the business cheerfully, and

with hearty affection towards it, great advantages
would follow.   What is forced cannot be modified ;
but here you may measure your concessions.

It is a consideration of great moment, that you
make the desired admission without altering the system
of your representation in the smallest degree, or in any
part.   You may leave that deliberation of a Parliamentary change or reform, if ever you should think fit
to engage in it, uncomplicated and unembarrassed with
the other question.   Whereas, if they are mixed and
confounded—as some people attempt to mix and confound them—no one can answer for the effects on the
constitution itself.

There is another advantage in taking up this
business singly and by an arrangement for the single
object.   It is that you may proceed by *degrees*.   We
must all obey the great law of change.   It is the most
powerful law of nature, and the means perhaps of its
conservation.   All we can do, and that human wisdom
can do, is to provide that the change shall proceed by
insensible degrees.   This has all the benefits which
may be in change, without any of the inconveniences
of mutation.   Everything is provided for as it arrives.
This mode will, on the one hand, prevent the *unfixing
old interests at once :* a thing which is apt to breed a
black and sullen discontent in those who are at once
dispossessed of all their influence and consideration.
This gradual course, on the other side, will prevent
men, long under depression, from being intoxicated

with a large draught of new power, which they always
abuse with a licentious insolence.   But wishing, as I
do, the change to be gradual and cautious, I would,
in my first steps, lean rather to the side of enlargement than restriction.

It is one excellence of our constitution, that all our
rights of provincial election regard rather property than
person.   It is another, that the rights which approach
more nearly to the personal are most of them corporate,
and suppose a restrained and strict education of seven
years in some useful occupation.   In both cases the
practice may have slid from the principle.   The standard
of qualification in both cases may be so low, or not so
judiciously chosen, as in some degree to frustrate the
end.   But all this is for your prudence in the case
before you.   You may raise a step or two the qualification of the Catholic voters.   But if you were to-
morrow to put the Catholic freeholder on the footing of
the most favoured forty-shilling Protestant dissenter,
you know that such is the actual state of Ireland, this
would not make a sensible alteration in almost any
one election in the kingdom.   The effect in their
favour, even defensively, would be infinitely slow.   But
it would be healing ; it would be satisfactory and protecting.   The stigma would be removed.   By admitting
settled, permanent substance in lieu of the numbers,
you would avoid the great danger of our time—that
of setting up number against property.   The numbers
ought never to be neglected, because (besides what is

T

due to them as men) collectively, though not individually, they have great property : they ought to have,
therefore, protection; they ought to have security; they
ought to have even consideration ; but they ought not
to predominate.

My dear sir, I have nearly done ; I meant to write
you a long letter, I have written a long dissertation. I
might have done it earlier and better. I might have
been more forcible and more clear, if I had not been
interrupted as I have been; and this obliges me not to
write to you in my own hand. Though my hand but
signs it, my heart goes with what I have written. Since
I could think at all, those have been my thoughts. You
know that thirty-two years ago they were as fully
matured in my mind as they are now. A letter of
mine to Lord Kenmare, though not by my desire, and
full of lesser mistakes, has been printed in Dublin.
It was written ten or twelve years ago, at the time
when I began the employment, which I have not yet
finished, in favour of another distressed people, injured
by those who have vanquished them, or stolen a dominion over them. It contained my sentiments then ;
you will see how far they accord with my sentiments
now. Time has more and more confirmed me in them
all. The present circumstances fix them deeper in my
mind.

I voted last session, if a particular vote could be
distinguished in unanimity, for an establishment of
the Church of England *conjointly* with the establish-

ment which was made some years before by Act of
Parliament, of the Roman Catholic, in the French conquered country of Canada.   At the time of making
this English ecclesiastical establishment, we did not
think it necessary for its safety to destroy the former
Gallican Church settlement.   In our first Act we settled
a government altogether monarchical, or nearly so.   In
that system the Canadian Catholics were far from
being deprived of the advantages or distinctions of
any kind which they enjoyed under their former
monarchy.   It is true that some people—and amongst
them one eminent divine—predicted at that time that
by this step we should lose our dominions in America.
He foretold that the Pope would send his indulgences
hither; that the Canadians would fall in with France,
would declare independence, and draw or force our
colonies into the same design.   The independence
happened according to his prediction, but in directly
the reverse order.   All our English Protestant countries revolted. They joined themselves to France :
and it so happened that Popish Canada was the only
place which preserved its fidelity—the only place in
which France got no footing—the only peopled colony
which now remains to Great Britain.   Vain are all
the prognostics taken from ideas and passions which
survive the state of things which gave rise to them.
When last year we gave a popular representation to
the same Canada by the choice of the landholders,
and an aristocratic representation at the choice of the

Crown, neither was the choice of the Crown nor the election of the landholders limited by a consideration of religion. We had no dread for the Protestant Church which we settled there, because we permitted the French Catholics, in the utmost latitude of the description, to be free subjects. They are good subjects, I have no doubt; but I will not allow that any French Canadian Catholics are better men or better citizens than the Irish of the same communion. Passing from the extremity of the west to the extremity almost of the east, I have been many years (now entering into the twelfth) employed in supporting the rights, privileges, laws, and immunities of a very remote people. I have not as yet been able to finish my task. I have struggled through much discouragement and much opposition, much obloquy, much calumny, for a people with whom I have no tie but the common bond of mankind. In this I have not been left alone. We did not fly from our undertaking because the people were Mahometans or pagans, and that a great majority of the Christians amongst them are Papists. Some gentlemen in Ireland, I dare say, have good reasons for what they may do, which do not occur to me. I do not presume to condemn them; but, thinking and acting as I have done towards these remote nations, I should not know how to show my face here or in Ireland, if I should say that all the Pagans, all the Mussulmen, and even all the Papists (since they must form the highest stage in the climax of evil) are worthy of a liberal and honourable condition, except those of one of the descriptions, which forms the majority of the inhabitants of the country in which you and I were born. If such are the Catholics of Ireland,—ill-natured and unjust people from our own data may be inclined not to think better of the Protestants of a soil which is supposed to infuse into its sects a kind of venom unknown in other places.

You hated the old system as early as I did. Your first juvenile lance was broken against that giant. I think you were even the first who attacked the grim phantom. You have an exceedingly good understanding, very good humour, and the best heart in the world. The dictates of that temper and that heart, as well as the policy pointed out by that understanding, led you to abhor the old code. You abhorred it, as I did, for its vicious perfection. For I must do it justice : it was a complete system, full of coherence and consistency, well digested and well composed in all its parts. It was a machine of wise and elaborate contrivance, and as well fitted for the oppression, impoverishment, and degradation of a people, and the debasement in them of human nature itself, as ever proceeded from the perverted ingenuity of man. It is a thing humiliating enough—that we are doubtful of the effect of the medicines we compound. We are sure of our poisons. My opinion ever was (in which I heartily agree with those that admired the old code) that it was so constructed, that if there was once a breach in any essential part of it, the ruin of the whole, or nearly of the whole, was at some time or other a certainty. For that reason I honour, and shall for ever honour and love you, and those who first caused it to stagger, crack, and gape. Others may finish; the beginners have the glory; and, take what part you please at this hour (I think you will take the best), your first services will never be forgotten by a grateful country. Adieu! Present my best regards to those I know, and as many as I know in our country I honour. There never was so much ability, nor, I believe, virtue in it. They have a task worthy of both. I doubt not they will perform it for the stability oᴸ the Church and State, and for the union and the separation of the people; for the union of the honest and peaceable of all sects; for their separation from all that is ill-intentioned and seditious in any of them.

BEACONSFIELD,
    3d January 1792.

VIII.

A LETTER to the RIGHT HON. EDMUND PERY.[1]

MY DEAR SIR,

I RECEIVED in due course your two very interesting and judicious letters, which gave me many new lights, and excited me to fresh activity in the important subject they related to. However, from that time I have not been perfectly free from doubt and uneasiness. I used a liberty with those letters, which perhaps, nothing can thoroughly justify, and which

---

[1] This letter is addressed to Mr. Pery (afterwards Lord Pery) then Speaker of the House of Commons of Ireland. It appears there had been much correspondence between that gentleman and Mr. Burke, on the subject of heads of a Bill (which had passed the Irish House of Commons in the summer of the year 1778, and had been transmitted by the Irish Privy Council of England) for the relief of his Majesty's Roman Catholic subjects in Ireland. The Bill contained a clause for exempting the Protestant Dissenters of Ireland from the Sacramental Test, which created a strong objection to the whole measure on the part of the English Government. Mr. Burke employed his most strenuous efforts to remove the prejudice which the king's ministers entertained againt the clause ; but the Bill was ultimately returned without it, and in that shape passed the Irish Parliament. (17th and 18 Geo. III. cap. 49.) In the subsequent Session, however, a separate Act was passed for the relief of the Protestant Dissenters of Ireland.

certainly nothing but the delicacy of the crisis, the
clearness of my intentions, and your great good nature
can at all excuse.   I might conceal this from you, but
I think it better to lay the whole matter before you,
and submit myself to your mercy; assuring you, at
the same time, that if you are so kind as to continue
your confidence on this, or to renew it upon any other
occasion, I shall never be tempted again to make so
bold and unauthorised a use of the trust you place in
me.   I will state to you the history of the business
since my last, and then you will see how far I am excusable by the circumstances.

On the 3d of July I received a letter from the
Attorney-General, dated the day before, in which, in a
very open and obliging manner, he desires my thoughts
of the Irish Toleration Bill, and particularly of the
Dissenters' Clause.   I gave them to him by the return
of the post at large; but as the time pressed, I kept no
copy of the letter.   The general drift was strongly to
recommend the *whole*, and principally to obviate the
objections to the part that related to the Dissenters,
with regard both to the general propriety and to the
temporary policy at this juncture.   I took likewise a
good deal of pains to state the difference which had
always subsisted with regard to the treatment of the
Protestant Dissenters in Ireland and in England, and
what I conceived the reason of that difference to be.
About the same time I was called to town for a day,
and I took an opportunity in Westminster Hall, of

urging the same points with all the force I was master
of to the Solicitor-General.   I attempted to see the
Chancellor for the same purpose, but was not fortunate
enough to meet him at home.   Soon after my return
hither on Tuesday, I received a very polite, and I may
say, friendly letter from him, wishing me (on supposition that I had continued in town) to dine with him
on that day, in order to talk over the business of the
Toleration Act then before him.   Unluckily I had
company with me, and was not able to leave them
until Thursday, when I went to town and called at his
house, but missed him.   However, in answer to his
letter I had before, and instantly on the receipt of it,
written to him at large, and urged such topics, both
with regard to the Catholics and Dissenters as I
imagined were the most likely to be prevalent with
him.   This letter I followed to town on Thursday.
On my arrival I was much alarmed with a report that
the Ministry had thoughts of rejecting the whole Bill.
Mr. M'Namara seemed apprehensive that it was a
determined measure, and there seemed to be but too
much reason for his fears.   Not having met the
Chancellor at home, either on my first visit or my
second after receiving his letter, and fearful that the
Cabinet should come to some unpleasant resolution, I
went to the Treasury on Friday.   There I saw Sir G.
Cooper.   I possessed him of the danger of a partial,
and the inevitable mischief of the total, rejection of the
Bill.   I reminded him of the understood compact be-

tween parties, upon which the whole scheme of the
Toleration, originating in the English Bill, was formed ;
of the fair part which the Whigs had acted in a business, which, though first started by them, was supposed
equally acceptable to all sides ; and the risk of which
they took upon themselves when others declined it.
To this I added such matter as I thought most fit to
engage Government, as Government—not to sport
with a singular opportunity which offered for the
union of every description of men amongst us, in
support of the common interest of the whole, and I
ended by desiring to see Lord North upon the subject.
Sir Grey Cooper showed a very right sense of the
matter, and in a few minutes after our conversation, I
went down from the Treasury Chambers to Lord
North's house. I had a great deal of discourse with
him. He told me that his ideas of toleration were
large ; but that, large as they were, they did not comprehend a promiscuous establishment, even in matters
merely civil !—that he thought the established religion
ought to be the religion of the State ; that, in this
idea, he was not for the repeal of the Sacramental
Test ; that indeed he knew the Dissenters in general
did not greatly scruple it ; but that very want of
scruple showed less zeal against the Establishment ;
and, after all, there could no provision be made by
human laws against those who made light of the tests
which were formed to discriminate opinions. On all
this he spoke with a good deal of temper. He did not,

indeed, seem to think the Test itself, which was rightly considered by Dissenters as in a manner dispensed with by an annual Act of Parliament, and which in Ireland was of a late origin, and of much less extent than here, a matter of much moment. The thing which seemed to affect him most was the offence that would be taken at the repeal by the leaders among the Church clergy here, on one hand, and on the other the steps which would be taken for its repeal in England in the next Session, in consequence of the repeal in Ireland. I assured him, with great truth, that we had no idea among the Whigs of moving the repeal of the Test. I confessed very freely, for my own part, that if it were brought in, I should certainly vote for it; but that I should neither use, nor did I think applicable, any arguments drawn from the analogy of what was done in other parts of the British dominions. We did not argue from analogy, even in this Island and United Kingdom. Presbytery was established in Scotland. It became no reason either for its religious or civil establishment here. In New England the Independent Congregational Churches had an established legal maintenance; whilst that country continued part of the British Empire, no argument in favour of Independency was adduced from the practice of New England. Government itself lately thought fit to establish the Roman Catholic religion in Canada; but they would not suffer an argument of analogy to be used for its

establishment anywhere else. These things were
governed, as all things of that nature are governed,
not by general maxims, but their own local and
peculiar circumstances. Finding, however, that though
he was very cool and patient, I made no great way in
the business of the Dissenters, I turned myself to try
whether, falling in with his maxims, some modification
might not be found, the hint of which I received from
your letter relative to the Irish Militia Bill, and the
point I laboured was so to alter the Clause as to
repeal the Test *quoad* Military and Revenue Offices.
For these being only subservient parts in the economy
and execution, rather than the administration of
affairs, the politic, civil, and judicial parts would still
continue in the hands of the Conformists to religious
establishments. Without giving any hopes, he however said, that this distinction deserved to be considered.

After this, I strongly pressed the mischief of rejecting the whole Bill; that a notion went abroad,
that Government was not at this moment very well
pleased with the Dissenters, as not very well affected
to the Monarchy; that in general, I conceived this
to be a mistake; but if it were not, the rejection of
a Bill in favour *of others*, because something in favour
of *them* was inserted, instead of humbling and mortify-
ing, would infinitely exalt them. For if the Legislature had no means of favouring those whom they
meant to favour, as long as the Dissenters could find
means to get themselves included, this would make

them, instead of their only being subject to restraint themselves, the arbitrators of the fate of others, and that, not so much by their own strength (which could not be prevented in its operation), as by the co-operation of those whom they opposed. In the conclusion I recommended, that if they wished well to the measure, which was the main object of the Bill, they must explicitly make it their own, and stake themselves upon it; that hitherto all their difficulties had arisen from their indecision and their wrong measures; and to make Lord North sensible of the necessity of giving a firm support to some part of the Bill, and to add weighty authority to my reasons, I read him your letter of the 10th of July. It seemed, in some measure, to answer the purpose which I intended. I pressed the necessity of the management of the affair, both as to conduct and as to gaining of men; and I renewed my former advice, that the Lord Lieutenant should be instructed to consult and co-operate with you in the whole affair. All this was apparently very fairly taken.

In the evening of that day I saw the Lord Chancellor. With him, too, I had much discourse. You know that he is intelligent, sagacious, systematic, and determined. At first he seemed of opinion that the relief contained in the Bill was so inadequate to the mass of oppression it was intended to remove, that it would be better to let it stand over until a more perfect and better digested plan could be settled.

This seemed to possess him very strongly. In order to combat this notion, and to show that the Bill—all things considered—was a very great acquisition, and that it was rather a preliminary than an obstruction to relief, I ventured to show him your letter. It had its effect. He declared himself roundly against giving anything to a confederacy, real or apparent, to distress Government; that if anything was done for Catholics or Dissenters, it should be done on its own separate merits, and not by way of bargain and compromise; that they should be each of them obliged to Government, not each to the other; that this would be a perpetual nursery of faction. In a word, he seemed so determined on not uniting these plans, that all I could say—and I said everything I could think of— was to no purpose. But when I insisted on the disgrace to Government which must arise from their rejecting a proposition recommended by themselves, because their opposers had made a mixture, separable too by themselves, I was better heard. On the whole, I found him well disposed.

As soon as I had returned to the country, this affair lay so much on my mind—and the absolute necessity of Government's making a serious business of it agreeably to the seriousness they professed and the object required—that I wrote to Sir G. Cooper tò remind him of the principles upon which we went in our conversation, and to press the plan which was suggested for carrying them into execution. He wrote to me on the 20th, and assured me " that Lord North had given all due attention and respect to what you said to him on Friday, and will pay the same respect to the sentiments conveyed in your letter. Everything you say or write on the subject undoubtedly demands it." Whether this was mere civility, or showed anything effectual in their intentions, time and the success of this measure will show. It is wholly with them, and if it should fail, you are a witness that nothing on our part has been wanting to free so large a part of our fellow-subjects and fellow-citizens from slavery, and to free Government from the weakness and danger of ruling them by force. As to my own particular part, the desire of doing this has betrayed me into a step which I cannot perfectly reconcile to myself. You are to judge how far in the circumstances it may be excused. I think it had a good effect. You may be assured that I made this communication in a manner effectually to exclude so false and groundless an idea as that I confer with you, any more than I confer with them, on any party principle whatsoever, or that in this affair we look farther than the measure which is in profession, and I am sure ought to be in reason, theirs. I am ever, with the sincerest affection and esteem, my dear sir, your most faithful and obedient humble servant,

EDMUND BURKE.

BEACONSFIELD, 18*th July* 1778.

I intended to have written sooner, but it has not been in my power.

To the Speaker of the
House of Commons of Ireland.

IX.

A LETTER to Thomas Burgh, Esq.[1]

My dear Sir,

I do not know in what manner I am to thank you
properly for the very friendly solicitude you have been
so good as to express for my reputation.   The concern
you have done me the honour to take in my affairs will
be an ample indemnity from all that I may suffer
from the rapid judgments of those who choose to form
their opinions of men—not from the life but from their
portraits in a newspaper.   I confess to you that my
frame of mind is so constructed—I have in me so little
of the constitution of a great man—that I am more

---

[1] Mr. Thomas Burgh, of *Old Town*, was a member of the House of
Commons in Ireland.

It appears from a letter written by this gentleman to Mr. Burke,
24th December 1779, and to which the following is an answer, that
the part Mr. Burke had taken in the discussion, which the affairs of
Ireland had undergone in the preceding sessions of Parliament in England (see note prefixed to *Two Letters to Gentlemen in Bristol*, and also
Speech at the Guildhall in Bristol), had been grossly misrepresented
and much censured in Ireland.

gratified with a very moderate share of approbation from those few who know me, than I should be with the most clamorous applause from those multitudes who love to admire at a due distance.

I am not, however, stoic enough to be able to affirm with truth, or hypocrite enough affectedly to pretend, that I am wholly unmoved at the difficulty which you and others of my friends in Ireland have found in vindicating my conduct towards my native country. It undoubtedly hurts me in some degree, but the wound is not very deep. If I had sought popularity in Ireland—when in the cause of that country I was ready to sacrifice, and did sacrifice, a much nearer, a much more immediate, and a much more advantageous popularity here,—I should find myself perfectly unhappy, because I should be totally disappointed in my expectations; because I should discover when it was too late (what common sense might have told me very early) that I risked the capital of my fame in the most disadvantageous lottery in the world. But I acted then as I act now—and as I hope I shall act always—from a strong impulse of right, and from motives in which popularity, either here or there, has but a very little part.

With the support of that consciousness I can bear a good deal of the coquetry of public opinion, which has her caprices, and must have her way—*Miseri quibus intentata nitet!* I, too, have had my holiday of popularity in Ireland. I have even heard of an intention

U

to erect a statue.[1]   I believe my intimate acquaintance know how little that idea was encouraged by me;
and I was sincerely glad that it never took effect.
Such honours belong exclusively to the tomb — the
natural and only period of human inconstancy with
regard either to desert or to opinion; for they are the
very same hands which erect, that very frequently
(and sometimes with reason enough) pluck down the
statue.   Had such an unmerited and unlooked-for
compliment been paid to me two years ago, the fragments of the piece might at this hour have the advantage of seeing actual service, while they were moving,
according to the law of projectiles, to the windows of
the Attorney-General, or of my old friend Monk
Mason.

   To speak seriously, let me assure you, my dear sir,
that though I am not permitted to rejoice at *all* its
effects, there is not one man on your side of the water
more pleased to see the situation of Ireland so prosperous as that she can afford to throw away her friends.
She has obtained, solely by her own efforts, the fruits
of a great victory, which I am very ready to allow
that the best efforts of her best well-wishers here could
not have done for her so effectually in a great number
of years, and perhaps could not have done at all.
I could wish, however, merely for the sake of her
own dignity, that in turning her poor relations and

---

[1] This intention was communicated to Mr. Burke in a letter from
Mr. Pery, the Speaker of the House of Commons in Ireland.

antiquated friends out of doors (though one of the most common effects of new prosperity), she had thought proper to dismiss us with fewer tokens of unkindness. It is true that there is no sort of danger in affronting men who are not of importance enough to have any trust of ministerial, of royal, or of national honour to surrender. The unforced and unbought services of humble men who have no medium of influence in great assemblies but through the precarious force of reason, must be looked upon with contempt by those who by their wisdom and spirit have improved the critical moment of their fortune, and have debated with authority against pusillanimous dissent and ungracious compliance at the head of 40,000 men.

Such feeble auxiliaries (as I talk of) to such a force employed against such resistance, I must own in the present moment, very little worthy of your attention. Yet, if one were to look forward, it scarcely seems altogether politic to bestow so much liberality of invective on the Whigs of this kingdom as I find has been the fashion to do both in and out of Parliament. That you should pay compliments in some tone or other, whether ironical or serious, to the minister from whose imbecility you have extorted what you could never obtain from his bounty, is not unnatural. In the first effusions of Parliamentary gratitude to that Minister for the early and voluntary benefits he has conferred upon Ireland, it might appear that you were wanting to the triumph of his surrender

if you did not lead some of his enemies captive before
him.   Neither could you feast him with decorum, if
his particular taste were not consulted.   A minister
who has never defended his measures in any other way
than by railing at his adversaries, cannot have his
palate made all at once to the relish of positive com-
mendation.   I cannot deny but that on this occasion
there was displayed a great deal of the good breeding
which consists in the accommodation of the entertain-
ment to the relish of the guest.

But that ceremony being past, it would not be unworthy of the wisdom of Ireland to consider what
consequences the extinguishing every spark of freedom
in this country may have upon your own liberties.
You are at this instant flushed with victory and full
of the confidence natural to recent and untried power.
We are in a temper equally natural, though very
different.   We feel as men do, who, having placed an
unbounded reliance on their force, have found it totally
to fail on trial.   We feel faint and heartless, and
without the smallest degree of self-opinion.   In plain
words, we are *cowed*.   When men give up their violence and injustice without a struggle, their condition
is next to desperate.   When no art, no management, no
argument is necessary to abate their pride and over-
come their prejudices, and their uneasiness only excites
an obscure and feeble rattling in their throat, their
final dissolution seems not far off.   In this miserable
state we are still further depressed by the overbearing

influence of the Crown. It acts with the officious
cruelty of a mercenary nurse, who, under pretence of
tenderness, stifles us with our clothes, and plucks the
pillow from our heads. *Injectu multæ vestis opprimi
senem jubet.* Under this influence we have so little
will of our own, that even in any apparent activity we
may be got to assume, I may say, without any violence
to sense and with very little to language, we are
merely passive. We have yielded to your demands
this session. In the last session we refused to prevent
them. In both cases—the passive and the active—our
principle was the same. Had the Crown pleased to
retain the spirit with regard to Ireland, which seems
to be now all directed to America, we should have
neglected our own immediate defence, and sent over
the last man of our militia to fight with the last man
of your volunteers.

To this influence the principle of action, the principle of policy, and the principle of union of the present
minority are opposed. These principles of the Opposition are the only thing which preserves a single symptom
of life in the nation. That Opposition is composed of
the far greater part of the independent property and
independent rank of the kingdom; of whatever is most
untainted in character, and of whatever ability remains
unextinguished in the people, and of all which tends to
draw the attention of foreign countries upon this. It is
now in its final and conclusive struggle. It has to struggle
against a force to which I am afraid it is not equal.

The *whole* kingdom of Scotland ranges with the venal, the unprincipled, and the wrong-principled of this; and if the kingdom of Ireland thinks proper to pass into the same camp, we shall certainly be obliged to quit the field. In that case, if I know anything of this country, another constitutional Opposition *can never* be formed in it; and if this be impossible, it will be at least as much so (if there can be degrees in impossibility) to have a constitutional Administration at any future time. The possibility of the former is the only security for the existence of the latter. Whether the present Administration be in the least like one, I must venture to doubt even in the honeymoon of the Irish fondness to Lord North, which has succeeded to all their slappings and scratchings.

If liberty cannot maintain its ground in this kingdom, I am sure that it cannot have any long continuance in yours. Our liberty might now and then jar, and strike a discord with that of Ireland. The thing is possible, but still the instruments might play in concert. But if ours be unstrung, yours will be hung up on a peg; and both will be mute for ever. Your new military force may give you confidence, and it serves well for a turn; but you and I know that it has not root. It is not perennial, and would prove but a poor shelter for your liberty when this nation, having no interest in its own, could look upon yours with the eye of envy and disgust. I cannot, therefore, help thinking and telling you what with great submission I think, that if the Parliament of

Ireland be so jealous of the spirit of our common constitution as she means to be, it was not so discreet to
mix with the panegyric on the minister so large a
portion of acrimony to the independent part of this
nation. You never received any sort of injury from
them, and you are grown to that degree of importance,
that the discourses in your Parliament will have a much
greater effect on our immediate fortune than our conversation can have upon yours. In the end they will
seriously affect both.

I have looked back upon our conduct and our public
conversations in order to discover what it is that can
have given you offence. I have done so because I am
ready to admit that to offend you without any cause
would be as contrary to true policy as I am sure it must
be to the inclinations of almost every one of us. About
two years ago Lord Nugent moved six propositions in
favour of Ireland, in the House of Commons. At the
time of the motions and during the debate, Lord North
was either wholly out of the House or engaged in other
matters of business or pleasantry in the remotest recesses
of the West Saxon corner. He took no part whatsoever
in the affair; but it was supposed his neutrality was
more inclined towards the side of favour. The mover
being a person in office was, however, the only indication that was given of such a leaning. We who supported the propositions, finding them better relished
than at first we looked for, pursued our advantage, and
began to open a way for more essential benefits to Ire-

land.   On the other hand, those who had hitherto
opposed them in vain redoubled their efforts, and
became exceedingly clamorous.   Then it was that Lord
North found it necessary to come out of his fastness,
and to interpose between the contending parties.   In
this character of mediator he declared that if anything
beyond the first six resolutions should be attempted, he
would oppose the whole ; but that if we rested there,
the original motions should have his support.   On this
a sort of convention took place between him and the
managers of the Irish business, in which the six resolutions were to be considered as an *uti possidetis*, and
to be held sacred.

By this time other parties began to appear.   A
good many of the trading towns and manufactures of
various kinds took the alarm.   Petitions crowded in
upon one another ; and the Bar was occupied by a
formidable body of Council.   Lord N. was staggered
by this new battery.   He is not of a constitution to
encounter such an opposition as had then risen, when
there were no other objects in view than those that
were then before the House.   In order not to lose
him we were obliged to abandon, bit by bit, the most
considerable part of the original agreement.

In several parts, however, he continued fair and
firm.   For my own part I acted, as I trust I commonly do, with decision.   I saw very well that the
things we had got were of no great consideration ; but
they were, even in their defects, somewhat leading.   I

was in hopes that we might obtain gradually, and by
parts, what we might attempt at once and in the whole
without success ; that one concession would lead to
another ; and that the people of England, discovering
by a progressive experience that none of the concessions
actually made were followed by the consequences they
had dreaded, their fears from what they were yet to
yield would considerably diminish. But that to which
I attached myself most particularly, was to fix *the
principle* of a free trade in all the ports of these
Islands, as founded in justice, and beneficial to the
whole ; but principally to this the seat of the supreme
power. And this I laboured to the utmost of my
might, upon general principles, illustrated by all the
commercial detail with which my little inquiries in
life were able to furnish me. I ought to forget such
trifling things as those, with all concerning myself ;
and possibly I might have forgotten them, if the Lord
Advocate of Scotland had not, in a very flattering
manner, revived them in my memory, in a full House
in this session. He told me that my arguments, such
as they were, had made him, at the period I allude to,
change the opinion with which he had come into the
House strongly impressed. I am sure that, at the
time, at least twenty more told me the same thing. I
certainly ought not to take their style of compliment
as a testimony to fact—neither do I. But all this
showed sufficiently, not what they thought of my
ability, but what they saw of my zeal. I could say

more in proof of the effects of that zeal, and of the
unceasing industry with which I then acted, both in
my endeavours which were apparent, and those that
were not so visible.   Let it be remembered that I
showed those dispositions while the Parliament of
England was in a capacity to deliberate, and in a
situation to refuse ; when there was something to be
risked here by being suspected of a partiality to
Ireland ; when there was an honourable danger
attending the profession of friendship to you, which
heightened its relish and made it worthy of a reception in manly minds.   But as for the awkward and
nauseous parade of debate without opposition, the
flimsy device of tricking out necessity, and disguising
it in the habit of choice, the shallow stratagem of
defending by argument what all the world must perceive is yielded to force—these are a sort of acts of
friendship which I am sorry that any of my countrymen should require of their real friends.   They are
things not *to my taste;* and if they are looked upon as
tests of friendship, I desire for one that I may be
considered as an enemy.

What party purpose did my conduct answer at
that time ?   I acted with Lord N.   I went to all the
ministerial meetings—and he and his associates in
office will do me the justice to say that, aiming at the
concord of the Empire, I made it my business to give
his concessions all the value of which they were capable,—whilst some of those who were covered with

his favours, derogated from them, treated them with
contempt, and openly threatened to oppose them.   If
I had acted with my dearest and most valued friends
—if I had acted with the Marquis of Rockingham, or
the Duke of Richmond, in that situation, I could not
have attended more to their honour, or endeavoured
more earnestly to give efficacy to the measures I had
taken in common with them.   The return which I, and
all who acted as I did, have met with from him, does
not make me repent the conduct which I then held.

As to the rest of the gentlemen with whom I have
the honour to act, they did not then, or at any other
time, make a party affair of Irish politics.   That matter
was always taken up without concert; but in general,
from the operation of our known liberal principles in
government, in commerce, in religion, in everything, it
was taken up favourably for Ireland.   Where some
local interests bore hard upon the members, they acted
on the sense of their constituents, upon ideas which,
though I do not always follow, I cannot blame.   However, two or three persons high in opposition, and high
in public esteem, ran great risks in their boroughs on
that occasion.   But all this was without any particular
plan.   I need not say that Ireland was in that affair
much obliged to the liberal mind and enlarged understanding of Charles Fox, to Mr. Thomas Townshend, to
Lord Middleton, and others.   On reviewing that affair,
which gave rise to all the subsequent manœuvres, I am
convinced that the whole of what has this day been

done might have then been effected. But then the minister must have taken it up as a great plan of national policy, and paid with his person in every lodgment of his approach. He must have used that influence to quiet prejudice, which he has so often used to corrupt principle; and I know that if he had, he must have succeeded. Many of the most active in opposition would have given him an unequivocal support. The Corporation of London, and the great body of the London West India merchants and planters which forms the greatest mass of that vast interest, were disposed to fall in with such a plan. They certainly gave no sort of discountenance to what was done, or what was proposed. But these are not the kind of objects for which our ministers bring out the heavy artillery of the State. Therefore, as things stood at that time, a great deal more was not practicable.

Last year another proposition was brought out for the relief of Ireland. It was started without any communication with a single person of activity in the country party, and, as it should seem, without any kind of concert with Government. It appeared to me extremely raw and undigested. The behaviour of Lord N. on the opening of that business was the exact transcript of his conduct on the Irish question in the former session. It was a mode of proceeding which his nature has wrought into the texture of his politics, and which is inseparable from them. He chose to absent himself on the proposition, and during the agitation of

that business, although the business of the House is
that alone for which he has any kind of relish, or, as I
am told, can be persuaded to listen to with any degree
of attention. But he was willing to let it take its
course. If it should pass without any considerable difficulty he would bring his acquiescence to tell
for merit in Ireland, and he would have the credit, out
of his indolence, of giving quiet to that country. If
difficulties should arise on the part of England, he knew
that the House was so well trained that he might at his
pleasure call us off from the hottest scent. As he acted
in his usual manner, and upon his usual principle,
opposition acted upon theirs, and rather generally supported the measure. As to myself, I expressed a disapprobation at the practice of bringing imperfect and
indigested projects into the House before means were
used to quiet the clamours which a misconception of
what we were doing might occasion at home, and before
measures were settled with men of weight and authority
in Ireland, in order to render our acts useful and
acceptable to that country. I said that the only thing
which could make the influence of the Crown (enormous without as well as within the House) in any
degree tolerable, was that it might be employed to give
something of order and system to the proceedings of a
popular assembly; that Government, being so situated
as to have a large range of prospect, and as it were a
bird's-eye view of everything, they might see distant
dangers and distant advantages, which were not so

visible to those who stood on the common level; they
might, besides, observe them from this advantage in
their relative and combined state, which people, locally
instructed and partially informed, could behold only in
an insulated and unconnected manner; but that for
many years past we suffered under all the evils, without any one of the advantages, of a Government influence; that the business of a minister, or of those who
acted as such, had been still further to contract the narrowness of men's ideas, to confirm inveterate prejudices,
to inflame vulgar passions, and to abet all sorts of popular absurdities, in order the better to destroy popular
rights and privileges; that, so far from methodising
the business of the House, they had let all things run
into an inextricable confusion, and had left affairs of
the most delicate policy wholly to chance.

After I had expressed myself with the warmth I felt
on seeing all government and order buried under the
ruins of liberty, and after I had made my protest against
the insufficiency of the propositions, I supported the
principle of enlargement, at which they aimed, though
short and somewhat wide of the mark; giving, as my
sole reason, that the more frequently these matters
came into discussion, the more it would tend to dispel
fears and to eradicate prejudices.

This was the only part I took. The detail was in
the hands of Lord Newhaven and Lord Beauchamp,
with some assistance from Earl Nugent and some independent gentlemen of Irish property. The dead weight

of the minister being removed, the House recovered its tone and elasticity. We had a temporary appearance of a deliberative character. The business was debated freely on both sides, and with sufficient temper. And the sense of the Members being influenced by nothing but what will naturally influence men unbought—their reason and their prejudices—these two principles had a fair conflict, and prejudice was obliged to give way to reason. A majority appeared on a division in favour of the propositions.

As these proceedings got out of doors, Glasgow and Manchester, and, I think, Liverpool began to move, but in a manner much more slow and languid than formerly. Nothing, in my opinion, would have been less difficult than entirely to have over-born their opposition. The London West India trade was, as on the former occasion, so on this, perfectly liberal, and perfectly quiet; and there is abroad so much respect for the united wisdom of the House, when supposed to act upon a fair view of a political situation, that I scarcely ever remember any considerable uneasiness out of doors, when the most active members, and those of most property and consideration in the Minority, have joined themselves to the Administration. Many factious people in the towns I mentioned began indeed to revile Lord North, and to reproach his neutrality as treacherous and ungrateful to those who had so heartily and so warmly entered into all his views with regard to America. That noble lord, whose decided character it is to give way to the latest

and nearest pressure without any sort of regard to distant consequences of any kind, thought fit to appear on
this signification of the pleasure of those his worthy
friends and partisans, and putting himself at the head
of the *Posse Scaccarii*, wholly regardless of the dignity
and consistency of our miserable House, drove the propositions entirely out of doors by a majority newly
summoned to duty.

In order to atone to Ireland for this gratification to
Manchester, he graciously permitted, or rather forwarded
two Bills—that for encouraging the growth of tobacco,
and that for giving a bounty on exportation of hemp
from Ireland.   They were brought in by two very
worthy members, and on good principles; but I was
sorry to see them; and after expressing my doubts of
their propriety, left the House.   Little also was said
upon them.   My objections were two; the first, that the
cultivation of those weeds (if one of them could be at
all cultivated to profit) was adverse to the introduction
of a good course of agriculture; the other, that the
encouragement given to them tended to establish that
mischievous policy of considering Ireland as a country
of staple, and a producer of raw materials.

When the rejection of the first propositions and the
acceptance of the last had jointly, as it was natural,
raised a very strong discontent in Ireland, Lord Rockingham, who frequently said that there never seemed a
more opportune time for the relief of Ireland than that
moment, when Lord North had rejected all rational

propositions for its relief, without consulting, I believe, any one living, did what he is not often very willing to do; but he thought this an occasion of magnitude enough to justify an extraordinary step. He went into the Closet, and made a strong representation on the matter to the king, which was not ill received, and I believe produced good effects. He then made the motion in the House of Lords which you may recollect, but he was content to withdraw all of censure which it contained on the solemn promise of Ministry that they would, in the recess of Parliament, prepare a plan for the benefit of Ireland, and have it in readiness to produce at the next meeting. You may recollect that Lord Gower became in a particular manner bound for the fulfilling this engagement. Even this did not satisfy; and most of the Minority were very unwilling that Parliament should be prorogued until something effectual on the subject should be done; particularly as we saw that the distresses, discontents, and armaments of Ireland were increasing every day, and that we are not so much lost to common sense as not to know the wisdom and efficacy of early concession in circumstances such as ours.

The session was now at an end. The ministers, instead of attending to a duty that was so urgent on them, employed themselves, as usual, in endeavours to destroy the reputation of those who were bold enough to remind them of it. They caused it to be industriously circulated through the nation that the distresses of Ireland were of a nature hard to be traced to the true source; that they

X

had been monstrously magnified; and that, in particular,
the official reports from Ireland had given the lie (that
was their phrase) to Lord Rockingham's representations.
And attributing the origin of the Irish proceedings wholly
to us, they asserted that everything done in Parliament
upon the subject was with a view of stirring up rebellion;
" that neither the Irish Legislature nor their constituents
had signified any dissatisfaction at the relief obtained in
the session preceding the last; that to convince both of
the impropriety of their *peaceable* conduct, opposition,
by making demands in the name of Ireland, pointed out
what she might extort from Great Britain; that the
facility with which relief was formerly granted, instead
of satisfying opposition, was calculated to create new
demands. These demands, as they *interfered* with the
commerce of Great Britain, were *certain* of being opposed—a circumstance which could not fail to create that
desirable confusion which suits the views of the party.
That they (the Irish) had long felt their own misery
without knowing well from whence it came. Our worthy
patriots, by *pointing out Great Britain* as the *cause of
Irish distress,* may have some chance of rousing Irish resentment." This I quote from a pamphlet, as perfectly
contemptible in point of writing, as it is false in its facts
and wicked in its design; but as it is written under the
authority of ministers by one of their principal literary
pensioners, and was circulated with great diligence, and,
as I am credibly informed, at a considerable expense to
the public, I use the words of that book to let you see

in what manner the friends and patrons of Ireland, the
heroes of your Parliament, represented all efforts for
your relief here, what means they took to dispose the
minds of the people towards that great object, and what
encouragement they gave to all who should choose to
exert themselves in your favour.   Their unwearied
endeavours were not wholly without success, and the
unthinking people in many places became ill affected
towards us on this account.   For the ministers proceeded in your affairs just as they did with regard
to those of America.   They always represented you as
a parcel of blockheads without sense, or even feeling;
that all your words were only the echo of faction here,
and (as you have seen above) that you had not understanding enough to know that your trade was cramped
by restrictive acts of the British Parliament, unless we
had, for factious purposes, given you the information.

They were so far from giving the least intimation of
the measures which have since taken place, that those
who were supposed the best to know their intentions
declared them impossible in the actual state of the two
kingdoms, and spoke of nothing but an Act of Union as
the only way that could be found of giving freedom of
trade to Ireland consistently with the interests of this
kingdom.   Even when the session opened Lord North
declared that he did not know what remedy to apply to
a disease, of the cause of which he was ignorant, and
Ministry not being then entirely resolved how far they
should submit to your energy, they, by anticipation, set

the above author, or some of his associates, to fill the
newspapers with invectives against us, as distressing the
minister by extravagant demands in favour of Ireland.

I need not inform you that everything they asserted
of the steps taken in Ireland as the result of our
machinations was utterly false and groundless. For
myself, I seriously protest to you that I neither wrote
a word or received a line upon any matter relative to
the trade of Ireland, or to the politics of it, from the
beginning of the last session to the day that I was
honoured with your letter. It would be an affront to the
talents in the Irish Parliament to say one word more.

What was done in Ireland during that period in and
out of Parliament never will be forgotten. You raised
an army new in its kind and adequate to its purposes.
It effected its end without its exertion. It was not
under the authority of law, most certainly, but it
derived from an authority still higher; and as they say
of faith that it is not contrary to reason but above it, so
this army did not so much contradict the spirit of the
law as supersede it. What you did in the legislative
body is above all praise. · By your proceeding with
regard to the supplies you revived the grand use and
characteristic benefit of Parliament, which was on the
point of being entirely lost amongst us. These sentiments I never concealed, and never shall, and Mr. Fox
expressed them with his usual power when he spoke on
the subject.

All this is very honourable to you. But in what

light must we see it? How are we to consider your
armament without commission from the Crown, when
some of the first people in *this* kingdom have been
refused arms at the time they did not only not reject,
but solicited the king's commissions? Here to arm and
embody would be represented as little less than high
treason if done on private authority. With you it
receives the thanks of a Privy Counsellor of Great
Britain, who obeys the Irish House of Lords in that
point with pleasure, and is made Secretary of State, the
moment he lands here, for his reward. You shortened
the credit given to the Crown to six months; you hung
up the public credit of your kingdom by a thread; you
refused to raise any taxes, whilst you confessed the
public debt and public exigencies to be great and
urgent beyond example. You certainly acted in a great
style, and on sound and invincible principles. But if
we, in the opposition which fills Ireland with such
loyal horrors, had even attempted what we never did
even attempt—the smallest delay or the smallest limitation of supply in order to a constitutional coercion of
the Crown—we should have been decried by all the
Court and Tory mouths of this kingdom as a desperate
faction, aiming at the direct ruin of the country, and to
surrender it bound hand and foot to a foreign enemy.
By actually doing what we never ventured to attempt,
you have paid your court with such address, and have
won so much favour with his Majesty and his Cabinet,
that they have, of their special grace and mere motion,

raised you to new titles; and, for the first time, in a speech from the throne, complimented you with the appellation of "faithful and loyal,"—and, in order to insult our low-spirited and degenerate obedience, have thrown these epithets and your resistance together in our teeth! What do you think were the feelings of every man who looks upon Parliament in a higher light than that of a market-overt for legalising a base traffic of votes and pensions, when he saw you employ such means of coercion to the Crown in order to coerce our Parliament through *that* medium? How much his Majesty is pleased with *his* part of the civility must be left to his own taste. But as to us, you declared to the world that you knew that the way of bringing us to reason was to apply yourselves to the true source of all our opinions, and the only motive to all our conduct! Now, it seems you think yourselves affronted, because a few of us express some indignation at the minister who has thought fit to strip us stark-naked, and expose the true state of our poxed and pestilential habit to the world! Think or say what you will in Ireland, I shall ever think it a crime hardly to be expiated by his blood. He might and ought, by a longer continuance, or by an earlier meeting of this Parliament, to have given us the credit of some wisdom in foreseeing and anticipating an approaching force. So far from it, Lord Gower, coming out of his own Cabinet, declares that one principal cause of his resignation was his not being able to prevail on the present minister to give any sort of

application to this business. Even on the late meeting
of Parliament nothing determinate could be drawn from
him or from any of his associates until you had actually
passed the short Money Bill, which measure they flattered themselves, and assured others, you would never
come up to. Disappointed in their expectation at seeing
the siege raised, they surrendered at discretion.

Judge, my dear sir, of our surprise at finding your
censure directed against those whose only crime was in
accusing the ministers of not having prevented your
demands by our graces, of not having given you the
natural advantages of your country in the most ample,
the most early, and the most liberal manner; and for
not having given away authority in such a manner as
to ensure friendship. That you should make the panegyric of the ministers is what I expected, because in
praising their bounty you paid a just compliment to
your own force. But that you should rail at us, either
individually or collectively, is what I can scarcely think
a natural proceeding. I can easily conceive that gentlemen might grow frightened at what they had done—that
they might imagine they had undertaken a business
above their direction—that having obtained a state of
independence for their country, they meant to take the
deserted helm into their own hands, and supply by
their very real abilities the total inefficacy of the
nominal Government. All these might be real, and
might be very justifiable motives for their reconciling
themselves cordially to the present Court system. But

I do not so well discover the reasons that could induce them, at the first feeble dawning of life in this country, to do all in their power to cast a cloud over it, and to prevent the least hope of our effecting the necessary reformations which are aimed at in our constitution and in our national economy.

But it seems I was silent at the passing the resolutions. Why—what had I to say? If I had thought them too much, I should have been accused of an endeavour to inflame England. If I should represent them as too little, I should have been charged with a design of fomenting the discontents of Ireland into actual rebellion. The Treasury Bench represented that the affair was a matter of State; they represented it truly. I therefore only asked whether they knew these propositions to be such as would satisfy Ireland; for if they were so, they would satisfy me. This did not indicate that I thought them too ample. In this our silence (however dishonourable to Parliament) there was one advantage; that the whole passed, as far as it is gone, with complete unanimity, and so quickly that there was no time left to excite any opposition to it out of doors. In the West India business, reasoning on what had lately passed in the Parliament of Ireland, and on the mode in which it was opened here, I thought I saw much matter of perplexity. But I have now better reason than ever to be pleased with my silence. If I had spoken, one of the most honest and able men [1]

[1] Mr. Grattan.

in the Irish Parliament would probably have thought
my observation an endeavour to sow dissension, which
he was resolved to prevent; and one of the most in-
genious and one of the most amiable men, that [1] ever
graced your or any House of Parliament, might have
looked on it as a chimera.   In the silence I observed I
was strongly countenanced (to say no more of it) by
every gentleman of Ireland that I had the honour of
conversing with in London.   The only word for that
reason, which I spoke, was to restrain a worthy county
member [2] who had received some communication from
a great trading place in the county he represents, which,
if it had been opened to the House, would have led to a
perplexing discussion of one of the most troublesome
matters that could arise in this business.   I got up to
put a stop to it; and I believe, if you knew what the
topic was, you would commend my discretion.

That it should be a matter of public discretion in
me to be silent on the affairs of Ireland is what, on all
accounts, I bitterly lament.   I stated to the House
what I felt; and I felt, as strongly as human sensibility
can feel, the extinction of my Parliamentary capacity
where I wished to use it most.   When I came into this
Parliament just fourteen years ago—into this Parliament then, in vulgar opinion at least, the presiding
Council of the greatest empire existing (and perhaps, all
things considered, that ever did exist),—obscure and a
stranger as I was, I considered myself as raised to the

[1] Mr. Hussey Burgh.   [2] Mr. Stanley, member for Lancashire.

highest dignity to which a creature of our species could
aspire.   In that opinion—one of the chief pleasures in
my situation—what was first and uppermost in my
thoughts was the hope, without injury to this country,
to be somewhat useful to the place of my birth and
education, which in many respects, internal and external,
I thought ill and impolitically governed.   But when I
found that the House, surrendering itself to the guid-
ance of an authority not grown out of an experienced
wisdom and integrity, but out of the accidents of Court
favour, had become the sport of the passions of men at
once rash and pusillanimous—that it had even got into
the habit of refusing everything to reason, and surrendering everything to force—all my power of obliging
either my country or individuals was gone, all the lustre
of my imaginary rank was tarnished, and I felt degraded
even by my elevation.   I said this, or something to this
effect.   If it gives offence to Ireland, I am sorry for it ;
it was the reason I gave for my silence, and it was, as
far as it went, the true one.

With you this silence of mine and of others was
represented as factious, and as a discountenance to the
measure of your relief.   Do you think us children ?   If
it had been our wish to embroil matters, and for the
sake of distressing Ministry to commit the two kingdoms in a dispute, we had nothing to do but (without
at all condemning the propositions) to have gone into
the commercial detail of the objects of them.   It could
not have been refused to us ; and you who know the

nature of business so well, must know that this would
have caused such delays, and given rise during that
delay to such discussions, as all the wisdom of your
favourite Minister could never have settled. But indeed you mistake your men. We tremble at the idea
of a disunion of these two nations. The only thing in
which we differ with you is this, that we do not think
your attaching yourselves to the Court, and quarrelling
with the independent part of this people, is the way to
promote the union of two free countries, or of holding
them together by the most natural and salutary ties.

You will be frightened when you see this long letter.
I smile, when I consider the length of it myself. I
never, that I remember, wrote any of the same extent.
But it shows me that the reproaches of the country
that I once belonged to, and in which I still have a
dearness of instinct more than I can justify to reason,
make a greater impression on me than I had imagined.
But parting words are admitted to be a little tedious,
because they are not likely to be renewed. If it will
not be making yourself as troublesome to others as I am
to you, I shall be obliged to you if you will show this,
at their greatest leisure, to the Speaker, to your excellent kinsman, to Mr. Grattan, Mr. Yelverton, and Mr.
Daly. All these I have the honour of being personally
known to except Mr. Yelverton, to whom I am only
known by my obligations to him. If you live in any
habits with my old friend the Provost, I shall be glad
that he too sees this, my humble apology.

Adieu! Once more accept my best thanks for the interest you take in me. Believe that it is received by a heart not yet so old as to have lost its susceptibility. All here give you the best old-fashioned wishes of the season, and believe me, with the greatest truth and regard, my dear sir, your most faithful and obliged humble servant,

EDMUND BURKE.

BEACONSFIELD, *New Year's Day*, 1780.

I am frightened at the trouble I give you and our friends; but I recollect that you are mostly lawyers, and habituated to read long tiresome papers, and where your friendship is concerned, without a fee. I am sure, too, that you will not act the lawyer in scrutinising too minutely every expression which my haste may make me use. I forgot to mention my friend O'Hara and others, but you will communicate it as you please.

X.

A LETTER to John Merlott, Esq.[1]

DEAR SIR,

I AM very unhappy to find that my conduct in the business of Ireland on a former occasion had made many to be cold and indifferent, who would otherwise have been warm in my favour. I really thought that events would have produced a quite contrary effect, and would have proved to all the inhabitants of Bristol that it was no desire of opposing myself to their wishes, but a certain knowledge of the necessity of their affairs, and a tender regard to their honour and interest, which induced me to take the part which I then took. They placed me in a situation which might enable me to discern what was fit to be done on a consideration of the relative circumstances of this country and all its neighbours. This was what you could not so well do yourselves; but you had a right to expect that I

---

[1] An eminent merchant in the City of Bristol, of which Mr Burke was one of the Representatives in Parliament. It relates to the same subject as the preceding letter.

should avail myself of the advantage which I derived from your favour. Under the impression of this duty and this trust, I had endeavoured to render by preventive graces and concessions every act of power at the same time an act of lenity — the result of English bounty, and not of English timidity and distress. I really flattered myself that the events which have proved beyond dispute the prudence of such a maxim, would have obtained pardon for me, if not approbation. But if I have not been so fortunate, I do most sincerely regret my great loss ; with this comfort, however, that if I have disobliged my constituents, it was not in pursuit of any sinister interest, or any party passion of my own, but in endeavouring to save them from disgrace, along with the whole community to which they and I belong. I shall be concerned for this, and very much so ; but I should be more concerned if, in gratifying a present humour of theirs, I had rendered myself unworthy of their former or their future choice. I confess that I could not bear to face my constituents at the next General Election if I had been a rival to Lord North in the glory of having refused some small, insignificant concessions in favour of Ireland, to the arguments and supplications of English Members of Parliament ; and in the very next Session, on the demand of 40,000 Irish bayonets, of having made a speech of two hours long to prove, that my former conduct was founded upon no one right principle either of policy, justice, or commerce. I never heard a more elaborate, more able, more convincing, and more shameful speech.   The debator obtained credit; but the statesman was disgraced for ever.   Amends were made for having refused small but timely concessions by an unlimited and untimely surrender, not only of every one of the objects of former restraints, but virtually of the whole legislative power itself, which had made them.   For it is not necessary to inform you that the unfortunate Parliament of this kingdom did not dare to qualify the very liberty she gave of trading with her *own* plantations, by applying, of her *own* authority, any one of the commercial regulations to the new traffic of Ireland, which bind us here under the several Acts of Navigation.   We were obliged to refer them to the Parliament of Ireland as conditions, just in the same manner, as if we were bestowing a privilege of the same sort on France and Spain, or any other independent power, and, indeed, with more studied caution than we should have used, not to shock the principle of their independence.   How the minister reconciled the refusal to reason, and the surrender to arms, raised in defiance of the prerogatives of the Crown to his master, I know not; it has probably been settled, in some way or other, between themselves.   But, however the king and his ministers may settle the question of his dignity and his rights, I thought it became me by vigilance and foresight to take care of yours; I thought I ought rather to lighten the ship in time than expose it to a total wreck.   The conduct pursued seemed to me without weight or judgment, and more fit for a member for Banbury than a member for Bristol. I stood, therefore, silent with grief and vexation on that day of the signal shame and humiliation of this degraded king and country. But it seems the pride of Ireland in the day of her power was equal to ours, when we dreamt we were powerful too. I have been abused there even for my silence, which was construed into a desire of exciting discontent in England. But, thank God, my letter to Bristol was in print; my sentiments on the policy of the measure were known and determined, and such as no man could think me absurd enough to contradict. When I am no longer a free agent, I am obliged in the crowd to yield to necessity; it is surely enough that I silently submit to power; it is enough that I do not foolishly affront the conqueror; it is too hard to force me to sing his praises, whilst I am led in triumph before him; or to make the panegyric of our own minister, who would put me neither in a condition to surrender with honour, or to fight with the smallest hope of victory. I was, I confess, sullen and silent on that day; and shall continue so, until I see some disposition to inquire into this and other causes of the national disgrace. If I suffer in my reputation for it in Ireland, I am sorry; but it neither does nor can affect me so nearly as my suffering in Bristol, for having wished to unite the interests of the two nations in a manner that would secure the supremacy of this.

Will you have the goodness to excuse the length of

this letter.   My earnest desire of explaining myself in
every point which may affect the mind of any worthy
gentleman in Bristol is the cause of it.   To yourself,
and to your liberal and manly notions, I know it is not
so necessary.   Believe me, my dear sir,—Your most
faithful and obedient humble Servant,

EDMUND BURKE.

BEACONSFIELD, *4th April* 1780.

To John Merlott, Esq., Bristol.

Y

XI.

A LETTER to WILLIAM SMITH, Esq.[1]

MY DEAR SIR,

YOUR letter is, to myself, infinitely obliging ; with regard to you, I can find no fault with it, except that of a tone of humility and disqualification, which neither your rank, nor the place you are in, nor the profession you belong to, nor your very extraordinary learning and talents, will, in propriety, demand, or perhaps admit. These dispositions will be still less proper, if you should feel them in the extent your modesty leads you to express them. You have certainly given by far too strong a proof of self-diffidence by asking the opinion of a man, circumstanced as I am, on the important subject of your letter. You are far more capable of forming just conceptions upon it than I can be. However, since you are pleased to command me to lay before you my thoughts, as materials upon

---

[1] Then a member of the Irish Parliament ; afterwards one of the Barons of the Court of Exchequer in Ireland.

which your better judgment may operate, I shall obey you; and submit them, with great deference, to your melioration or rejection.

But first permit me to put myself in the right. I owe you an answer to your former letter. It did not desire one; but it deserved it. If not for an answer, it called for an acknowledgment. It was a new favour; and indeed I should be worse than insensible if I did not consider the honours you have heaped upon me with no sparing hand, with becoming gratitude. But your letter arrived to me at a time, when the closing of my long and last business in life, a business extremely complex, and full of difficulties and vexations of all sorts, occupied me in a manner which those who have not seen the interior as well as exterior of it, cannot easily imagine. I confess that in the crisis of that rude conflict, I neglected many things that well deserved my best attention—none that deserved it better, or have caused me more regret in the neglect, than your letter. The instant that business was over, and the House had passed its judgment on the conduct of the managers, I lost no time to execute what for years I had resolved on; it was to quit my public station, and to seek that tranquillity in my very advanced age, to which, after a very tempestuous life, I thought myself entitled. But God has thought fit (and I unfeignedly acknowledge His justice) to dispose of things otherwise. So heavy a calamity has fallen upon me as to disable me for business, and to disqualify me for repose. The

existence I have, I do not know that I can call life.
Accordingly I do not meddle with any one measure of
Government, though, for what reasons I know not, you
seem to suppose me deeply in the secret of affairs. I
only know, so far as your side of the water is concerned,
that your present excellent Lord Lieutenant (the best
man in every relation that I have ever been acquainted
with) has perfectly pure intentions with regard to
Ireland; and, of course, that he wishes cordially well
to those who form the great mass of its inhabitants;
and who, as they are well or ill managed, must form an
important part of its strength or weakness. If with
regard to that great object he has carried over any
ready-made system, I assure you it is perfectly unknown
to me; I am very much retired from the world, and
live in much ignorance. This, I hope, will form my
humble apology, if I should err in the notions I entertain of the question, which is soon to become the subject
of your deliberations. At the same time, accept it as an
apology for my neglects.

You need make no apology for your attachment to
the religious description you belong to. It proves (as
in you it is sincere) your attachment to the great points
in which the leading divisions are agreed, when the
lesser, in which they differ, are so dear to you. I shall
never call any religious opinions, which appear important to serious and pious minds, things of no consideration. Nothing is so fatal to religion as indifference, which is, at least, half infidelity. As long as men

hold charity and justice to be essential integral parts of
religion, there can be little danger from a strong attachment to particular tenets in faith. This I am
perfectly sure is your case; but I am not equally
sure that either zeal for the tenets of faith, or the
smallest degree of charity or justice, have much influenced the gentlemen who, under pretexts of zeal,
have resisted the enfranchisement of their country.
My dear son, who was a person of discernment, as
well as clear and acute in his expressions, said in a
letter of his which I have seen, " that in order to grace
their cause, and to draw some respect to their persons,
they pretend to be bigots." But here I take it we have
not much to do with the theological tenets on the
one side of the question or the other. The point itself
is practically decided. That religion is owned by the
State. Except in a settled maintenance, it is protected.
A great deal of the rubbish, which, as a nuisance, long
obstructed the way, is removed. One impediment
remained longer, as a matter to justify the proscription of the body of our country, after the rest had
been abandoned as untenable ground. But the business of the pope (that mixed person of politics and
religion), has long ceased to be a bugbear; for some
time past he has ceased to be even a colourable pretext.
This was well known when the Catholics of these
kingdoms, for our amusement, were obliged on oath to
disclaim him in his political capacity; which implied
an allowance for them to recognise him in some sort of

ecclesiastical superiority. It was a compromise of the old dispute.

For my part, I confess, I wish that we had been less eager in this point. I don't think, indeed, that much mischief will happen from it if things are otherwise properly managed. Too nice an inquisition ought not to be made into opinions that are dying away of themselves. Had we lived a hundred and fifty years ago, I should have been as earnest and anxious as anybody for this sort of abjuration ; but, living at the time in which I live, and obliged to speculate forward instead of backward, I must fairly say I could well endure the existence of every sort of collateral aid, which opinion might, in the now state of things, afford to authority. I must see much more danger than in my life I have seen, or than others will venture seriously to affirm that they see in the pope aforesaid (though a foreign power, and with his long tail of etceteras), before I should be active in weakening any hold which Government might think it prudent to resort to in the management of that large part of the king's subjects. I do not choose to direct all my precautions to the part where the danger does not press, and to leave myself open and unguarded where I am not only really but visibly attacked.

My whole politics at present centre in one point, and to this the merit or demerit of every measure (with me) is referable ; that is, what will most promote or depress the cause of Jacobinism. What is Jacobinism ? It is an attempt (hitherto but too successful) to eradicate prejudice out of the minds of men for the purpose of putting all power and authority into the hands of the persons capable of occasionally enlightening the minds of the people. For this purpose the Jacobins have resolved to destroy the whole frame and fabric of the old societies of the world, and to regenerate them after their fashion. To obtain an army for this purpose they everywhere engage the poor by holding out to them as a bribe the spoils of the rich. This I take to be a fair description of the principles and leading maxims of the enlightened of our day, who are commonly called Jacobins.

As the grand prejudice, and that which holds all the other prejudices together, the first, last, and middle object of their hostility is religion. With that they are at inexpiable war. They make no distinction of sects. A Christian as such is to them an enemy. What then is left to a real Christian (Christian as a believer and as a statesman) but to make a league between all the grand divisions of that name—to protect and to cherish them all, and by no means to proscribe in any manner, more or less, any member of our common party? The divisions which formerly prevailed in the Church, with all their overdone zeal, only purified and ventilated our common faith, because there was no common enemy arrayed and embattled to take advantage of their dissensions; but now nothing but inevitable ruin will be the consequence of our quarrels. I think we may dispute, rail, persecute, and provoke the Catholics out of

their prejudices; but it is not in ours they will take
refuge.   If anything is, one more than another, out of
the power of man, it is to *create* a prejudice.   Somebody
has said that a king may make a nobleman, but he cannot make a gentleman.

All the principal religions in Europe stand upon one
common bottom.   The support that the whole or the
favoured parts may have in the secret dispensations of
Providence it is impossible to tell; but, humanly speaking, they are all *prescriptive* religions.   They have all
stood long enough to make prescription and its chain of
legitimate prejudices their mainstay.   The people, who
compose the four grand divisions of Christianity, have
now their religion as a habit, and upon authority, and
not on disputation,—as all men who have their religion
derived from their parents, and the fruits of education,
must have it, however the one, more than the other,
may be able to reconcile his faith to his own reason, or
to that of other men.   Depend upon it they must all be
supported, or they must all fall in the crash of a common ruin.   The Catholics are the far more numerous
part of the Christians in your country; and how can
Christianity (that is now the point in issue) be supported
under the persecution, or even under the discountenance
of the greater number of Christians?   It is a great truth,
and which in one of the debates I stated as strongly as
I could to the House of Commons in the last session,
that if the Catholic religion is destroyed by the infidels,
it is a most contemptible and absurd idea that this or

any Protestant Church can survive that event. Therefore my humble and decided opinion is, that all the three religions, prevalent more or less in various parts of these islands, ought all, in subordination to the legal establishments as they stand in the several countries, to be all countenanced, protected, and cherished; and that in Ireland particularly the Roman Catholic religion should be upheld in high respect and veneration; and should be, in its place, provided with all the means of making it a blessing to the people who profess it; that it ought to be cherished as a good (though not as the most preferable good, if a choice was now to be made), and not tolerated as an inevitable evil. If this be my opinion as to the Catholic religion as a sect, you must see that I must be to the last degree averse to put a man, upon that account, upon a bad footing with relation to the privileges which the fundamental laws of this country give him as a subject. I am the more serious on the positive encouragement to be given to this religion (always, however, as secondary), because the serious and earnest belief and practice of it by its professors forms, as things stand, the most effectual barrier, if not the sole barrier, against Jacobinism. The Catholics form the great body of the lower ranks of your community, and no small part of those classes of the middling that come nearest to them. You know that the seduction of that part of mankind from the principles of religion, morality, subordination, and social order is the great object of the Jacobins. Let them grow lax, sceptical, careless, and indifferent with regard to religion, and so sure as we have an existence, it is not a zealous Anglican or Scottish Church principle, but direct Jacobinism, which will enter into that breach. Two hundred years dreadfully spent in experiments to force that people to change the form of their religion have proved fruitless. You have now your choice, for full four-fifths of your people, of the Catholic religion or Jacobinism. If things appear to you to stand on this alternative, I think you will not be long in making your option.

You have made, as you naturally do, a very able analysis of powers, and have separated, as the things are separable, civil from political powers. You start, too, a question whether the civil can be secured without some share in the political. For my part, as abstract questions, I should find some difficulty in an attempt to resolve them. But as applied to the state of Ireland, to the form of our commonwealth, to the parties that divide us, and to the dispositions of the leading men in those parties, I cannot hesitate to lay before you my opinion, that whilst any kind of discouragements and disqualifications remain on the Catholics, a handle will be made by a factious power utterly to defeat the benefits of any civil rights they may apparently possess. I need not go to very remote times for my examples. It was within the course of about a twelvemonth that, after Parliament had been led into a step quite unparalleled in its records,—after they had resisted all concession, and even hearing, with an obstinacy equal to anything that could have actuated a party domination in the second or eighth of Queen Anne,—after the strange adventure of the grand juries,—and after Parliament had listened to the sovereign pleading for the emancipation of his subjects ;—it was after all this that such a grudging and discontent was expressed as must justly have alarmed, as it did extremely alarm, the whole of the Catholic body; and I remember but one period in my whole life (I mean the savage period between 1761 and 1767) in which they have been more harshly or contumeliously treated than since the last partial enlargement. And thus I am convinced it will be by paroxysms, as long as any stigma remains on them, and whilst they are considered as no better than half citizens. If they are kept such for any length of time they will be made whole Jacobins. Against this grand and dreadful evil of our time (I do not love to cheat myself or others) I do not know any solid security whatsoever. But I am quite certain that what will come nearest to it is to interest as many as you can in the present order of things, religiously, civilly, politically, by all the ties and principles by which mankind are held. This is like to be the effectual policy—I am sure it is honourable policy ; and it is better to fail, if fail we must, in the paths of direct and manly than of low and crooked wisdom.

As to the capacity of sitting in Parliament, after all the capacities for voting, for the army, for the navy, for the professions, for civil offices, it is a dispute *de lanâ*

caprinâ, in my poor opinion,—at least on the part of
those who oppose it.   In the first place, this admission
to office, and this exclusion from Parliament, on the
principle of an exclusion from political power, is the
very reverse of the principle of the English Test Act.
If I were to form a judgment from experience rather
than theory, I should doubt much whether the capacity
for, or even the possession of, a seat in Parliament did
really convey much of power to be properly called political.   I have sat there, with some observation, for nine
and twenty years or thereabouts.   The power of a
member of Parliament is uncertain and indirect; and if
power rather than splendour and fame were the object,
I should think that any of the principal clerks in office,
to say nothing of their superiors (several of whom are
disqualified by law for seats in Parliament) possesses far
more power than nine-tenths of the members of the
House of Commons.   I might say this of men who
seemed from their fortunes, their weight in their country,
and their talents, to be persons of figure there; and
persons, too, not in opposition to the prevailing party in
government.

But be they what they will, on a fair canvass of the
several prevalent Parliamentary interests in Ireland, I
cannot, out of the three hundred members, of whom the
Irish Parliament is composed, discover that above three,
or at the utmost four, Catholics would be returned to the
House of Commons.   But suppose they should amount
to thirty, that is, to a tenth part (a thing I hold impos-

sible for a long series of years, and never very likely to happen), what is this to those who are to balance them in the one house, and the clear and settled majority in the other? for I think it absolutely impossible that, in the course of many years, above four or five peers should be created of that communion. In fact, the exclusion of them seems to me only to mark jealousy and suspicion, and not to provide security in any way. But I return to the old ground. The danger is not there; these are things long since done away. The grand controversy is no longer between you and them. Forgive this length. My pen has insensibly run on. You are yourself to blame if you are much fatigued. I congratulate you on the auspicious opening of your session. Surely Great Britain and Ireland ought to join in wreathing a never fading garland for the head of Grattan. Adieu! my dear sir—good nights to you! I never can have any.—Yours always most sincerely.

EDMUND BURKE.

29th January 1795.
Twelve at night.

XII.

A SECOND LETTER to Sir Hercules Langrishe.

My dear Sir,

If I am not as early as I ought to be in my acknow-
ledgments for your very kind letter, pray do me the
justice to attribute my failure to its natural and but too
real cause,—a want of the most ordinary power of exertion, owing to the impressions made upon an old and
infirm constitution by private misfortune and by public
calamity. It is true I make occasional efforts to rouse
myself to something better, but I soon relapse into
that state of languor which must be the habit of my
body and understanding to the end of my short and
cheerless existence in this world.

I am sincerely grateful for your kindness in connecting the interest you take in the sentiments of an old
friend with the able part you take in the service of your
country. It is an instance among many of that happy
temper which has always given a character of amenity
to your virtues, and a good-natured direction to your
talents.

Your speech on the Catholic question I read with much satisfaction. It is solid, it is convincing, it is eloquent, and it ought on the spot to have produced that effect which its reason, and that contained in the other excellent speeches on the same side of the question, cannot possibly fail (though with less pleasant consequences) to produce hereafter. What a sad thing it is that the grand instructor, time, has not yet been able to teach the grand lesson of his own value, and that in every question of moral and political prudence it is the choice of the moment which renders the measure serviceable or useless, noxious or salutary!

In the Catholic question I considered only one point. Was it, at the time and in the circumstances, a measure which tended to promote the concord of the citizens? I have no difficulty in saying it was, and as little in saying that the present concord of the citizens was worth buying at a critical season, by granting a few *capacities* which probably no one man now living is likely to be served or hurt by. When any man tells *you* and *me* that if these places were left in the discretion of a Protestant Crown, and these memberships in the discretion of protestant electors or patrons, we should have a Popish official system and a Popish representation capable of overturning the Establishment, he only insults our understandings. When any man tells this to *Catholics* he insults their understandings, and he galls their feelings. It is not the question of the places and seats, it is the real hostile disposition and the *pretended*

fears, that leave stings in the minds of the people. I
really thought that in the total of the late circumstances
with regard to persons, to things, to principles, and to
measures, was to be found a conjuncture favourable to
the introduction and to the perpetuation of a general
harmony, producing a general strength, which to that
hour Ireland was never so happy as to enjoy. My
sanguine hopes are blasted, and I must consign my feelings on that terrible disappointment to the same patience
in which I have been obliged to bury the vexation
I suffered on the defeat of the other great, just, and honourable causes in which I have had some share, and
which have given more of dignity than of peace and
advantage to a long laborious life. Though, perhaps, a
want of success might be urged as a reason for making
me doubt of the justice of the part I have taken, yet
until I have other lights than one side of the debate
has furnished me, I must see things, and feel them too,
as I see and feel them. I think I can hardly overrate
the malignity of the principles of Protestant ascendency
as they affect Ireland ; or of Indianism as they affect
these countries, and as they affect Asia ; or of Jacobinism, as they affect all Europe and the state of human
society itself. The last is the greatest evil ; but it really
combines with the others, and flows from them. Whatever breeds discontent at this time will produce that
great master-mischief most infallibly. Whatever tends
to persuade the people that the *few*, called by whatever
name you please, religious or political, are of opinion

that their interest is not compatible with that of the
many, is a great point gained to Jacobinism.   Whatever
tends to irritate the talents of a country, which have at
all times, and at these particularly, a mighty influence
on the public mind, is of infinite service to that formidable cause.   Unless where heaven has mingled uncom-
mon ingredients of virtue in the composition—*quos
meliore luto finxit præcordia Titan*—talents naturally
gravitate to Jacobinism.   Whatever ill-humours are
afloat in the State, they will be sure to discharge themselves in a mingled torrent in the *cloacâ maximâ* of
Jacobinism.   Therefore people ought well to look about
them.   First, the physicians are to take care that they
do nothing to irritate this epidemical distemper.   It is
a foolish thing to have the better of the patient in a
dispute.   The complaint, or its cause, ought to be removed, and wise and lenient arts ought to precede the
measures of vigour.   They ought to be the *ultima,* not
the *prima,* not the *tota* ratio of a wise government.
God forbid that on a worthy occasion authority should
want the means of force, or the disposition to use it.
But where a prudent and enlarged policy does not precede it, and attend it too, where the hearts of the better
sort of people do not go with the hands of the soldiery,
you may call your constitution what you will, in effect
it will consist of three parts (orders, if you please)—
cavalry, infantry, and artillery,—and of nothing else or
better.

I agree with you in your dislike of the discourses in

z

Francis Street; but I like as little some of those in
College Green. I am even less pleased with the temper that predominated in the latter, as better things
might have been expected in the regular family mansion
of public discretion, than in a new and hasty assembly
of unexperienced men, congregated under circumstances
of no small irritation. After people have taken your
tests, prescribed by yourselves as proofs of their allegiance, to be marked as enemies, traitors, or at best as
suspected and dangerous persons, and that they are not
to be believed on their oaths, we are not to be surprised
if they fall into a passion, and talk, as men in a passion
do, intemperately and idly.

The worst of the matter is this—you are partly
leading, partly driving, into Jacobinism that description of your people whose religious principles—Church
polity and habitual discipline—might make them an invincible dyke against that inundation. This you have a
thousand mattocks and pickaxes lifted up to demolish.
You make a sad story of the Pope !—*O seri studiorum !*
—It will not be difficult to get many called Catholics to
laugh at this fundamental part of their religion. Never
doubt it. You have succeeded in part; and you may
succeed completely. But in the present state of men's
minds and affairs, do not flatter yourselves that they
will piously look to the head of our Church in the place
of that Pope whom you make them forswear; and out
of all reverence to whom you bully, and rail, and buffoon
them. Perhaps you may succeed in the same manner

with all the other tenets of doctrine and usages of discipline amongst the Catholics.   But what security have
you that in the temper, and on the principles on which
they have made this change, they will stop at the exact
sticking places you have marked in *your* articles ? You
have no security for anything, but that they will become what are called *Franco-Jacobins*, and reject the
whole together. No converts now will be made in a
considerable number from one of our sects to the other
upon a really religious principle. Controversy moves
in another direction.

Next to religion, *property* is the great point of Jacobin
attack. Here many of the debaters in your majority,
and their writers, have given the Jacobins all the assistance their hearts can wish. When the Catholics desire
places and seats, you tell them that this is only a pretext (though Protestants might suppose it just *possible*
for men to like good places and snug boroughs for their
own merits) ; but that their real view is to strip Protestants of their property. To my certain knowledge
till those Jacobin lectures were opened in the House of
Commons, they never dreamt of any such thing ; but
now, the great professors may stimulate them to inquire
(on the new principles) into the foundation of that property, and of all property. If you treat men as robbers,
why robbers, sooner or later, they will become.

A third point of Jacobin attack is on *old traditionary
constitutions*. You are apprehensive for yours, which
leans from its perpendicular, and does not stand firm

on its theory.   I like Parliamentary reforms as little as
any man who has boroughs to sell for money or for
peerages in Ireland.   But it passes my comprehension
in what manner it is that men can be reconciled to the
practical merits of a constitution, the theory of which
is in litigation, by being *practically* excluded from any
of its advantages.   Let us put ourselves in the place of
these people, and try an experiment of the effects of
such a procedure on our own minds.   Unquestionably
we should be perfectly satisfied when we were told that
Houses of Parliament, instead of being places of refuge
for popular liberty, were citadels for keeping us in order
as a conquered people.   These things play the Jacobin
game to a nicety.   Indeed, my dear sir, there is not a
single particular in the Francis Street declamations,
which has not, to your and to my certain knowledge,
been taught by the jealous ascendants, sometimes by
doctrine, sometimes by example, always by provocation.
Remember the whole of 1781 and 1782—in Parliament
and out of Parliament—at this very day, and in the
worst acts and designs, observe the tenor of the objections with which the College Green orators of the
ascendency reproach the Catholics.   You have observed,
no doubt, how much they rely on the affair of Jackson.
Is it not pleasant to hear Catholics reproached for a
supposed connection—with whom ?—with Protestant
clergymen, with Protestant gentlemen ! — with Mr.
Jackson !—with Mr. Rowan, etc. etc. !   But *egomet
mi ig nosco.*   Conspiracies and treasons are privileged

pleasures, not to be profaned by the impure and un-
hallowed touch of Papists.   Indeed, all this will do
perhaps well enough with detachments of dismounted
cavalry and fencibles from England.   But let us not
say to Catholics, by way of *argument*, that they are to
be kept in a degraded state because some of them are
no better than many of us Protestants.   The thing I
most disliked in some of their speeches (those I mean of
the Catholics) was what is called the spirit of liberality,
so much and so diligently taught by the ascendants,
by which they are made to abandon their own particular interests, and to merge them in the general discontents of the country.   It gave me no pleasure to hear
of the dissolution of the committee.   There were in it a
majority, to my knowledge, of very sober well-intentioned
men ; and there were none in it but such who, if not
continually goaded and irritated, might be made useful
to the tranquillity of the country.   It is right always to
have a few of every description, through whom you may
quietly operate on the many, both for the interests of
the description, and for the general interest.   Excuse
me, my dear friend, if I have a little tried your patience.
You have brought this trouble on yourself, by your
thinking of a man forgot, and who has no objection to
be forgot, by the world.   These things we discussed together four or five and thirty years ago.   We were then,
and at bottom ever since, of the same opinion on the
justice and policy of the whole, and of every part, of the
penal system.   You and I and everybody must now

and then ply and bend to the occasion, and take what can be got. But very sure I am that whilst there remains in the law any principle whatever which can furnish to certain politicians an excuse for raising an opinion of their own importance as necessary to keep their fellow-subjects in order, the obnoxious people will be fretted, harassed, insulted, provoked to discontent and disorder, and practically excluded from the partial advantages from which the letter of the law does not exclude them.

Adieu! my dear sir, and believe me very truly yours,

EDMUND BURKE.

BEACONSFIELD, 26*th May* 1795.

XIII.

A LETTER to RICHARD BURKE, Esq.[1]

MY DEAR SON,

WE are all again assembled in town to finish the last, but the most laborious, of the tasks which have been imposed upon me during my Parliamentary service. We are as well as, at our time of life, we can expect to be. We have indeed some moments of anxiety about you. You are engaged in an undertaking similar in its principle to mine. You are engaged in the relief of an oppressed people.[2] In that service you must necessarily excite the same sort of passions in those who have exercised and who wish to continue that oppression that I have had to struggle with in this long labour. As your

[1] Of this letter the first part appears to have been originally addressed by Mr. Burke to his son in the manner in which it is now printed, but to have been left unfinished ; after whose death he probably designed to have given the substance of it, with additional observations, to the public in some other form ; but never found leisure or inclination to finish it.

[2] Richard Burke acted as agent for the Roman Catholics of Ireland, with the approbation of his father. He died in 1794.

father has done, you must make enemies of many of the rich, of the proud, and of the powerful. I and you began in the same way. I must confess that if our place was of our choice, I could wish it had been your lot to begin the career of your life with an endeavour to render some more moderate and less invidious service to the public. But being engaged in a great and critical work, I have not the least hesitation about your having hitherto done your duty as becomes you. If I had not an assurance not to be shaken from the character of your mind, I should be satisfied on that point by the cry that is raised against you. If you had behaved, as they call it, discreetly, that is, faintly and treacherously in the execution of your trust, you would have had, for a while, the good word of all sorts of men, even of many of those whose cause you had betrayed ; and whilst your favour lasted, you might have coined that false reputation into a true and solid interest to yourself. This you are well apprised of; and you do not refuse to travel that beaten road from an ignorance, but from a contempt of the objects it leads to.

When you choose an arduous and slippery path, God forbid that any weak feelings of my declining age, which calls for soothings and supports, and which can have none but from you, should make me wish that you should abandon what you are about, or should trifle with it. In this House we submit, though with troubled minds, to that order which has connected all great duties with toils and with perils, which has conducted the road to glory through the regions of obloquy and reproach, and which will never suffer the disparaging alliance of spurious, false, and fugitive praise with genuine and permanent reputation. We know that the power which has settled that order, and subjected you to it by placing you in the situation you are in, is able to bring you out of it with credit and with safety. His will be done. All must come right. You may open the way with pain, and under reproach. Others will pursue it with ease and with applause.

I am sorry to find that pride and passion, and that sort of zeal for religion which never shows any wonderful heat but when it afflicts and mortifies our neighbour, will not let the ruling description perceive that the privilege for which your clients contend, is very nearly as much for the benefit of those who refuse it as those who ask it. I am not to examine into the charges that are daily made on the Administration of Ireland. I am not qualified to say how much in them is cold truth, and how much rhetorical exaggeration. Allowing some foundation to the complaint, it is to no purpose that these people allege that their Government is a job in its administration. I am sure it is a job in its constitution ; nor is it possible, a scheme of polity, which, in total exclusion of the body of the community, confines (with little or no regard to their rank or condition in life) to a certain set of favoured citizens the rights which formerly belonged to the whole, should not, by the operation of the same selfish and narrow

principles, teach the persons who administer in that
Government to prefer their own particular but well-
understood private interest to the false and ill-calcu-
lated private interest of the monopolising Company
they belong to. Eminent characters, to be sure, overrule places and circumstances. I have nothing to say
to that virtue which shoots up in full force by the
native vigour of the seminal principle, in spite of the
adverse soil and climate that it grows in. But, speaking of things in their ordinary course, in a country of
monopoly there *can* be no patriotism. There may be a
party spirit—but public spirit there can be none. As
to a spirit of liberty, still less can it exist, or anything
like it. A liberty made up of penalties! a liberty made
up of incapacities! a liberty made up of exclusion and
proscription, continued for ages, of four fifths, perhaps,
of the inhabitants of all ranks and fortunes! In what
does such liberty differ from the description of the
most shocking kind of servitude?

But it will be said in that country some people are
free—why, this is the very description of despotism.
*Partial freedom is privilege and prerogative, and not
liberty.* Liberty, such as deserves the name, is an
honest, equitable, diffusive, and impartial principle. It
is a great and enlarged virtue, and not a sordid, selfish,
and illiberal vice. It is the portion of the mass of the
citizens; and not the haughty license of some potent
individual, or some predominant faction.

If anything ought to be despotic in a country, it is

its government; because there is no cause of constant operation to make its yoke unequal.   But the dominion of a party must continually, steadily, and by its very essence, lean upon the prostrate description.   A constitution formed so as to enable a party to overrule its very government, and to overpower the people too, answers the purposes neither of government nor of freedom.   It compels that power which ought and often would be disposed *equally* to protect the subjects, to fail in its trust, to counteract its purposes, and to become no better than the instrument of the wrongs of a faction. Some degree of influence must exist in all governments. But a government which has no interest to please the body of the people, and can neither support them, nor with safety call for their support, nor is. of power to sway the domineering faction, can only exist by corruption ; and taught by that monopolising party, which usurps the title and qualities of the public, to consider the body of the people as out of the constitution, they will consider those who are in it in the light in which they choose to consider themselves.   The whole relation of government and of freedom will be a battle or a traffic.

This system, in its real nature, and under its proper appellations, is odious and unnatural, especially when a constitution is admitted, which not only, as all constitutions do profess, has a regard to the good of the multitude, but in its theory makes profession of their power also.   But of late this scheme of theirs has been

new christened—*honestum nomen imponitur vitio.* A
word has been lately struck in the mint of the Castle of
Dublin ; thence it was conveyed to the Tholsel, or City
Hall, where, having passed the touch of the Corporation,
so respectably stamped and vouched, it soon became
current in Parliament, and was carried back by the
Speaker of the House of Commons in great pomp, as an
offering of homage from whence it came. The word is
Ascendency. It is not absolutely new. But the sense
in which I have hitherto seen it used, was to signify an
influence obtained over the minds of some other person
by love and reverence, or by superior management and
dexterity. It had, therefore, to this its promotion no
more than a moral, not a civil or political use. But I
admit it is capable of being so applied ; and if the Lord
Mayor of Dublin, and the Speaker of the Irish Parliament, who recommend the preservation of the Protestant ascendency, mean to employ the word in that
sense—that is, if they understand by it the preservation
of the influence of that description of gentlemen over
the Catholics by means of an authority derived from
their wisdom and virtue, and from an opinion they raise
in that people of a pious regard and affection for their
freedom and happiness, it is impossible not to commend
their adoption of so apt a term into the family of
politics. It may be truly said to enrich the language.
Even if the Lord Mayor and Speaker mean to insinuate
that this influence is to be obtained and held by flattering their people, by managing them, by skilfully adapt-

ing themselves to the humours and passions of those
whom they would govern, he must be a very untoward
critic who would cavil even at this use of the word,
though such cajoleries would perhaps be more prudently
practised than professed.   These are all meanings laudable, or at least tolerable.   But when we look a little
more narrowly, and compare it with the plan to which
it owes its present technical application, I find it has
strayed far from its original sense.   It goes much
farther than the privilege allowed by Horace.   It is
more than *parcè detortum.*   This Protestant ascendency
means nothing less than an influence obtained by virtue,
by love, or even by artifice and seduction ; full as little
an influence derived from the means by which ministers
have obtained an influence, which might be called without straining an *ascendency* in public assemblies in
England, that is, by a liberal distribution of places and
pensions, and other graces of Government.   This last is
wide indeed of the signification of the word.   New
ascendency is the old mastership.   It is neither more
nor less than the resolution of one set of people in Ireland to consider themselves as the sole citizens in the
commonwealth, and to keep a dominion over the rest
by reducing them to absolute slavery under a military
power ; and thus fortified in their power, to divide the
public estate, which is the result of general contribution, as a military booty solely amongst themselves.

The poor word ascendency, so soft and melodious in
its sound, so lenitive and emollient in its first usage, is

now employed to cover to the world the most rigid, and
perhaps not the most wise, of all plans of policy. The
word is large enough in its comprehension. I cannot
conceive what mode of oppression in civil life, or what
mode of religious persecution may not come within the
methods of preserving an *ascendency*. In plain old
English, as they apply it, it signifies *pride and dominion*
on the one part of the relation, and on the other *subserviency and contempt*—and it signifies nothing else.
The old words are as fit to be set to music as the new;
but use has long since affixed to them their true signification, and they sound, as the other will, harshly and
odiously to the moral and intelligent ears of mankind.

This ascendency, by being a *Protestant* ascendency,
does not better it from the combination of a note or two
more in this anti-harmonic scale. If Protestant ascendency means the prescription from citizenship of by far
the major part of the people of any country, then Protestant ascendency is a bad thing, and it ought to have
no existence. But there is a deeper evil. By the use
that is so frequently made of the term, and the policy
which is engrafted on it, the name Protestant becomes
nothing more or better than the name of a persecuting
faction, with a relation of some sort of theological
hostility to others, but without any sort of ascertained
tenets of its own, upon the ground of which it persecutes
other men; for the patrons of this Protestant ascendency neither do, nor can by anything positive, define or
describe what they mean by the word Protestant. It

is defined, as Cowley defines wit, not by what it is,˙but by what it is not. It is not the Christian religion as professed in the churches holding communion with Rome—the majority of Christians ; that is all which, in the latitude of the term, is known about the signification. This makes such persecutors ten times worse than any of that description that hitherto have been known in the world. The old persecutors, whether Pagan or Christian, whether Arian or Orthodox, whether Catholics, Anglicans, or Calvinists, actually were, or at least had the decorum to pretend to be, strong dogmatists. They pretended that their religious maxims were clear and ascertained, and so useful that they were bound for the eternal benefit of mankind to defend or diffuse them, though by any sacrifices of the temporal good of those who were the objects of their system of experiment.

The bottom of this theory of persecution is false. It is not permitted to us to sacrifice the temporal good of any body of men to our own ideas of the truth and falsehood of any religious opinions. By making men miserable in this life, they counteract one of the great ends of charity, which is, inasmuch as in us lies, to make men happy in every period of their existence, and most in what most depends upon us. But give to these old persecutors their mistaken principle, in their reasoning they are consistent, and in their tempers they may be even kind and good-natured. But whenever a faction would render millions of mankind miserable, some

millions of the race co-existent with themselves, and
many millions in their succession, without knowing, or
so much as pretending to ascertain, the doctrines of their
own school (in which there is much of the lash and
nothing of the lesson), the errors which the persons in
such a faction fall into are not those that are natural to
human imbecility, nor is the least mixture of mistaken
kindness to mankind an ingredient in the severities they
inflict. The whole is nothing but pure and perfect
malice. It is indeed a perfection in that kind belonging to beings of a higher order than man, and to them
we ought to leave it.

This kind of persecutors, without zeal, without
charity, know well enough that religion, to pass by all
questions of the truth or falsehood of any of its
particular systems (a matter I abandoned to the theo-
logians on all sides) is a source of great comfort to us
mortals in this our short but tedious journey through
the world. They know that to enjoy this consolation,
men must believe their religion upon some principle or
other, whether of education, habit, theory, or authority.
When men are driven from any of those principles on
which they have received religion, without embracing
with the same assurance and cordiality some other
system, a dreadful void is left in their minds, and a
terrible shock is given to their morals. They lose their
guide, their comfort, their hope. None but the most cruel
and hard-hearted of men, who had banished all natural
tenderness from their minds, such as those beings of

iron, the atheists, could bring themselves to any persecution like this.   Strange it is, but so it is, that men, driven by force from their habits in one mode of religion, have, by contrary habits under the same force, often quietly settled in another.   They suborn their reason to declare in favour of their necessity.   Man and his conscience cannot always be at war.   If the first races have not been able to make a pacification between the conscience and the convenience, their descendants come generally to submit to the violence of the laws without violence to their minds.   As things stood formerly, they possessed a *positive* scheme of direction and of consolation.   In this men may acquiesce. The harsh methods in use with the old class of persecutors were to make converts—not apostates only.   If they perversely hated other sects and factions, they loved their own inordinately.   But in this Protestant persecution there is anything but benevolence at work. What do the Irish statutes ?   They do not make a conformity to the *established* religion, and to its doctrines and practices, the condition of getting out of servitude. No such thing.   Let three millions of people but abandon all that they and their ancestors have been taught to believe sacred, and to forswear it publicly in terms the most degrading, scurrilous, and indecent for men of integrity and virtue, and to abuse the whole of their former lives, and to slander the education they have received,—and nothing more is required of them. There is no system of folly or impiety, or blasphemy, or atheism, into which they may not throw themselves, and which they may not profess openly, and as a system consistently with the enjoyment of all the privileges of a free citizen in the happiest constitution in the world.

Some of the unhappy assertors of this strange scheme say they are not persecutors on account of religion. In the first place they say what is not true. For what else do they disfranchise the people? If the man gets rid of a religion through which their malice operates, he gets rid of all their penalties and incapacities at once. They never afterwards inquire about him. I speak here of their pretexts, and not of the true spirit of the transaction in which religious bigotry, I apprehend, has little share. Every man has his taste, but I think, if I were so miserable and undone as to be guilty of premeditated and continued violence towards any set of men, I had rather that my conduct was supposed to arise from wild conceits concerning their religious advantages, than from low and ungenerous motives relative to my own selfish interest. I had rather be thought insane in my charity than rational in my malice. This much, my dear son, I have to say of this Protestant persecution, that is, a persecution of religion itself.

A very great part of the mischiefs that vex the world, arises from words. People soon forget the meaning, but the impression and the passion remain. The word Protestant is the charm that locks up in the dungeon of servitude three millions of your people. It is not amiss to consider this spell of potency, this abracadabra that is hung about the necks of the unhappy, not to heal, but to communicate disease. We sometimes hear of a Protestant *religion,* frequently of a Protestant *interest.* We hear of the latter the most frequently, because it has a positive meaning. The other has none. We hear of it the most frequently, because it has a word in the phrase, which well or ill understood, has animated to persecution and oppression at all times infinitely more than all the dogmas in dispute between religious factions. These are indeed well formed to perplex and torment the intellect, but not half so well calculated to inflame the passions and animosities of men.

I do readily admit that a great deal of the wars, seditions, and troubles of the world did formerly turn upon the contention between *interests* that went by the names of Protestant and Catholic. But I imagined that at this time no one was weak enough to believe, or impudent enough to pretend, that questions of Popish and Protestant opinions or interest are the things by which men are at present menaced with crusades by foreign invasion, or with seditions, which shake the foundations of the State at home. It is long since all this combination of things has vanished from the view of intelligent observers. The existence of quite another system of opinions and interests is now plain to the grossest sense. Are these the questions that raise a flame in the minds of men at this day? If ever the Church and the constitution of England should fall in these islands (and they will fall together), it is not Presbyterian discipline, nor Popish hierarchy that will rise upon their ruins. It will not be the Church of Rome, nor the Church of Scotland, nor the Church of Luther, nor the Church of Calvin. On the contrary, all these Churches are menaced, and menaced alike. It is the new fanatical religion now in the heat of its first ferment of the rights of man, which rejects all establishments, all discipline, all ecclesiastical, and in truth, all civil order, which will triumph, and which will lay prostrate your Church; which will destroy your distinctions, and which will put all your properties to auction, and disperse you over the earth. If the present establishment should fall, it is this religion which will triumph in Ireland and in England, as it has triumphed in France. This religion, which laughs at creeds and dogmas and confessions of faith, may be fomented equally amongst all descriptions and all sects, amongst nominal Catholics, and amongst nominal Churchmen, and amongst those Dissenters, who know little and care less about a Presbytery, or any of its discipline, or any of its doctrine.

Against this new, this growing, this exterminatory system, all these Churches have a common concern to defend themselves. How the enthusiasts of this rising sect rejoice to see you of the old Churches play their game, and stir and rake the cinders of animosities sunk in their ashes, in order to keep up the execution of their plan for your common ruin!

I suppress all that is in my mind about the blindness of those of our clergy, who will shut their eyes to a thing which glares in such manifest day. If some wretches amongst an indigent and disorderly part of the populace raise a riot about tithes, there are of these gentlemen ready to cry out that this is an overt act of a treasonable conspiracy. Here the bulls and the pardons, and the crusade and the Pope, and the thunders of the Vatican, are everywhere at work. There is a plot to bring in a foreign power to destroy the Church. Alas! it is not about Popes, but about potatoes, that the minds of this unhappy people are agitated. It is not from the spirit of zeal, but the spirit of whisky, that these wretches act. Is it then not conceived possible that a poor clown can be unwilling, after paying three pounds rent to a gentleman in a brown coat, to pay fourteen shillings to one in a black coat, for his acre of potatoes, and tumultuously to desire some modification of the charge without being supposed to have no other motive than a frantic zeal for being thus double-taxed to another set of landholders and another set of priests. Have men no self-interest? no avarice? no repugnance to public imposts? Have they no sturdy and restive minds, no undisciplined habits? Is there nothing in the whole mob of irregular passions which might precipitate some of the common people in some places to quarrel with a legal, because they feel it to be a burthensome imposition! According to these gentlemen, no offence can be committed by Papists but from zeal to their religion.

To make room for the vices of Papists, they clear the
house of all the vices of men. Some of the common
people (not one, however, in ten thousand) commit
disorders. Well! punish them as you do, and as you
ought to punish them for their violence against the just
property of each individual clergyman as each individual suffers. Support the injured rector or the injured
impropriator in the enjoyment of the estate of which
(whether on the best plan or not) the laws have put
him in possession. Let the crime and the punishment
stand upon their own bottom. But now we ought all
of us—clergymen most particularly—to avoid assigning
another cause of quarrel in order to infuse a new source
of bitterness into a dispute which personal feelings on
both sides will of themselves make bitter enough, and
thereby involve in it by religious descriptions, men who
have individually no share whatsoever in those irregular
acts. Let us not make the malignant fictions of our
own imaginations, heated with factious controversies,
reasons for keeping men that are neither guilty nor
justly suspected of crime, in a servitude equally dishonourable and unsafe to religion and to the State.
When men are constantly accused, but know themselves not to be guilty, they must naturally abhor their
accusers. There is no character, when malignantly
taken up and deliberately pursued, which more naturally excites indignation and abhorrence in mankind—
especially in that part of mankind which suffers from it.

I do not pretend to take pride in an extravagant

attachment to any sect. Some gentlemen in Ireland affect that sort of glory. It is to their taste. Their piety, I take it for granted, justifies the fervour of their zeal, and may palliate the excess of it. Being myself no more than a common layman, commonly informed in controversies, leading only a very common life, and having only a common citizen's interest in the Church or in the State, yet to you I will say, in justice to my own sentiments, that not one of those zealots for a Protestant interest wishes more sincerely than I do—perhaps not half so sincerely—for the support of the Established Church in both these kingdoms. It is a great link towards holding fast the connection of religion with the State, and for keeping these two islands, in their present critical independence of constitution, in a close connection of *opinion and affection*. I wish it well, as the religion of the greater number of the primary landed proprietors of the kingdom with whom all establishments of Church and State, for strong political reasons, ought, in my opinion, to be warmly connected. I wish it well, because it is more closely combined than any other of the Church systems with the *Crown*, which is the stay of the mixed constitution, because it is, as things now stand, the sole connecting *political* principle between the constitutions of the two independent kingdoms. I have another, and infinitely a stronger reason for wishing it well—it is that in the present time I consider it as one of the main pillars of the Christian religion itself. The body and substance

of every religion I regard much more than any of the
forms and dogmas of the particular sects. Its fall
would leave a great void which nothing else of which
I can form any distinct idea, might fill. I respect the
Catholic hierarchy and the Presbyterian republic. But
I know that the hope or the fear of establishing either
of them is in these kingdoms equally chimerical, even
if I preferred one or the other of them to the Establishment, which certainly I do not.

These are some of my reasons for wishing the support of the Church of Ireland as by law established.
These reasons are founded as well on the absolute as
on the relative situation of that kingdom. But is it
because I love the Church, and the king, and the
privileges of Parliament, that I am to be ready for any
violence, or any injustice, or any absurdity, in the
means of supporting any of these powers, or all of
them together? Instead of prating about Protestant
ascendencies, Protestant Parliaments ought, in my opinion, to think at last of becoming Patriot Parliaments.

The Legislature of Ireland, like all legislatures,
ought to frame its laws to suit the people and the
circumstances of the country, and not any longer to
make it their whole business to force the nature, the
temper, and the inveterate habits of a nation to a
conformity to speculative systems concerning any kind
of laws. Ireland has an established government, and
a religion legally established, which are to be preserved. It has a people, who are to be preserved too,

and to be led by reason, principle, sentiment, and interest to acquiesce in that Government. Ireland is a country under peculiar circumstances. The people of Ireland are a very mixed people ; and the quantities of the several ingredients in the mixture are very much disproportioned to each other. Are we to govern this mixed body as if it were composed of the most simple elements, comprehending the whole in one system of benevolent legislation ? or are we not rather to provide for the several parts according to the various and diversified necessities of the heterogeneous nature of the mass ? Would not common reason and common honesty dictate to us the policy of regulating the people in the several descriptions of which they are composed, according to the natural ranks and classes of an orderly civil society, under a common protecting sovereign, and under a form of constitution favourable at once to authority and to freedom ; such as the British constitution boasts to be, and such as it is, to those who enjoy it ?

You have an ecclesiastical establishment, which, though the religion of the prince, and of most of the first class of landed proprietors, is not the religion of the major part of the inhabitants, and which consequently does not answer to *them* any one purpose of a religious establishment. This is a state of things which no man in his senses can call perfectly happy. But it is the state of Ireland. Two hundred years of experiment show it to be unalterable. Many a fierce struggle has passed between the parties. The result is—you cannot make the people Protestants—and they cannot shake off a Protestant government. This is what experience teaches, and what all men of sense, of all descriptions, know. To-day the question is this —are we to make the best of this situation, which we cannot alter? The question is—shall the condition of the body of the people be alleviated in other things, on account of their necessary suffering from their being subject to the burthens of two religious establishments, from one of which they do not partake the least, living or dying, either of instruction or of consolation; or shall it be aggravated by stripping the people thus loaded of everything, which might support and indemnify them in this state, so as to leave them naked of every sort of right, and of every name of franchise; to outlaw them from the constitution, and to cut off (perhaps) three millions of plebeian subjects, without reference to property, or any other qualification, from all connection with the popular representation of the kingdom?

As to religion, it has nothing at all to do with the proceeding. Liberty is not sacrificed to a zeal for religion; but a zeal for religion is pretended and assumed to destroy liberty. The Catholic religion is completely free. It has no establishment; but it is recognised, permitted, and, in a degree, protected by the laws. If a man is satisfied to be a slave, he may be a Papist with perfect impunity. He may say mass, or hear it, as he pleases; but he must consider him-

self as an outlaw from the British constitution. If
the constitutional liberty of the subject were not the
thing aimed at, the direct reverse course would be
taken. The franchise would have been permitted, and
the mass exterminated. But the conscience of a man
left, and a tenderness for it hypocritically pretended,
is to make it a trap to catch his liberty.

So much is this the design that the violent partisans
of this scheme fairly take up all the maxims and arguments, as well as the practices by which tyranny has
fortified itself at all times. Trusting wholly in their
strength and power (and upon this they reckon as always
ready to strike wherever they wish to direct the storm),
they abandon all pretext of the general good of the
community. They say that if the people, under any
given modification, obtain the smallest portion or particle
of constitutional freedom, it will be impossible for them
to hold their property. They tell us that they act only
on the defensive. They inform the public of Europe
that their estates are made up of forfeitures and confiscations from the natives; that, if the body of people
obtain votes, any number of votes, however small, it
will be a step to the choice of members of their own
religion; that the House of Commons, in spite of the
influence of nineteen parts in twenty of the landed
interest now in their hands, will be composed in the
whole or in far the major part of Papists; that this
Popish House of Commons will instantly pass a law to
confiscate all their estates, which it will not be in their

power to save even by entering into that Popish party
themselves, because there are prior claimants to be
satisfied; that as to the House of Lords, though neither
Papists nor Protestants have a share in electing them,
the body of the peerage will be so obliging and disinterested as to fall in with this exterminatory scheme,
which is to forfeit all their estates, the largest part of the
kingdom; and, to crown all, that his Majesty will give
his cheerful assent to this causeless act of attainder of his
innocent and faithful Protestant subjects; that they will
be, or are to be left, without house or land, to the dreadful resource of living by their wits, out of which they are
already frightened by the apprehension of this spoliation
with which they are threatened; that, therefore, they
cannot so much as listen to any arguments drawn from
equity or from national or constitutional policy; the
sword is at their throats; beggary and famine at their
door. See what it is to have a good look-out, and to
see danger at the end of a sufficiently long perspective!

This is indeed to speak plain, though to speak nothing very new. The same thing has been said in all
times and in all languages. The language of tyranny
has been invariable; the general good is inconsistent
with my personal safety. Justice and liberty seem so
alarming to these gentlemen, that they are not ashamed
even to slander their own titles, to calumniate and call
in doubt their right to their own estates, and to consider
themselves as novel disseizors, usurpers, and intruders,
rather than lose a pretext for becoming oppressors of

their fellow-citizens, whom they (not I) choose to describe themselves as having robbed.

Instead of putting themselves in this odious point of light, one would think they would wish to let Time draw his oblivious veil over the unpleasant modes by which lordships and demeans have been acquired in their's, and almost in all other countries upon earth. It might be imagined that when the sufferer (if a sufferer exist) had forgot the wrong, they would be pleased to forget it too ; that they would permit the sacred name of possession to stand in the place of the melancholy and unpleasant title of grantees of confiscation, which, though firm and valid in law, surely merits the name that a great Roman jurist gave to a title at least as valid in his nation as confiscation would be either in his or in ours.—*Tristis et luctuosa successio.*

Such is the situation of every man who comes in upon the ruin of another—his succeeding, under this circumstance, is *tristis et luctuosa successio.* If it had been the fate of any gentleman to profit by the confiscation of his neighbour, one would think he would be more disposed to give him a valuable interest under him in his land ; or to allow him a pension, as I understand one worthy person has done, without fear or apprehension, that his benevolence to a ruined family would be construed into a recognition of the forfeited title. The public of England the other day acted in this manner towards Lord Newburgh, a Catholic. Though the estate had been vested by law in the greatest of the public charities, they have given him a pension from his confiscation. They have gone farther in other cases. On the last Rebellion in 1745, in Scotland, several forfeitures were incurred. They had been disposed of by Parliament to certain laudable uses. Parliament reversed the method which they had adopted in Lord Newburgh's case, and in my opinion did better; they gave the forfeited estates to the successors of the forfeiting proprietors, chargeable in part with the uses. Is this, or anything like this, asked in favour of any human creature in Ireland? It is bounty; it is charity; wise bounty and politic charity; but no man can claim it as a right. Here no such thing is claimed as right, or begged as charity. The demand has an object as distant from all considerations of this sort as any two extremes can be. The people desire the privileges inseparably annexed, since Magna Charta, to the freehold, which they have by descent, or obtain as the fruits of their industry. They call for no man's estate ; they desire not to be dispossessed of their own.

But this melancholy and invidious title is a favourite (and like favourites, always of the least merit) with those who possess every other title upon earth along with it. For this purpose they revive the bitter memory of every dissension which has torn to pieces their miserable country for ages. After what has passed in 1782, one would not think that decorum, to say nothing of policy, would permit them to call up, by magic charms, the grounds, reasons, and principles of those terrible confiscatory and exterminatory periods. They would not set men upon calling from the quiet sleep of death any Samuel, to ask him by what act of arbitrary monarchs; by what inquisitions of corrupted tribunals, and tortured jurors; by what fictitious tenures, invented to dispossess whole unoffending tribes and their chieftains! They would not conjure up the ghosts from the ruins of castles and churches, to tell for what attempt to struggle for the independence of an Irish Legislature, and to raise armies of volunteers, without regular commissions from the Crown, in support of that independence, the estates of the old Irish nobility and gentry had been confiscated. They would not wantonly call on those phantoms to tell by what English Acts of Parliament, forced upon two reluctant kings, the lands of their country were put up to a mean and scandalous auction in every goldsmith's shop in London; or chopped to pieces, and cut into rations, to pay the mercenary soldiery of a regicide usurper. They would not be so fond of titles under Cromwell, who, if he avenged an Irish rebellion against the sovereign authority of the Parliament of England, had himself rebelled against the very Parliament whose sovereignty he asserted, full as much as the Irish nation, which he was sent to subdue and confiscate, could rebel against that Parliament, or could rebel against the king, against whom both he and the Parliament which he served, and which he betrayed, had both of them rebelled.

The gentlemen who hold the language of the day

know perfectly well that the Irish in 1641 pretended at least that they did not rise against the king, nor in fact did they, whatever constructions law might put upon their act. But full surely they rebelled against the authority of the Parliament of England, and they openly professed so to do. Admitting (I have now no time to discuss the matter) the enormous and unpardonable magnitude of this their crime, they rued it in their persons, and in those of their children and their grandchildren, even to the fifth and sixth generations. Admitting, then, the enormity of this unnatural rebellion in favour of the independence of Ireland, will it follow that it must be avenged for ever? Will it follow that it must be avenged on thousands, and perhaps hundreds of thousands, of those whom they can never trace, by the labours of the most subtle metaphysician of the traduction of crimes, or the most inquisitive genealogist of proscription, to the descendant of any one concerned in that nefarious Irish rebellion against the Parliament of England?

If, however, you could find out these pedigrees of guilt, I do not think the difference would be essential. History records many things which ought to make us hate evil actions; but neither history, nor morals, nor policy, can teach us to punish innocent men on that account. What lesson does the iniquity of prevalent factions read to us? It ought to lesson us into an abhorrence of the abuse of our own power in our own day; when we hate its excesses so much in other persons and in other times. To that school true statesmen ought to be satisfied to leave mankind. They ought not to call from the dead all the discussions and litigations which formerly inflamed the furious factions which had torn their country to pieces; they ought not to rake into the hideous and abominable things which were done in the turbulent fury of an injured, robbed, and persecuted people, and which were afterwards cruelly revenged in the execution, and as outrageously and shamefully exaggerated in the representation, in order, an hundred and fifty years after, to find some colour for justifying them in the eternal proscription and civil excommunication of a whole people.

Let us come to a later period of those confiscations, with the memory of which the gentlemen, who triumph in the Acts of 1782, are so much delighted. The Irish again rebelled against English Parliament in 1688, and the English Parliament again put up to sale the greatest part of their estates. I do not presume to defend the Irish for this rebellion ; nor to blame the English Parliament for this confiscation. The Irish, it is true, did not revolt from King James's power. He threw himself upon their fidelity, and they supported him to the best of their feeble power. Be the crime of that obstinate adherence to an abdicated sovereign against a prince whom the Parliaments of Ireland and Scotland had recognised what it may, I do not mean to justify this rebellion more than the former. It might,

however, admit some palliation in them. In generous
minds, some small degree of compassion might be
excited for an error, where they were misled, as Cicero
says to a conqueror, *quâdam specie et similitudine pacis*,
not without a mistaken appearance of duty, and for
which the guilty have suffered by exile abroad, and
slavery at home, to the extent of their folly or their
offence. The best calculators compute that Ireland
lost 200,000 of her inhabitants in that struggle. If
the principle of the English and Scottish resistance at
the Revolution is to be justified (as sure I am it is),
the submission of Ireland must be somewhat extenuated.
For if the Irish resisted King William, they resisted
him on the very same principle that the English and
Scotch resisted King James. The Irish Catholics must
have been the very worst and the most truly unnatural
of rebels, if they had not supported a prince whom
they had seen attacked, not for any designs against
their religion, or *their* liberties, but for an extreme
partiality for their sect; and who, far from trespassing
on *their* liberties and properties, secured both them and
the independence of their country in much the same
manner that we have seen the same things done at
the period of 1782—I trust the last Revolution in
Ireland.

That the Irish Parliament of King James did in
some particulars, though feebly, imitate the rigour
which had been used towards the Irish, is true enough.
Blameable enough they were for what they had done,

though under the greatest possible provocation.   I shall
never praise confiscations or counter-confiscations as
long as I live.   When they happen by necessity, I shall
think the necessity lamentable and odious.   I shall
think that anything done under it ought not to pass into
precedent, or to be adopted by choice, or to produce any
of those shocking retaliations which never suffer dissensions to subside.   Least of all would I fix the
transitory spirit of civil fury by perpetuating and
methodising it in tyrannic government.   If it were permitted to argue with power, might one not ask these
gentlemen whether it would not be more natural, instead of wantonly mooting these questions concerning
their property as if it were an exercise in law, to found
it on the solid rock of prescription?—the soundest, the
most general, and the most recognised title between
man and man that is known in municipal or in public
jurisprudence—a title in which not arbitrary institutions but the eternal order of things gives judgment—
a title which is not the creature but the master of
positive law—a title which, though not fixed in its
term, is rooted in its principle, in the law of nature
itself, and is indeed the original ground of all known
property; for all property in soil will always be traced
back to that source, and will rest there.   The miserable
natives of Ireland, who ninety-nine in a hundred are
tormented with quite other cares, and are bowed down
to labour for the bread of the hour, are not, as gentlemen
pretend, plodding with antiquaries for titles of centuries

ago to the estates of the great Lords and Squires for whom they labour. But if they were thinking of the titles which gentlemen labour to beat into their heads, where can they bottom their own claims but in a presumption and a proof that these lands had at some time been possessed by their ancestors? These gentlemen— for they have lawyers amongst them—know as well as I that in England we have had always a prescription or limitation, as all nations have, against each other. The Crown was excepted; but that exception is destroyed, and we have lately established a sixty years' possession as against the Crown. All titles terminate in prescription, in which (differently from Time in the fabulous instances) the son devours the father, and the last prescription eats up all the former.

.   .   .   .

XIV.

A LETTER on the AFFAIRS of IRELAND, written in the year 1797.[1]

DEAR SIR,

IN the reduced state of body, and in the dejected state of mind, in which I find myself at this very advanced period of my life, it is a great consolation to me to know that a cause I ever had so very near my heart is taken up by a man of your activity and talents.

It is very true that your late friend, my ever dear and honoured son, was in the highest degree solicitous about the final event of a business which he also had pursued for a long time with infinite zeal and no small degree of success. It was not above half-an-hour before he left me for ever that he spoke with considerable earnestness on this very subject. If I had needed any incentives to do my best for freeing the body of

[1] The name of the person to whom this letter was addressed does not appear on the manuscript, nor has the letter been found to which it was written as an answer. The letter was dictated from Mr. Burke's couch at Bath, to which place he had gone by the advice of his physicians in March 1797. His health was now rapidly declining; the vigour of his mind remained unimpaired.

my country from the grievances under which they labour, this alone would certainly call forth all my endeavours.

The person who succeeded to the Government of Ireland about the time of that afflicting event had been all along of my sentiments and yours upon this subject; and far from needing to be stimulated by me, that incomparable person and those in whom he strictly confided even went before me in their resolution to pursue the great end of Government, the satisfaction and concord of the people, with whose welfare they were charged. I cannot bear to think on the causes by which this great plan of policy, so manifestly beneficial to both kingdoms, has been defeated.

Your mistake with regard to me lies in supposing that I did not, when his removal was in agitation, strongly and personally represent to several of his Majesty's Ministers, to whom I could have the most ready access, the true state of Ireland, and the mischiefs which sooner or later must arise from subjecting the mass of the people to the capricious and interested domination of an exceeding small faction and its dependencies.

That representation was made the last time, or very nearly the last time, that I have ever had the honour of seeing those Ministers. I am so far from having any credit with them on this or any other public matters, that I have reason to be certain if it were known that any person in office in Ireland, from the highest to the lowest, were influenced by my opinions and disposed to act upon them, such an one would be instantly turned out of his employment. You have formed to my person a flattering, yet in truth a very erroneous opinion of my power with those who direct the public measures. I never have been directly or indirectly consulted about anything that is done. The judgment of the eminent and able persons who conduct public affiairs is undoubtedly superior to mine, but self-partiality induces almost every man to defer something to his own. Nothing is more notorious than that I have the misfortune of thinking that no one capital measure relative to political arrangements, and still less that a new military plan for the defence of either kingdom in this arduous war, has been taken upon any other principle than such as must conduct us to inevitable ruin.

In the state of my mind, so discordant with the tone of Ministers, and still more discordant with the tone of Opposition, you may judge what degree of weight I am likely to have with either of the parties who divide this kingdom ; even though I were endowed with strength of body, or were possessed of any active situation in the Government, which might give success to my endeavours. But the fact is, since the day of my unspeakable calamity, except in the attentions of a very few old and compassionate friends, I am totally out of all social intercourse. My health has gone down very rapidly ; and I have been brought hither with very faint hopes of life, and enfeebled to such a degree, as those who had

known me some time ago, could scarcely think credible.
Since I came hither, my sufferings have been greatly
aggravated, and my little strength still further reduced ;
so that, though I am told the symptoms of my disorder
begin to carry a more favourable aspect, I pass the far
larger part of the twenty-four hours, indeed almost the
whole, either in my bed, or lying upon the couch, from
which I dictate this.   Had you been apprised of this
circumstance, you could not have expected anything, as
you seem to do, from my active exertions.   I could do
nothing, if I was still stronger, not even "*Si meus
adforet Hector.*"

There is no hope for the body of the people of Ireland, as long as those who are in power with you shall
make it the great object of their policy to propagate an
opinion on this side of the water, that the mass of their
countrymen are not to be trusted by their Government ;
and that the only hold which England has upon Ireland
consists in preserving a certain very small number of
gentlemen in full possession of a monopoly of that kingdom.   This system has disgusted many others besides
Catholics and Dissenters.

As to those who on your side are in the Opposition
to Government, they are composed of persons, several
of whom I love and revere.   They have been irritated
by a treatment too much for the ordinary patience of
mankind to bear into the adoption of schemes, which,
however *argumentatively* specious, would go *practically*
to the inevitable ruin of the kingdom.   The Opposition

always connects the emancipation of the Catholics with these schemes of reformation ; indeed it makes the former only a member of the latter project.   The gentlemen who enforce that opposition, are, in my opinion, playing the game of their adversaries with all their might ; and there is no third party in Ireland (nor in England neither) to separate things that are in themselves so distinct, I mean the admitting people to the benefits of the constitution, and the change in the form of the constitution itself.

As every one knows, that a great part of the constitution of the Irish House of Commons was formed about the year 1614, expressly for bringing that House into a state of dependence ; and that the new representative was at that time seated and installed by force and violence ; nothing can be more impolitic than for those who wish the House to stand on its present basis (as for one, I most sincerely do), to make it appear to have kept too much the principle of its first institution, and to continue to be as little a virtual, as it is an actual representative of the Commons. It is the *degeneracy* of such an institution, *so vicious in its principle*, that is to be wished for.   If men have the real benefit of a *sympathetic* representation, none but those who are heated and intoxicated with theory will look for any other.   This sort of representation, my dear sir, must wholly depend, not on the force with which it is upheld, but upon the *prudence* of those who have influence upon it.   Indeed, without some such prudence in the use of authority, I do not know, at least in the present time, how any power can long continue.

If it be true that both parties are carrying things to extremities in different ways, the object which you and I have in common, that is to say, the union and concord of our country, *on the basis of the actual representation,* without risking those evils which any change in the form of our Legislature must inevitably bring on, can never be obtained. On the part of the Catholics (that is to say, of the body of the people of the kingdom) it is a terrible alternative, either to submit to the yoke of declared and insulting enemies; or to seek a remedy in plunging themselves into the horrors and crimes of that Jacobinism, which unfortunately is not disagreeable to the principles and inclinations of, I am afraid, the majority of what we call the Protestants of Ireland. The Protestant part of that kingdom is represented by the Government itself to be, by whole counties, in nothing less than open rebellion. I am sure that it is everywhere teeming with dangerous conspiracy.

I believe it will be found that though the principles of the Catholics, and the incessant endeavours of their clergy, have kept them from being generally infected with the systems of this time, yet, whenever their situation brings them nearer into contact with the Jacobin Protestants, they are more or less infected with their doctrines.

It is a matter for melancholy reflection ; but I am fully convinced that many persons in Ireland would be glad that the Catholics should become more and more infected with the Jacobin madness, in order to furnish new arguments for fortifying them in their monopoly. On any other ground it is impossible to account for the late language of your men in power. If statesmen (let me suppose for argument), upon the most solid political principles, conceive themselves obliged to resist the wishes of the far more numerous, and, as things stand, not the worst part of the community, one would think they would naturally put their refusal as much as possible upon temporary grounds ; and that they would act towards them in the most conciliatory manner, and would talk to them in the most gentle and soothing language ; for refusal in itself is not a very gracious thing, and, unfortunately, men are very quickly irritated out of their principles.   Nothing is more discouraging to the loyalty of any description of men than to represent to them that their humiliation and subjection make a principal part in the funda- mental and invariable policy, which regards the con- junction of these two kingdoms. This is not the way to give them a warm interest in that conjunction.

My poor opinion is, that the closest connection be- tween Great Britain and Ireland is essential to the wellbeing, I had almost said to the very being of the two kingdoms. For that purpose I humbly conceive, that the whole of the superior, and what I should call

imperial politics ought to have its residence here; and
that Ireland, locally, civilly, and commercially independent, ought politically to look up to Great Britain
in all matters of peace or of war; in all those points to
be guided by her : and, in a word, with her to live and
to die.   At bottom, Ireland has no other choice—I mean
no other rational choice.

I think, indeed, that Great Britain would be ruined
by the separation of Ireland ; but as there are degrees
even in ruin, it would fall the most heavily on Ireland.
By such a separation Ireland would be the most completely undone country in the world, the most wretched,
the most distracted, and, in the end, the most desolate
part of the habitable globe.   Little do many people in
Ireland consider how much of its prosperity has been
owing to, and still depends upon, its intimate connection
with this kingdom.   But, more sensible of this great
truth than perhaps any other man, I have never conceived, or can conceive, that the connection is strengthened
by making the major part of the inhabitants of your
country believe that their ease, and their satisfaction,
and their equalisation with the rest of their fellow-
subjects of Ireland, are things adverse to the principles
of that connection ; or that their subjection to a small
monopolising junto, composed of one of the smallest of
their own internal factions, is the very condition upon
which the harmony of the two kingdoms essentially
depends.   I was sorry to hear that this principle, or
something not unlike it, was publicly and fully avowed

by persons of great rank and authority in the House of Lords in Ireland.

As to a participation on the part of the Catholics in the privileges and capacities which are withheld, without meaning wholly to depreciate their importance, if I had the honour of being an Irish Catholic I should be content to expect satisfaction upon that subject with patience, until the minds of my adversaries, few but powerful, were come to a proper temper; because if the Catholics did enjoy without fraud, chicane, or partiality, some fair portion of those advantages which the law, even as now the law is, leaves open to them; and if the rod were not shaken over them at every turn, their present condition would be tolerable—as compared with their former condition it would be happy. But the most favourable laws can do very little towards the happiness of a people when the disposition of the ruling power is adverse to them. Men do not live upon blotted paper. The favourable or the hostile mind of the ruling power is of far more importance to mankind, for good or evil, than the black letter of any statute. Late Acts of Parliament, whilst they fixed at least a temporary bar to the hopes and progress of the larger description of the nation, opened to them certain subordinate objects of equality; but it is impossible that the people should imagine that any fair measure of advantage is intended to them, when they hear the laws by which they were admitted to this limited qualification publicly reprobated as excessive and inconsiderate. They must think that there is a hankering after the old penal and persecuting code. Their alarm must be great when that declaration is made by a person in very high and important office in the House of Commons, and as the very first specimen and auspice of a new Government.

All this is very unfortunate. I have the honour of an old acquaintance, and entertain, in common with you, a very high esteem for the few English persons who are concerned in the Government of Ireland ; but I am not ignorant of the relation these transitory ministers bear to the more settled Irish part of your Administration. It is a delicate topic, upon which I wish to say but little ; though my reflections upon it are many and serious. There is a great cry against English influence. I am quite sure that it is Irish influence that dreads the English habits.

Great disorders have long prevailed in Ireland. It is not long since that the Catholics were the suffering party from those disorders. I am sure they were not protected as the case required. Their sufferings became a matter of discussion in Parliament. It produced the most infuriated declamation against them that I have ever read. An inquiry was moved into the facts. The declamation was at least tolerated, if not approved. The inquiry was absolutely rejected. In that case what is left for those who are abandoned by Government but to join with the persons who are capable of injuring them or protecting them, as they

oppose or concur in their designs? This will produce
a very fatal kind of union amongst the people, but
it is a union which an unequal administration of justice
tends necessarily to produce.

If anything could astonish one at this time, it is the
war that the rulers in Ireland think it proper to carry
on against the person whom they call the pope, and
against all his adherents, whenever they think they
have the power of manifesting their hostility. Without
in the least derogating from the talents of your theological politicians, or from the military abilities of your
commanders (who act on the same principles) in Ireland,
and without derogating from the zeal of either, it
appears to me that the Protestant Directory of Paris,
as statesmen, and the Protestant hero, Bonaparte, as
a general, have done more to destroy the said pope
and all his adherents, in all their capacities, than the
junto in Ireland have ever been able to effect. You
must submit your *fasces* to theirs, and at best be contented to follow with songs of gratulation, or invectives,
according to your humour, the triumphal car of those
great conquerors. Had that true Protestant *Hoche*,
with an army not infected with the slightest tincture of
Popery, made good his landing in Ireland, he would
have saved you from a great deal of the trouble which
is taken to keep under a description of your fellow-
citizens, obnoxious to you from their religion. It would
not have a month's existence, supposing his success.
This is the alliance which, under the appearance of

hostility, we act as if we wished to promote. All is well, provided we are safe from Popery.

It was not necessary for you, my dear sir, to explain yourself to *me* (in justification of your good wishes to your fellow-citizens), concerning your total alienation from the principles of the Catholics. I am more concerned in what we agree than in what we differ. You know the impossibility of our forming any judgment upon the opinions, religious, moral, or political, of those who in the largest sense are called Protestants ; at least as these opinions and tenets form a qualification for holding any civil, judicial, military, or even ecclesiastical situation. I have no doubt of the orthodox opinion of many, both of the clergy and laity, professing the established religion in Ireland, and of many, even amongst the dissenters, relative to the great points of the Christian faith : but that orthodoxy concerns them only as *individuals*. As a *qualification* for employment, we all know that in Ireland it is not necessary that they should profess any religion at all ; so that the war that we make is upon certain theological tenets, about which scholastic disputes are carried on *æquo Marte* by controvertists on their side, as able and as learned, and perhaps as well intentioned, as those are who fight the battle on the other part. To them I would leave those controversies. I would turn my mind to what is more within its competence, and has been more my study (though for a man of the world I have thought of those things)—I mean the moral, civil, and political good of the countries we belong to, and in which God has appointed your station and mine. Let every man be as pious as he pleases, and in the way that he pleases ; but it is agreeable neither to piety nor to policy to give exclusively all manner of civil privileges and advantages to a *negative* religion,—such is the Protestant without a certain creed—and at the same time to deny those privileges to men whom we know to agree to an iota in every one *positive* doctrine, which all of us who profess the religion authoritatively taught in England hold ourselves, according to our faculties, bound to believe. The Catholics of Ireland (as I have said) have the whole of our *positive* religion ; our difference is only a negation of certain tenets of theirs. If we strip ourselves of *that* part of Catholicism we abjure Christianity. If we drive them from that holding, without engaging them in some other positive religion (which you know by our qualifying laws we do not), what do we better than to hold out to them terrors on the one side, and bounties on the other, in favour of that which, for anything we know to the contrary, may be pure Atheism?

You are well aware that when a man renounces the Roman religion there is no civil inconvenience or incapacity whatsoever which shall hinder him from joining any new or old sect of Dissenters, or of forming a sect of his own invention upon the most antichristian principles. Let Mr. Thomas Paine obtain a pardon (as on change of Ministry he may), there is nothing to hinder him from setting up a church of his own in the

2 c

very midst of you. He is a natural-born British
subject. His French citizenship does not disqualify
him, at least upon a peace. This Protestant Apostle is
as much above all suspicion of Popery as the greatest
and most zealous of your Sanhedrim in Ireland can
possibly be. On purchasing a qualification (which his
friends of the Directory are not so poor as to be unable
to effect) he may sit in Parliament; and there is no
doubt that there is not one of your tests against Popery
that he will not take as fairly and as much *ex animo*
as the best of your zealous statesmen. I push this point
no farther, and only adduce this example (a pretty strong
one, and fully in point) to show what I take to be the
madness and folly of driving men, under the existing
circumstances, from any *positive* religion whatever into
the irreligion of the times and its sure concomitant
principles of anarchy.

When religion is brought into a question of civil and
political arrangement, it must be considered more politically than theologically, at least by us, who are nothing
more than mere laymen. In that light the case of the
Catholics of Ireland is peculiarly hard, whether they be
laity or clergy. If any of them take part, like the
gentleman you mention, with some of the most ac-
credited Protestants of the country, in projects, which
cannot be more abhorrent to your nature and disposition
than they are to mine; in that case, however few these
Catholic factions, who are united with factious Protestants, may be—(and very few they are now, whatever

shortly they may become)—on their account the whole
body is considered as of suspected fidelity to the Crown,
and as wholly undeserving of its favour.   But if, on the
contrary, in those districts of the kingdom where their
numbers are the greatest, where they make, in a manner,
the whole body of the people (as, out of cities, in three-
fourths of the kingdom they do), these Catholics show
every mark of loyalty and zeal in support of the
Government, which at best looks on them with an evil
eye; then their very loyalty is turned against their
claims.   They are represented as a contented and happy
people; and that it is unnecessary to do anything more
in their favour.   Thus the factious disposition of a few
among the Catholics, and the loyalty of the whole mass,
are equally assigned as reasons for not putting them on
a *par* with those Protestants, who are asserted by the
Government itself, which frowns upon Papists, to be in
a state of nothing short of actual rebellion, and in a
strong disposition to make common cause with the
worst foreign enemy that these countries have ever had
to deal with.   What in the end can come of all this?

As to the Irish Catholic Clergy, their condition is
likewise most critical: if they endeavour by their influence to keep a dissatisfied laity in quiet, they are in
danger of losing the little credit they possess, by being
considered as the instruments of a Government adverse
to the civil interests of their flock.   If they let things
take their course, they will be represented as colluding
with sedition, or at least tacitly encouraging it.   If they

remonstrate against persecution, they propagate rebellion. Whilst Government publicly avows hostility to that people, as a part of a regular system, there is no road they can take, which does not lead to their ruin.

If nothing can be done on your side of the water, I promise you that nothing will be done here. Whether in reality or only in appearance, I cannot positively determine; but you will be left to yourselves by the ruling powers here. It is thus ostensibly and above-board; and in part, I believe, the disposition is real. As to the people at large in this country, I am sure they have no disposition to intermeddle in your affairs. They mean you no ill whatever; and they are too ignorant of the state of your affairs to be able to do you any good. Whatever opinion they have on your subject is very faint and indistinct; and if there is anything like a formed notion, even that amounts to no more than a sort of humming, that remains on their ears, of the burthen of the old song about Popery. Poor souls, they are to be pitied, who think of nothing but dangers long passed by; and but little of the perils that actually surround them.

I have been long, but it is almost a necessary con-sequence of dictating, and that by snatches, as a relief from pain gives me the means of expressing my senti-ments. They can have little weight as coming from me; and I have not power enough of mind or body to bring them out with their natural force. But I do not wish to have it concealed that I am of the same opinion to my last breath, which I entertained when my faculties

were at the best; and I have not held back from men
in power in this kingdom, to whom I have very good
wishes, any part of my sentiments on this melancholy
subject, so long as I had means of access to persons of
their consideration.

I have the honour to be, etc.

PRIVATE LETTERS

LETTER to the DUKE of PORTLAND.

MY DEAR LORD,

YOUR great goodness and condescension have always
encouraged me to take great liberties with you.   I have
done so with the less scruple, as your own excellent
understanding will always enable you to improve the
imperfect hints that others may throw out to you, or
to control them where they are extravagant and ill-
conceived.

In my present state of mind, and what is likely to
be long my state of mind, nothing could induce me to
intrude any opinion of mine, except I thought the matter
was of great importance to your and Lord Fitzwilliam's
reputation.

I wish everything you do to be not only right, but
so splendidly right, that faction and malice may not be
able to carp at it.   It will not do for you to be vulgar,
commonplace ministers.

I have already ventured, through Mr. Windham, to

submit to your better judgment, and with my reasons
in writing, my poor thoughts upon an event then likely
to take place,—the death of Hely Hutchinson.   That
event, I find, has happened.   He held two important
offices, upon the proper or improper disposal of which
a great deal will depend ;—the provostship, and the
Secretaryship of State.   The former of these it was a
shameful job to give him ; but it will be even more so,
after all the consequences which attended it, again to
break through the statutes without a reason as strong
as that which gave ground to the statute itself, which
most assuredly does not exist.   On the contrary, no
choice can exist, out of the University, so good as that
which is furnished within its own walls.   Three or four
of the senior Fellows are men of the first order ;—the
others may be so also, for anything I hear to the contrary.   I have not the honour of what may be called an
acquaintance with any of them.   Dr. Murray,[1] the vice-
provost, who has filled that place with the highest
honour, and stands therefore next in designation for the
provostship, I do not recollect ever to have seen.   I
should be sorry, when I was recommending to ministers
not to give way to their own partialities, to insinuate
into them any partiality of mine.

This office ought not to be considered as a thing in
the mass of promiscuous patronage, and which may as
well be given to one man as to another.

[1] Dr. Murray was appointed Provost during Lord Fitzwilliam's
Lieutenancy, in January 1795.

I hear that the Bishop of Cloyne[1] is to be recommended to it. The Irish bishoprics are all valuable things ; this of Cloyne is amongst the best of those valuable things, and the road to the highest, by translation, is open to him ; and nothing but an odious, and, at this time, a portentous avarice and rapacity could induce any of the Episcopal bench to seize upon this corporate office, the undoubted right of others, and which is fitted to be exercised by one who is practised in its particular corporate duties. If a check is not put upon them, they will be ruined by this mean, secular spirit.

Your Grace holds a most honourable office,—that of chancellor of one of our Universities. Your Grace's showing a manly and inflexible firmness in defence of the legal and equitable rights of another, against the unwarrantable use of a dispensing power, will do you infinite honour. It will be, I know, highly pleasing to the University of Dublin, which, about a twelvemonth ago, sent over a deputation to remonstrate against an unstatutable arrangement proposed for the succession to the provostship. They justly considered it as a gross and unmerited affront (as it was) to their body.

Your Grace, by being where you are, is abundantly concerned that Government, at all times, but eminently at this time, ought to be kept in awe and reverence from opinion ; and by the manner in which public

[1] Dr. Bennet, promoted by the Earl of Westmorland to the see of Cork and Ross in 1790, and translated by him to that of Cloyne in 1794.

trusts are bestowed ; and not to leave obedience to be
enforced by the pillory, the gallows, and the transport-
vessel. No one thing is just now more necessary than
the education of youth ; the least suspicion of any part
of it being converted into a job will ruin all.

As to Mr. Hutchinson's other office, your Grace will
pardon me a suggestion on the subject. As the first
ought to be kept out of the line of patronage, this of the
office of secretaryship ought (always supposing common
qualification) to be kept strictly within it. Whilst it
was a sinecure pension, it might be given on the principle of any other pension, during life, or as Government
thought fit ; though, in my opinion, infinite caution
ought to be used in giving anything in Ireland for life.
But now, I hear the office is in a considerable degree
effective, and may be made the means of great embar-
rassment to Government. I hope your Grace will stand
in the gap, and not suffer the present Lord-Lieutenant to
job it out of the hands of his successor. If great care
is not used, Lord Fitzwilliam will find himself invested
on every side. English Government, if they are suffered
to go on there as they have gone on, will not be left
even the miserable shadow of authority which it now
seems to possess. God bless you and guide you ; everything appears to me, in this season, to be serious and
alarming in the highest degree. Office, to which men
like you can only be called by an imperious duty,
cannot afford to be conducted, as formerly it might, with
impunity, by fancy, liking, or momentary expediency.

Again excuse the liberty of zeal and affection. I am as a man dead ; and dead men, in their written opinions, are heard with patience. I have now no one earthly interest of my own. I have no other way than this of showing my gratitude for your long-continued kindness to me and to my poor brother. Alas ! he and my son are gone, and can no longer call for the protection of any mortal.

I am ever, with the most affectionate and cordial attachment to your person, your honour, and your best interests,—My dear Lord, your Grace's most sincere, but most unhappy friend,

EDM. BURKE.

September 14, 1794.

LETTER to the REV. DR. HUSSEY.

MY DEAR SIR,

I HAVE received your two letters—the first in answer to mine about Hylan ;[1] the second, chiefly employed in the account of the deserved confidence which the Catholics of Ireland, and most of the other descriptions in our country, repose in Earl Fitzwilliam. I thank you for both of them, as I do for all the other marks I have received of your good opinion and friendship.

I must always be proud of the partiality you have

---

[1] A Catholic soldier who had been ill-treated. See p. 426.

shown to me, and to him who was dearer to me than I
am to myself.   I am no flatterer, though to commend
with justice is, I hope, more agreeable to my nature
than with the same justice to censure.   However, that
must be done sometimes.   I have always loved your
public spirit, your regard to your country, your attachment to its Government, your singular disinterestedness,
and that very rare union you have made of the enlightened statesman with the ecclesiastic.   I once spoke
my sentiments very freely upon that subject to Mr.
Pitt.   From what had come to his own knowledge he
did not seem at all to dissent from my notions, though
his arrangements did not permit him at that time to
make that use of your services which I proposed.
Wherever you are you will be useful.   I am sure you
are so in Ireland.   I am charmed with what you tell
me of the alienation of the Catholics from the grand
evil of our time, and their resolution to resist with all
their might the attempts of Jacobinism from without
and from within.   I am more rejoiced at this, as few
things have been left undone by their enemies to irritate
them into the frenzy of that malignant fever.   I am
confident that the wisdom, the temper, and the firm
magnanimity of Lord Fitzwilliam, will prevent their
ever being provoked or seduced to their own or the
general ruin.

You tell me that some of the old gentry murmur at
your having been at all at the Castle, though you have
never been at levee or drawing-room of the Lord Lieu-

tenant or the Secretary, and never went to the Castle but when you were sent for. I trust that neither the Government nor you will be in the smallest degree affected by the creaking which some of the old worm-eaten furniture makes at its removal. But if (which I am far from thinking) any of the new household stuff should make the same noise in warping by its un-seasoned greenness, which the other does in falling to pieces by its corruption, they may be assured that this fermentable sap portends the dry rot at no very remote distance. The being of Government depends upon keeping the Catholics from a mischievous presumption, and from a mean depression. No man is more con-vinced than you are that they and public order have a common cause. A licentious popular arrogance would, along with their credit and happiness, subvert the foun-dations of that order. On the other hand, if you lose dignity and courage, you lose the means of preserving that order and everything else. The advances you have hitherto made have been wholly owing to your having preserved that medium, which is only to be found in a calm and temperate firmness,—the remotest thing in the world from that false and adulterate moderation, which is nothing else but a mode of delivering deluded men, without a struggle, to the violence and intem-perance of their enemies.

Above all things, take care that, without being ob-trusive (which is meanness in another mode) nothing should carry the appearance of skulking, or of being

ashamed of your cause.   If any one is ashamed of you,
or afraid of your contact, it is clear that you can derive
no essential service from such a person.   The leading
Catholics will be polite, attentive, forbearing, humble,
and to a degree even submissive, to the ascendency,
particularly to every man in office and in Parliament.
But I have one favour to ask of them, which I hope
they will grant to my tried attachment, which is, that
they will be true to themselves, and that they will not
pass by in silence any one act of outrage, oppression,
and violence that they may suffer, without a complaint
and a proceeding suitable to the nature of the wrong.

If Lord Fitzwilliam was to live for half a century,
and to continue in station as long as he lived, I should
not pray to God for a greater security to you for everything that you hold dear ; for in that time his virtues (the
greatest and unmixed that I have known in man) would
bring the leading men of the nation into habits of
moderation, lenity, equity, and justice, which the
practice of some hundreds of years, and the narrow
hard-heartedness of a monopoly, have in a manner
banished from the minds of too many of them.   For it
is plain that the late change in the laws has not made
any alteration in their tempers, except that of aggravat-
ing their habitual pride by resentment and vexation.
They have resolved to make one among the many unhappy discoveries of our times.   It is this—that neither
the laws nor the dispositions of the chief executive
magistrate are able to give security to the people when-

ever certain leading men in the country and in office
are against them. They have actually made the discovery ; and a dreadful one it is for things, laws, and
subjects. This is what makes all ideas of *ascendency*
in particular factions, whether distinguished by party-
names taken from theology or from politics, so mischievous as they have been. Wherever such factions
predominate in such a manner that they come to link
(which, without loss of time, they are sure to do) a
pecuniary and personal interest with the licentiousness
of a party domination, nothing can secure those that
are under it. If this was not clear enough upon a consideration of the nature of things and the nature of
men, the late proceedings in Ireland subsequent to the
repeal of the penal laws would leave no doubt of it.
For (besides not suffering individual Catholics to derive
the smallest benefit from the capacities which the laws
had granted to them) a more fierce, insolent, and con-
tumelious persecution had not (except in the time
between '61 and '66) been carried on against them
during the long period of my memory. This religious
persecution, like most others, has been carried on under
the pretext of their being bad subjects and disaffected
to the Government. I think it very possible that to a
degree the ascendants were sincere. The understanding
is soon debauched over to the passions; and our
opinions very easily follow our wishes. When we are
once ill-inclined to any men, or set of men, we readily
believe any evil of him or them that is inconvenient to

our hostile designs. Besides, in that they have another
excuse. Knowing and feeling that they are themselves
attached to the cause of Government only on account
of the profit they derive from their connection with it,
it cannot enter into their conceptions how any man
can be other than a *rebel* who is not brought into an
obedience to law and authority. They are excusable,
and may do the worst of things without being the worst
of men. But it is not the less, but the more necessary
that you should guard against such implacable and
unprincipled enemies by an unremitting vigilance and
a severe distrust. In the same manner that you never
give the smallest credit to your enemies, in that proportion you are to cherish and support your real
friends who were such at the time of trial; and indeed
to wish well to all such as, without malice, went with
the fashion and the crowd, but have since shown
gentle and placable dispositions. Well, to know your
friends and your enemies is almost the whole history of
political prudence. This brings me to the business of
Hylan, on occasion of which I took the liberty of opening my correspondence with you. I refer you to the
letter I wrote to you on that occasion. I wrote it in
the first emotions which that cruel and infamous affair
produced in my mind, and I have not altered my
opinions in reflecting on the subject. In my poor
opinion, the Catholic committee is bound in honour, in
duty, and in common sense (if that affair is such as I
imagine it to be), not to suffer a veil to be thrown over

it, or to compromise it in the smallest degree. You
mention that more noise would have been made about
it if it had not been from respect to Lord F. If this
business had been done by his Excellency's orders, or
under his countenance, to be sure, to hush it up, however improper, would be to show respect to him. But
as this was not the case, I do not feel how it can be to
honour any Government to suppose it concerned in the
impunity of oppression. Were I in that place, I should
feel myself turned out of my situation the moment I
was deprived of the power of being just and of protecting the people under my care from the tumult of the
multitude and the insolence of the rich and powerful;
for, in the name of God, for what else are governors and
governments appointed ? I am (you will believe, whatever others may) beyond all men, perhaps, a friend to
a lenient course; but my lenities are not for pride,
cruelty, and oppression, but for those who are likely to
suffer from these vices in action under royal or aristocratic or democratic power. I would not put my
melilot plaister on the back of the hangman, but on the
skin of the person who has been torn by his whips.
Your departed friend[1] was a wise person, of a penetrat-
ing and sagacious mind, and one who, by reading and
observation, had made himself perfect master of the
state of Ireland from the beginning of the sixteenth
century to this hour. I wish you to look at the letter
of his which he wrote when he was last in Cork, in

---

[1] Richard Burke junior.

answer to an insidious paper circulated, and for some small time with effect, to delude the Irish Catholics. It is printed by Byrne, in Dublin. The spirit of that letter I wish to guide and direct the body of our country in all things. He was your true friend. He was not your friend because he was your law-counsel and active agent; but he was your counsel and agent because he was your friend. Think it is he that speaks to you from the church of Beaconsfield, in which you, and the Duke of Portland, and Windham, and the Comte de Coigny, and O'Connor, and the Earl of Inchiquin, and Adey, laid the purest body that ever was informed by a rational soul. *He* would say to you, "Do not stifle the affair of Hylan! Pursue it with Government, with the courts of justice, with Parliament, with the public!" My dear sir, I am tired and sadly sunk. I will write to you more fully on the other subject of your letter to-morrow. Adieu!—Ever affectionately yours,   EDMUND BURKE.

BEACONSFIELD, *February* 4, 1795.

LETTER to REV. DR. HUSSEY.

MY DEAR SIR,

I DON'T know exactly why I am so unwilling to write by the post. I have little to say that might not be known to the world; at the same time, there is something unpleasant in talking the confidential language of

2 D

friendship in the public theatre. It is still worse to
put it into the power of any one to make unfaithful
representations of it, or to make it the subject of
malicious comments. I thank you for your letter; it
is full of that good sense and good temper, as well as of
that fortitude, which are natural to you. Since persons
of so much greater authority than I am, and of so much
better judgment, are of opinion you ought to stay, it
was clearly right for you to remain at all risks. Indeed,
if it could be done with tolerable safety, I wished you
to watch over the cradle of those seminaries on which
the future weal or woe of Ireland essentially depends.
For you, I dread the revolutionary tribunal of Drog-
heda. For the country, if some proper mode of education is not adopted, I tremble for the spread of Atheism
amongst the Catholics. I do not like the style of the
meeting[1] in Francis Street. The tone was wholly
Jacobinical. In Parliament, the language of your
friends (one only excepted) was what it ought to be.
But that one speech, though full of fire and animation,
was not warmed with the fire of heaven. I am sorry
for it. I have seen that gentleman but once. He is
certainly a man of parts; but one who has dealt too
much in the philosophy of France. Justice, prudence,
tenderness, moderation, and Christian charity, ought to
become the measures of tolerance; and not a cold
apathy, or indeed, rather a savage hatred, to all religion,

[1] The assembly of the Roman Catholics held April 9, 1795, in
Francis Street chapel.

and an avowed contempt of all those points on which
we differ and on those about which we agree. If what
was said in Francis Street was in the first heat it might
be excused. They were given to understand that a
change of administration, short only of a revolution in
violence, was made, only on account of a disposition in
a Lord-Lieutenant to favour Catholics. Many provoking
circumstances attended the business ; not the least of
them was, that they saw themselves delivered over to
their enemies, on no other apparent ground of merit
than that they were such. All this is very true ; but
under every provocation they ought not to be irritated
by their enemies out of their principles and out of
their senses. The language of the day went plainly to
a separation of the two kingdoms. God forbid that
anything like it should ever happen ! They would both
be ruined by it ; but Ireland would suffer most and
first. The thing, however, is impossible. Those who
should attempt that improbability would be undone.
If ever the arms, which, indirectly, these orators seem
to menace, were to be taken up, surely the threat of
such a measure is not wise, as it could add nothing to
their strength, but would give every possible advantage
to their enemies. It is a foolish language, adopted from
the United Irishmen, that their grievances originate
from England. The direct contrary. It is an ascendency which some of their own factions have obtained
here that has hurt the Catholics with this Government.
It is not as an English Government that Ministers act

in that manner, but as assisting a party in Ireland.
When they talk of dissolving themselves as a Catholic
body, and mixing their grievances with those of their
country, all I have to say is, that they lose their own
importance as a body by this amalgamation; and they
sink real matters of complaint in those which are
factious and imaginary.   For, in the name of God, what
grievance has Ireland, as Ireland, to complain of with
regard to Great Britain; unless the protection of the
most powerful country upon earth—giving all her
privileges, without exception, in common to Ireland,
and reserving to herself only the painful pre-eminence
of tenfold burdens, be a matter of complaint.   The
subject, as a subject, is as free in Ireland as he is in
England.   As a member of the empire, an Irishman has
every privilege of a natural-born Englishman, in every
part of it, in every occupation, and in every branch of
commerce.   No monopoly is established against him
anywhere; and the great staple manufacture of Ireland
is not only not prohibited, not only not discouraged, but
it is privileged in a manner that has no example.   The
provision trade is the same; nor does Ireland, on her
part, take a single article from England but what she
has with more advantage than she could have it from
any nation upon earth.   I say nothing of the immense
advantage she derives from the use of the English
capital.   In what country upon earth is it that a
quantity of linens, the moment they are lodged in the
warehouse, and before the sale, would entitle the Irish

merchant or manufacturer to draw bills on the terms,
and at the time, in which this is done by the ware-
houseman on London ?   Ireland, therefore, as Ireland,
whether it be taken civilly, constitutionally, or commercially, suffers no grievance.   The Catholics, as
Catholics, do; and what can be got by joining their real
complaint to a complaint which is fictitious, but to make
the whole pass for fiction and groundless pretence ?   I
am not a man for construing with too much rigour the
expressions of men under a sense of ill-usage.   I know
that much is to be given to passion; and I hope I am
more disposed to accuse the person who provokes
another to anger, than the person who gives way to
natural feelings in hot language.   If this be all, it is no
great matter; but, if anger only brings out a plan that
was before meditated, and laid up in the mind, the thing
is more serious.   The tenor of the speeches in Francis
Street, attacking the idea of an incorporating union
between the two kingdoms, expressed principles that
went the full length of a separation, and of a dissolution
of that union which arises from their being under the
same crown.   That Ireland would, in that case, come to
make a figure amongst the nations, is an idea which has
more of the ambition of individuals in it than of a sober
regard to the happiness of a whole people.   But if a
people were to sacrifice solid quiet to empty glory, as on
some occasions they have done—under the circumstances
of Ireland, *she*, most assuredly, never would obtain that
independent glory, but would certainly lose all her

tranquillity, all her prosperity, and even that degree of
lustre which she has, by the very free and very honourable connection she enjoys with a nation the most
splendid and the most powerful upon earth.   Ireland,
constitutionally, is independent; *politically*, she never
can be so.   It is a struggle against nature.   She must
be protected, and there is no protection to be found for
her, but either from France or England.   France, even
if (under any form she may assume) she were disposed
to give the same liberal and honourable protection to
Ireland, has not the means of either serving or hurting
her that are in the hands of Great Britain.   She might
make Ireland (supposing that kind of independence
could be maintained, which for a year I am certain it
could not) a dreadful thorn in the side of this kingdom;
but Ireland would dearly buy that malignant and
infernal satisfaction, by a dependence upon a power,
either despotic, as formerly, or anarchical, as at present.
We see well enough the kind of liberty which she
either enjoys herself or is willing to bestow on others.
This I say with regard to the scheme of those who call
themselves United Irishmen; that is to say, of those
who, without any regard to religion, club all kinds of
discontents together, in order to produce all kinds of
disorders.   But to speak to Catholics, as such, it is plain
that whatever security they enjoy for their religion, as
well as for the many solid advantages which, even
under the present restrictions, they are entitled to,
depends wholly upon their connection with this king-

dom. France is an enemy to all religion; but eminently, and with a peculiar malignity, an enemy to the Catholic religion, which they mean, if they can, to extirpate throughout the globe. It is something perverse, and even unnatural, for Catholics to hear even the sound of a connection with France; unless, under the colour and pretext of a religious description, they should, as some have done in this country, form themselves into a mischievous political faction. Catholics, as things now stand, have all the splendid abilities and much of the independent property in Parliament in their favour, and every Protestant (I believe with very few exceptions) who is really a Christian. Should they alienate these men from their cause, their choice is amongst those who, indeed, may have ability, but not wisdom or temper in proportion; and whose very ability is not equal, either in strength or exercise, to that which they lose. They will have to choose men of desperate property, or of no property, and men of no religious and no moral principle. Without a Protestant connection of some kind or other they cannot go on; and here are the two sorts of descriptions of Protestants between whom they have an option to make. In this state of things their situation, I allow, is difficult and delicate. If the better part lies by in a sullen silence, they still cannot hinder the more factious part both from speaking and from writing; and the sentiments of those who are silent will be judged by the effusions of the people, who do not wish to conceal thoughts that the

sober part of mankind will not approve. On the other
hand, if the better and more temperate part come forward
to disclaim the others, they instantly make a breach in
their own party, of which a malignant enemy will take
advantage to crush them all. They will praise the
sober part, but they will grant them nothing they shall
desire; nay, they will make use of their submission as
a proof that sober men are perfectly satisfied in remaining prostrate under their oppressive hands. These are
dreadful dilemmas; and they are such as ever will arise
when men in power are possessed with a crafty malignant disposition, without any real wisdom or enlarged
policy.

However, as in every case of difficulty, there is a
better way of proceeding and a worse; and that some
medium may be found between an abject, and, for
that reason, an imprudent submission, and a contu-
macious, absurd resistance,—what I would humbly suggest is, that on occasion of the declamations in the
newspaper, they should make, not an apology (for that
is dishonourable and dangerous), but a strong charge on
their enemies for defamation; disclaiming the tenets,
practices, and designs, impudently attributed to them,
and asserting, in cool, modest, and determined language,
their resolution to assert the privileges to which, as good
citizens and good subjects, they hold themselves entitled, without being intimidated or wearied out by the
opposition of the monopolists of the kingdom. In this
there will be nothing mean or servile, or which can

carry any appearance of the effect of fear, but the contrary. At the same time it will remove the prejudices which, on this side of the water as well as on yours, are propagated against you with so much systematic pains. I think the committee would do well to do something of this kind in their own name. I trust those men of great ability in that committee, who incline to think that the Catholics ought to melt down their cause into the general mass of uncertain discontents and unascertained principles, will, I hope, for the sake of agreeing with those whom, I am sure, they love and respect among their own brethren, as well as for the sake of the kingdom at large, waive that idea (which I do not deny to be greatly provoked) of dissolving the Catholic body before the objects of its union are obtained, and turning the objects of their relief into a national quarrel. This, I am satisfied on recollection, they will think not irrational. The course taken by the enemy often becomes a fair rule of action. You see, by the whole turn of the debate against them, that their adversaries endeavoured to give this colour to the contest, and to make it hinge on this principle. The same policy cannot be good for you and your enemies. Sir George Shee, who is so good to take this, waits, or I should say more on this point. I should say something, too, of the colleges. I long much to hear how you go on. I have, however, said too much. If Grattan, by whom I wish the Catholics to be wholly advised, thinks differently from me, I wish the whole unsaid.

You see Lord Fitzwilliam sticks nobly to his text, and neither abandons his cause nor his friends, though he has few indeed to support him.   When you can, pray let me hear from you.   Mrs. Burke and myself, in this lonely and disconsolate house, never cease to think of you as we ought to do.   I send some prints to Dublin; but, as your house is not there, I reserve a memorial of my dear Richard for your return.   I am ever, my dear sir, faithfully and affectionately, your miserable friend,

EDM. BURKE.

BEACONSFIELD, *May* 18, 1795.

LETTER to THOMAS KEOGH, Esq.

SIR,

I AM so much out of the world that I am not surprised every one should be ignorant of, as he is uninterested in, the state of my health, my habits of life, or anything else that belongs to me.

Your obliging letter of the 20th of July was delivered to me at Bath, to which place I was driven by urgent necessity, as my only chance of preserving a life which did not then promise a month's duration. I was directed to suspend all application to business, even to the writing of a common letter, as it was thought that I had suffered by some such application, and by the attendant anxiety, before and about that time. I returned from Bath not well, but much recovered from the state in which I had been ; and I continued in the

same condition of convalescence for a month or six
weeks longer.   Soon after I began gradually to decline,
and at this moment I do not find myself very materially
better or stronger than when I was sent to Bath.

I am obliged to you for the offer which you made
in that letter of conveying anything from me to Ireland ; but I really thought you had known that I have
no kind of correspondence or communication with that
country, and that for a good while I had not taken any
part whatsoever in its affairs.   I believe you must
have observed, when last I had the honour of seeing
you in London, how little any opinions of mine are
likely to prevail with persons in power here,—even with
those with whom I had formerly a long and intimate
connection.   I never see any of his Majesty's ministers,
except one gentleman who, from mere compassion, has
paid me some visits in this my retreat, and has endeavoured, by his generous sympathy, to soothe my pains
and my sorrows ; but that gentleman has no concern in
Irish affairs, nor is, I believe, consulted about them.   I
cannot conceive how you or anybody can think that
any sentiments of mine are called for, or even admitted,
when it is notorious that there is nothing at home or
abroad, in war or in peace, that I have the good fortune
to be at all pleased with.   I ought to presume that
they who have a great public trust, who are of distinguished abilities, and who are in the vigour of their
life, behold things in a juster point of view than I am
able to see them, however my self-partiality may make

me too tenacious of my own opinion. I am in no degree of confidence with the great leader either of Ministry or Opposition.

In a general way, I am but too well acquainted with the distracted state of Ireland, and with the designs of the public enemy pointed at that kingdom. I have my own thoughts upon the causes of those evils. You do me justice in saying in your letter of July that I am a true Irishman. Considering, as I do, England as my country, of long habit, of obligation, and of establishment, and that my primary duties are hers, I cannot conceive how a man can be a genuine Englishman, without being at the same time a true Irishman, though fortune should have made his birth on this side the water. I think the same sentiments ought to be reciprocal on the part of Ireland, and, if possible, with much stronger reason. Ireland cannot be separated one moment from England without losing every source of her present prosperity, and even hope of her future. I am very much afflicted, deeply and bitterly afflicted, to see that a very small faction.in Ireland should arrogate it to itself to be the whole of that great kingdom. I am more afflicted in seeing that a very minute part of that small faction should be able to persuade any person here, that on the support of their power the connection of the two kingdoms essentially depends. This strange error, if persevered in (as I am afraid it will), must accomplish the ruin of both countries. At the same time I must as bitterly regret that any persons who suffer

by the predominance of that corrupt fragment of a faction should totally mistake the cause of their evils as
well as their remedy—if a remedy can be at all looked
for; which, I confess, I am not sanguine enough to
expect in any event, or from the exertions of any person;
and least of all from exertions of mine, even if I had
either health or prospect of life commensurate to so
difficult an undertaking.   I say, I do regret that the
conduct of those who suffer should give any advantage
to those who are resolved to tyrannise.   I do believe that
this conduct has served only as a pretext for aggravat-
ing the calamities of that party, which, though superior
in number, is from many circumstances much inferior
in force.

I believe there are very few cases which will justify
a revolt against the established government of a
country, let its constitution be what it will, and even
though its abuses should be great and provoking; but
I am sure there is no case in which it is justifiable,
either to conscience or to prudence, to menace resistance
when there is no means of effecting it, nor perhaps in
the major part any disposition.   You know the state of
that country better than I can pretend to do, but I
could wish, if there was any use in retrospect, that
those menaces had been forborne, because they have
caused a real alarm in some weak though well-intentioned minds; and because they furnish the bold and
crafty with pretences for exciting a persecution of a
much more fierce and terrible nature than I ever

remember, even when the country was under a system
of laws apparently less favourable to its tranquillity
and good government, at the same time that sober exertion has lessened in the exact proportion in which
flashy menaces increased.   Pusillanimity (as it often
does) has succeeded to rage and fury.   Against all
reason, experience, and observation, many persons in
Ireland have taken it into their heads that the influence
of the Government here has been the cause of the mis-
demeanour of persons in power in that country, and
that they are suffering under the yoke of a British
dominion.   I must speak the truth—I must say that
all the evils of Ireland originate within itself; that it
is the boundless credit which is given to an Irish cabal
that produces whatever mischiefs both countries may
feel in their relation.   England has hardly anything
to do with Irish government.   I heartily wish it were
otherwise ;   but the body of the people of England, even
the most active politicians, take little or no concern in
the affairs of Ireland.   They are, therefore, by the minister of this country, who fears upon that account no
responsibility here, and who shuns all responsibility
in Ireland, abandoned to the direction of those who are
actually in possession of its internal government; this
has been the case more eminently for these five or six
last years ; and it is a system, if it deserves that name,
not likely to be altered.

I conceive that the last disturbances, and those the
most important, and which have the deepest root, do

not originate, nor have they their greatest strength, among the Catholics ; but there is, and ever has been, a strong republican Protestant faction in Ireland, which has persecuted the Catholics as long as persecution would answer their purpose; and now the same faction would dupe them to become accomplices in effectuating the same purposes; and thus, either by tyranny or seduction, would accomplish their ruin. It was with grief I saw last year, with the Catholic delegates, a gentleman who was not of their religion, or united to them in any avowable bond of a public interest, acting as their secretary, in their most confidential concerns. I afterwards found that this gentleman's name was implicated in a correspondence with certain Protestant conspirators and traitors, who were acting in direct connection with the enemies of all government and religion. He might be innocent ; and I am very sure that those who employed and trusted him were perfectly ignorant of his treasonable correspondences and designs, if such he had ; but as he has thought proper to quit the king's dominions about the time of the investigation of that conspiracy, unpleasant inferences may have been drawn from it. I never saw him but once, which was in your company, and at that time knew nothing of his connections, character, or dispositions.

I am never likely to be called upon for my advice in this, or in any business ; and after having once almost forcibly obtruded myself into it, and having found no sort of good effect from my uncalled-for inter-ference, I shall certainly, though I should have better health than I can flatter myself with, never again thrust myself into those intricate affairs.   Persons of much greater abilities, rank, and consequence than I am, and who had been called by their situation to those affairs, have been totally overwhelmed by the domineering party in Ireland, and have been disgraced and ruined, as far as independence, honour, and virtue can be ruined and disgraced.   However, if your leisure permits you to pay a visit to this melancholy infirmary, I shall certainly receive any information with which you are pleased to furnish me; but merely as news, and what may serve to feed the little interest I take in this world.   You will excuse my having used the hand of a confidential friend in this letter, for indeed I suffer much by stooping to write. —— I have the honour to be, etc.

EDMUND BURKE.

BEACONSFIELD, *November* 17, 1796.

LETTER to REV. DR. HUSSEY.

MY DEAR SIR,

THIS morning I received your letter of the 30th of November from Maynooth.   I dictate my answer from my couch, on which I am obliged to lie for a good part of the day.   I cannot conceal from you, much less can I conceal from myself, that in all probability I am not long for this world. Indeed, things are in such a situation, independently of the domestic wound, that I never could have less reason for regret in quitting the world than at this moment ; and my end will be, by several, as little regretted.

I have no difficulty at all in communicating to you, or, if it were any use, to mankind at large, my sentiments and feelings on the dismal state of things in Ireland ; but I find it difficult indeed to give you the advice you are pleased to ask, as to your own conduct in your very critical situation.

You state, what has long been but too obvious, that it seems the unfortunate policy of the hour to put to the far largest portion of the king's subjects in Ireland the desperate alternative between a thankless acquiescence under grievous oppression, or a refuge in Jacobinism, with all its horrors and all its crimes. You prefer the former dismal part of the choice. There is no doubt but that you would have reason, if the election of one of these evils was at all a security against the other. But they are things very alliable, and as closely connected as cause and effect. That Jacobinism which is speculative in its origin, and which arises from wantonness and fulness of bread, may possibly be kept under by firmness and prudence. The very levity of character which produces it may extinguish it. But Jacobinism, which arises from penury and irritation, from scorned loyalty and rejected allegiance, has much deeper roots. They take their nourishment from the bottom of human

2 E

nature, and the unalterable constitution of things, and
not from humour and caprice, or the opinions of the day
about privileges and liberties.   These roots will be shot
into the depths of hell, and will at last raise up their
proud tops to heaven itself.   This radical evil may baffle
the attempts of heads much wiser than those are, who,
in the petulance and riot of their drunken power, are
neither ashamed nor afraid to insult and provoke those
whom it is their duty, and ought to be their glory, to
cherish and protect.

So then, the little wise men of the west, with every
hazard of this evil, are resolved to persevere in the manly
and well-timed resolution of a war against Popery.   In
the principle, and in all the proceedings, it is perfectly
suited to their character.   They begin this last series of
their offensive operations by laying traps for the consciences of poor foot-soldiers.   They call these wretches
to their church (empty of a volunteer congregation), not
by the bell, but by the whip.   This ecclesiastic military
discipline is happily taken up, in order to form an army
of well-scourged Papists into a firm phalanx for the
support of the Protestant religion.   I wish them joy of
this their valuable discovery in theology, politics, and
the art military.   Fashion governs the world, and it is
the fashion in the great French empire of pure and perfect Protestantism, as well as in the little busy meddling
province of servile imitators, that apes at a humble distance the tone of its capital, to make a crusade against
you poor Catholics.   But whatever may be thought in

Ireland of its share of a war against the Pope in that out-lying part of Europe, the zealous Protestant, Bonaparte, has given his late Holiness far more deadly blows, in the centre of his own power, and in the nearest seats of his influence, than the Irish Directory [1] can arrogate to itself within its own jurisdiction, from the utmost efforts of its political and military skill. I have my doubts (they may perhaps arise from my ignorance) whether the glories of the night expeditions, in surprising the cabin fortresses in Louth and Meath, or whether the slaughter and expulsion of the Catholic weavers by another set of zealots in Armagh, or even the proud trophies of the late potato field [2] in that county, are quite to be compared with the Protestant victories on the plains of Lombardy, or to the possession of the flat of Bologna, or to the approaching sack of Rome, where, even now, the Protestant commissaries give the law. In all this business Great Britain, to us merely secular politicians, makes no great figure ; but let the glory of Great Britain shift for itself as it may. All is well, provided Popery is crushed.

This war against Popery furnishes me with a clue that leads me out of a maze of perplexed politics, which,

[1] By the "Irish Directory," Mr. Burke means the Protestant ascendency party, then in power in Ireland.

[2] Mr. Burke alludes to popular disturbances in Louth and Meath, and the very questionable means taken by the Irish Government to suppress them ; to the attacks on the Catholics in Armagh by Orangemen ; and probably to the "Battle of the Diamond," in that county, in September 1795.

without it, I could not in the least understand.   I now can account for the whole.   Lord Malmesbury is sent to prostrate the dignity of the English monarchy at Paris, that an Irish, Popish common soldier may be whipt in, to give an appearance of habitation, to a deserted Protestant Church in Ireland.   Thus we balance the account—defeat and dishonour abroad; oppression at home.   We sneak to the regicides, but we boldly trample on our poor fellow-citizens.   But all is for the Protestant cause.

The same ruling principle explains the rest.   We have abdicated the crown of Corsica, which had been newly soldered to the crown of Great Britain and to the crown of Ireland, lest the British diadem should look too like the Pope's triple crown.   We have run away from the people of Corsica, and abandoned them without capitulation of any kind in favour of those of them who might be our friends ; but then it was for their having capitulated with us for Popery, as a part of their constitution.   We made amends for our sins by our repentance, and for our apostasy from Protestantism by a breach of faith with Popery.   We have fled, overspread with dirt and ashes, but with hardly enough of sackcloth to cover our nakedness.   We recollected that this island (together with its yews [1] and its other salubrious productions) had given birth to the illustrious champion of the Protestant world, Bonaparte.   It was therefore not fit (to use the favourite French expression) that the cradle of this reli-

---

[1] Sic tua Cyrnæas fugiant examina taxos.   Virg. Ecl. ix. 30.

gious hero should be polluted by the feet of the British
renegade slaves who had stipulated to support Popery
in that island, whilst his friends and fellow-missionaries
are so gloriously employed in extirpating it in another.
Our policy is growing every day into more and more
consistency. We have showed our broad back to the
Mediterranean ; we have abandoned, too, the very hope
of an alliance in Italy ; we have relinquished the Levant
to the Jacobins; we have considered our trade as nothing ;
our policy and our honour went along with it. But all
these objects were well sacrificed to remove the very
suspicion of giving any assistance to that abomination
the Pope, in his insolent attempts to resist a truly Protestant power resolved to humble the Papal tiara, and to
prevent his pardons and dispensations from being any
longer the standing terror of the wise and virtuous Directory of Ireland ; who cannot sit down with any tolerable
comfort to an innocent little job, whilst his bulls are
thundering through the world. I ought to suppose that
the arrival of General Hoche is eagerly expected in
Ireland ; for he, too, is a most zealous Protestant, and he
has given proof of it, by the studied cruelties and insults
by which he put to death the old Bishop of Dol,[1] whom
(but from the mortal fear I am in lest the suspicion of
Popery should attach upon me) I should call a glorious
martyr, and should class him amongst the most venerable prelates that have appeared in this century. It is
to be feared, however, that the zealots will be disap-

[1] In Bretagne.

pointed in their pious hopes by the season of the year
and the bad condition of the Jacobin navy, which may
keep him this winter from giving his brother Protestants
his kind assistance in accomplishing with you what the
other friend of the cause, Bonaparte, is doing in Italy ;
and what the masters of these two pious men, the Protestant Directory of France, have so thoroughly accomplished in that, the most Popish, but unluckily, whilst
Popish, the most cultivated, the most populous, and the
most flourishing of all countries—the Austrian Netherlands.

When I consider the narrowness of the views, and
the total want of human wisdom displayed in our
western crusade against Popery, it is impossible to
speak of it but with every mark of contempt and
scorn. Yet one cannot help shuddering with horror
when one contemplates the terrible consequences that
are frequently the results of craft united with folly
placed in an unnatural elevation. Such ever will be
the issue of things when the mean vices attempt
to mimic the grand passions. Great men will never do
great mischief but for some great end. For this, they
must be in a state of inflammation, and, in a manner, out
of themselves. Among the nobler animals, whose
blood is hot, the bite is never poisonous, except when
the creature is mad ; but in the cold-blooded reptile
race, whose poison is exalted by the chemistry of their
icy complexion, their venom is the result of their
health, and of the perfection of their nature. Woe to

the country in which such snakes, whose *primum mobile* is their belly, obtain wings, and from serpents become dragons. It is not that these people want natural talents, and even a good cultivation; on the contrary, they are the sharpest and most sagacious of mankind in the things to which they apply. But, having wasted their faculties upon base and unworthy objects, in anything of a higher order they are far below the common rate of two-legged animals.

I have nothing more to say just now upon the Directory in Ireland, which, indeed, is alone worth any mention at all. As to the half-dozen (or half-score as it may be) of gentlemen, who, under various names of authority, are sent from hence to be the subordinate agents of that low order of beings, I consider them as wholly out of the question. Their virtues or their vices, their ability or their weakness, are matters of no sort of consideration. You feel the thing very rightly. All the evils of Ireland originate within itself. That unwise body, the United Irishmen, have had the folly to represent those evils as owing to this country, when, in truth, its chief guilt is in its total neglect, its utter oblivion, its shameful indifference, and its entire ignorance of Ireland, and of everything that relates to it, and not in any oppressive disposition towards that unknown region. No such disposition exists. English Government has farmed out Ireland, without the reservation of a pepper-corn rent in power or influence, public or individual, to the little narrow

faction that domineers there. Through that alone they
see, feel, hear, or understand, anything relative to that
kingdom. Nor do they any way interfere, that I know
of, except in giving their countenance, and the sanction
of their names, to whatever is done by that junto.

Ireland has derived some advantage from its independence on the Parliament of this kingdom, or rather,
it did derive advantage from the arrangements that
were made at the time of the establishment of that
independence. But human blessings are mixed, and I
cannot but think that even these great blessings were
bought dearly enough when, along with the weight of
the authority, they have totally lost all benefit from the
superintendence of the British Parliament. Our pride
of England is succeeded by fear. It is little less than
a breach of order even to mention Ireland in the House
of Commons of Great Britain. If the people of Ireland
were to be flayed alive by the predominant faction, it
would be the most critical of all attempts, so much as
to discuss the subject in any public assembly upon this
side of the water. If such a faction should hereafter
happen, by its folly or its iniquity, or both, to promote
disturbances in Ireland, the force paid by this kingdom
(supposing our own insufficient) would infallibly be
employed to redress them. This would be right enough,
and indeed our duty, if our public councils at the same
time possessed and employed the means of inquiring
into the merits of that cause, in which their blood and
treasure were to be laid out. By a strange inversion of

the order of things, not only the largest part of the
natives of Ireland are thus annihilated, but the Parliament of Great Britain itself is rendered no better than
an instrument in the hands of an Irish faction. This is
ascendency with a witness! In what all this will end
it is not impossible to conjecture, though the exact
time of the accomplishment cannot be fixed with the
same certainty as you may calculate an eclipse.

As to your particular conduct, it has undoubtedly
been that of a good and faithful subject, and of a man
of integrity and honour. You went to Ireland this
last time, as you did the first time, at the express
desire of the English minister of that department, and
at the request of the Lord-Lieutenant himself. You
were fully aware of the difficulties that would attend
your mission; and I was equally sensible of them.
Yet you consented, and I advised, that you should obey
the voice of what we considered an indispensable duty.
We regarded, as the great evil of the time, the growth
of Jacobinism, and we were very well assured that,
from a variety of causes, no part of these countries was
more favourable to the growth and progress of that evil
than our unfortunate country. I considered it as a tolerably good omen that Government would do nothing
further to foment and promote the Jacobin malady that
they called upon you, a strenuous and steady Royalist, an
enlightened and exemplary clergyman, a man of birth
and respectable connexions in the country, a man well-
informed and conversant in State affairs, and in the

general politics of the several courts of Europe, and intimately and personally habituated in some of those courts. I regretted indeed that the ministry had declined to make any sort of use of the reiterated informations you had given them of the designs of their enemies, and had taken no notice of the noble and disinterested offers which, through me, were made for employing you to save Italy and Spain to the British alliance. But this being past, and Spain and Italy lost, I was in hopes that they were resolved to put themselves in the right at home, by calling upon you; that they would leave, on their part, no cause or pretext for Jacobinism, except in the seditious disposition of individuals; but I now see that, instead of profiting by your advice and services, they will not so much as take the least notice of your written representations, or permit you to have access to them, on the part of those whom it was your business to reconcile to Government, as well as to conciliate Government towards them. Having rejected your services as a friend of Government, and in some sort in its employment, they will not even permit to you the natural expression of those sentiments which every man of sense and honesty must feel, and which every plain and sincere man must speak, upon this vile plan of abusing military discipline, and perverting it into an instrument of religious persecution. You remember with what indignation I heard of the scourging of the soldier at Carrick for adhering to his religious opinions. It was at the time when

Lord Fitzwilliam went to take possession of a short-
lived Government in Ireland.

He could not live long in power, because he was a
true patriot, a true friend of both countries, a steady
resister of Jacobinism in every part of the world. On
this occasion he was not of my opinion. He thought,
indeed, that the sufferer ought to be relieved and discharged, and I think he was so ; but, as to punishment
to be inflicted on the offenders, he thought more lenient
measures, comprehended in a general plan to prevent
such evils in future, would be the better course. My
judgment, such as it was, had been that punishment
ought to attach, so far as the laws permitted, upon every
evil action of subordinate power, as it arose. That such
acts ought at least to be marked with the displeasure of
Government, because general remedies are uncertain in
their operation when obtained ; but that it is a matter
of general uncertainty whether they can be obtained at
all. For a time *his* appeared to be the better opinion.
Even after he was cruelly torn from the embraces of the
people of Ireland, when the militia and other troops
were encamped (if I recollect right) at Loughlinstown,
you yourself, with the knowledge and acquiescence of
Government, publicly performed your function to the
Catholics then in service. I believe, too, that all the
Irish, who had composed the foreign corps taken into
British pay, had their regular chaplains. But we see
that things are returning fast to their old corrupted
channels. There they will continue to flow.

If any material evil had been stated to have arisen
from this liberty, that is, if sedition, mutiny, disobedi-
ence of any kind to command, had been taught in their
chapels, there might have been a reason for not only
forcing the soldiers into churches where better doctrines
were taught, but for punishing the teachers of disobedi-
ence and sedition.   But I have never heard of any such
complaint.   It is a part, therefore, of the systematic ill-
treatment of Catholics.   This system never will be
abandoned, as long as it brings advantage to those who
adopt it.   If the country enjoys a momentary quiet, it
is pleaded as an argument in favour of the good effect
of wholesome rigours.   If, on the contrary, the country
grows more discontented, and if riots and disorders
multiply, new arguments are furnished for giving a
vigorous support to the authority of the Directory, on
account of the rebellious disposition of the people.   So
long, therefore, as disorders in the country become pretexts for adding to the power and emolument of a junto,
means will be found to keep one part of it, or other, in
a perpetual state of confusion and disorder.   This is the
old traditionary policy of that sort of men.   The discontents which, under them, break out amongst the people,
become the tenure by which they hold their situation.

I do not deny that in these contests the people, however oppressed, are frequently much to blame; whether
provoked to their excesses or not, undoubtedly the law
ought to look to nothing but the offence, and punish it.
The redress of grievances is not less necessary than the

punishment of disorders, but it is of another resort. In
punishing, however, the law ought to be the only rule.
If it is not of sufficient force; a force consistent with its
general principles ought to be added to it. The first
duty of a State is to provide for its own conservation.
Until that point is secured it can preserve and protect
nothing else. But, if possible, it has greater interest
in acting according to strict law than even the subject
himself. For, if the people see that the law is violated
to crush them, they will certainly despise the law.
They, or their party, will be easily led to violate it,
whenever they can, by all the means in their power.
Except in cases of direct war, whenever Government
abandons law it proclaims anarchy. I am well aware
(if I cared one farthing, for the few days I have to live,
whether the vain breath of men blow hot or cold about
me) that they who censure any oppressive proceeding
of Government are exciting the people to sedition and
revolt. If there be any oppression, it is very true, or if
there be nothing more than the lapses which will
happen to human infirmity at all times, and in the
exercise of all power, such complaints would be wicked
indeed. These lapses are exceptions implied, an allowance for which is a part of the understood covenant by
which power is delegated by fallible men to other men
that are not infallible ; but, whenever a hostile spirit on
the part of Government is shown, the question assumes
another form. This is no casual error, no lapse, no
sudden surprise ; nor is it a question of civil or political

liberty. What contemptible stuff it is to say that a
man who is lashed to church against his conscience
would not discover that the whip is painful, or that he
had a conscience to be violated, unless I told him so!
Would not a penitent offender, confessing his offence and
expiating it by his blood, when denied the consolation
of religion at his last moments, feel it as no injury to
himself; or that the rest of the world would feel so
horrible and impious an oppression with no indignation,
unless I happened to say it ought to be reckoned
amongst the most barbarous acts of our barbarous times?
Would the people consider the being taken out of their
beds, and transported from their family and friends,
to be an equitable, and legal, and charitable proceeding, unless I should say that it was a violation of
justice and a dissolution, *pro tanto*, of the very compact
of human society? If a House of Parliament, whose
essence it is to be the guardian of the laws, and a sympathetic protector of the rights of the people, and
eminently so of the most defenceless, should not only
countenance but applaud this very violation of all law,
and refuse even to examine into the grounds of the
necessity upon the allegation of which the law was so
violated, would this be taken for a tender solicitude for
the welfare of the poor, and a true proof of the representative capacity of the House of Commons, unless I
should happen to say (what I do say) that the House
had not done its duty, either in preserving the sacred
rules of law, or in justifying the woeful and humiliating

privilege of necessity ?   They may indemnify and
reward others.   They might contrive, if I was within
their grasp, to punish me, or, if they thought it worth
their while, to stigmatise me by their censures ; but who
will indemnify them for the disgrace of such an act ?
Who will save them from the censures of posterity ?
What act of oblivion will cover them from the wakeful
memory, from the notices and issues of the grand
remembrancer—the God within ?   Would it pass with
the people who suffer from the abuse of lawful power,
when at the same time they suffer from the use of law-
less violence of factions amongst themselves, that Government had done its duty, and acted leniently in not
animadverting on one of those acts of violence, if I did
not tell them that the lenity with which Government
passes by the crimes and oppressions of a favourite
faction was itself an act of the most atrocious cruelty ?
If a Parliament should hear a declamation attributing
the sufferings of those who are destroyed by these riotous
proceedings to their misconduct, and then to make them
self-felonious, and should in effect refuse an inquiry into
the fact, is no inference to be drawn from thence, unless
I tell men in high places that these proceedings, taken
together, form not only an encouragement to the abuse
of power, but to riot, sedition, and a rebellious spirit,
which, sooner or later, will turn upon those that
encourage it ?

I say little of the business of the potato field,
because I am not acquainted with the particulars.   If

any persons were found in arms against the king,
whether in a field of potatoes, or of flax, or of turnips,
they ought to be attacked by a military power, and
brought to condign punishment by course of *law*. If
the county in which the rebellion was raised was not in
a temper fit for the execution of justice, a law ought to
be made, such as was made with regard to Scotland, in
the suppression of the Rebellion of '45, to try the delinquents. There would be no difficulty in convicting
men who were found "*flagranto delicte.*" But I hear
nothing of all this. No law, no trial, no punishment
commensurate to rebellion, nor of a known proportion
to any lesser delinquency, nor any discrimination of the
more or the less guilty. Shall you and I find fault
with the proceedings of France, and be totally indifferent to the proceedings of Directories at home?
You and I hate Jacobinism as we hate the gates of hell.
Why? Because it is a system of oppression. What
can make us in love with oppression because the
syllables "*Jacobin*" are not put before the "*ism*," when
the very same things are done under the "*ism*" pre-
ceded by any other name in the Directory of Ireland?

I have told you, at a great length for a letter,—very
shortly for the subject and for my feelings on it,—my
sentiments of the scene in which you have been called
to act. On being consulted, you advised the sufferers
to quiet and submission; and, giving Government full
credit for an attention to its duties, you held out, as an
inducement to that submission, some sort of hope of

redress.   You tried what your reasons and your credit
would do to effect it.   In consequence of this piece of
service to Government you have been excluded from all
communication with the Castle; and perhaps you may
thank yourself that you are not in Newgate.   You have
done a little more than, in your circumstances, I should
have done.   You are, indeed, very excusable from your
motives; but it is very dangerous to hold out to an
irritated people any hopes that we are not pretty sure
of being able to realise.   The doctrine of passive obedience, as a doctrine, it is unquestionably right to teach,
but to go beyond that is a sort of deceit; and the
people who are provoked by their oppressors do not
readily forgive their friends, if, whilst the first persecute,
the other appear to deceive them.   These friends lose
all power of being serviceable to that Government in
whose favour they have taken an ill-considered step;
therefore, my opinion is that, until the Castle shall
show a greater disposition to listen to its true friends
than hitherto it has done, it would not be right in you
any further to obtrude your services.   In the meantime,
upon any new application from the Catholics, you
ought to let them know, simply and candidly, how you
stand.

The Duke of Portland sent you to Ireland, from a
situation in this country of advantage and comfort to
yourself, and no small utility to others.   You explained
to him, in the clearest manner, the conduct you were
resolved to hold.   I do not know that your writing to

2 F

him will be of the smallest advantage. I rather think
not ; yet I am far from sure that you do not owe to him
and yourself to represent to his Grace the matters
which in substance you have stated to me.

If anything else should occur to me, I shall, as you
ask it, communicate my thoughts to you. In the meantime, I shall be happy to hear from you as often as you
find it convenient. You never can neglect the great
object of which you are so justly fond; and let me beg
of you not to let slip out of your mind the idea of the
auxiliary studies and acquirements which I recommended to you, to add to the merely professional pursuits of your young clergy ; and, above all, I hope that
you will use the whole of your influence among the
Catholics to persuade them to a greater indifference
about the political objects which at present they have
in view. It is not but that I am aware of their importance, or that I wish them to be abandoned; but
that they would follow opportunities, and not attempt
to force anything. I doubt whether the privileges they
now seek, or have lately sought, are compassable. The
struggle would, I am afraid, only lead to those very
disorders which are made pretexts for further oppression
of the oppressed. I wish the leading people amongst
them would give the most systematic attention to prevent frequent communication with their adversaries.
There are a part of them proud, insulting, capricious,
and tyrannical. These, of course, will keep at a
distance. There are others of a seditious temper, who

would make them at first the instruments, and in the end the victims, of their factious temper and purposes. Those that steer a middle course are truly respectable, but they are very few. Your friends ought to avoid all imitation of the vices of their proud lords. To many of these they are themselves sufficiently disposed. I should therefore recommend to the middle ranks of that description,—in which I include not only all merchants, but all farmers and tradesmen,—that they would change as much as possible those expensive modes of living, and that dissipation, to which our countrymen in general are so much addicted. It does not at all become men in a state of persecution. They ought to conform themselves to the circumstances of a people whom Government is resolved not to consider as upon a par with their fellow-subjects. Favour, they will have none. They must aim at other resources ; and to make themselves independent in *fact*, before they aim at a *nominal* independence. Depend upon it, that, with half the privileges of the others, joined to a different system of manners, they would grow to a degree of importance, to which, without it, no privileges could raise them, much less any intrigues or factious practices. I know very well that such a discipline, among so numerous a people, is not easily introduced, but I am sure it is not impossible. If I had youth and strength, I would go myself over to Ireland to work on that plan ; so certain I am that the well-being of all descriptions in the kingdom, as well as of themselves, depends upon a reformation amongst the Catholics. The work will be new, and slow in its operation, but it is certain in its effect. There is nothing which will not yield to perseverance and method. Adieu! my dear sir. You have full liberty to show this letter to all those (and they are but very few) who may be disposed to think well of my opinions. I did not care, so far as regards myself, whether it were read on the 'Change; but with regard to you, more reserve may be proper; but of that you will be the best judge.

December 1796.

LETTER to the RIGHT HON. WM. WINDHAM.

MY DEAR FRIEND,

. . . IRELAND is in a truly unpleasant situation. The Government is losing the hearts of the people, if it has not quite lost them, by the falsehood of its maxims, and their total ignorance in the art of governing. The Opposition in that country, as well as in this, is running the whole course of Jacobinism, and losing credit amongst the sober people, as the other loses credit with the people at large. It is a general bankruptcy of reputation in both parties. They must be singularly unfortunate who think to govern by dinners and bows, and who mistake the oil which facilitates the motion for the machine itself. It is a terrible thing for Government to put its confidence in a handful of people of fortune, separate from all holdings and dependencies. A full levée is not a complete army. I know very well that when they disarm a whole province they think that all is well; but to take away arms is not to destroy disaffection. It has cast deep roots in the principles and habits of the majority amongst the lower and middle classes of the whole Protestant part of Ireland. The Catholics who are intermingled with them are more or less tainted. In the other parts of Ireland (some in Dublin only excepted) the Catholics, who are in a manner the whole people, are as yet sound; but they may be provoked, as all men easily may be, out of their principles. I do not allude to the granting or withholding the matters of privilege, etc., which are in discussion between them and the Castle. In themselves, I consider them of very little moment, the one way or the other. But the principle is what sticks with me; which principle is the avowal of a direct, determined hostility to those who compose the infinitely larger part of the people, and that part upon whose fidelity, let what will be thought of it, the whole strength of Government ultimately rests. But I have done with this topic, and perhaps for ever, though I receive letters from the fast friends of the Catholics to solicit Government here to consider their true interests. Neglect, contumely, and insult, were never the ways of keeping friends; and they add nothing to force against an enemy. . . .

EDM. BURKE.

BATH, *March* 30, 1796.

LETTER to Dr. Laurence.

My dear Laurence,

I am satisfied that there is nothing like a fixed intention of making a real change of system in Ireland; but that they vary from day to day as their hopes are more or less sanguine from the Luttrellade. The system of military government is mad in the extreme—merely as a system, but still worse in the mad hands in which it is placed. But my opinion is, that if Windham has not been brought into an absolute relish of this scheme, he has been brought off from any systematical dislike to it. When I object to the scheme of any military government, you do not imagine that I object to the use of the military arm in its proper place and order; but I am sure that so long as this is looked upon as principal, it will become the sole reliance of Government— and that from its apparent facility, everything whatsoever belonging to real civil policy in the management of a people will be postponed, if not totally set aside. The truth is, the government of Ireland grows every day more and more difficult; and, consequently, the incapacity of the jobbers there every day more and more evident; but as long as they can draw upon England for indefinite aids of men and sums of money, they will go on with more resolution than ever in their jobbing system.   Things must take their course.[1] . . . Yours ever,

E. B.

BEACONSFIELD, *June* 5, 1797.

[1] Mr. Burke died on the 9th of July 1797, aged sixty-seven.

THE END.

The Cresset Library

Cover: *View from Capel Street, looking over Essex Bridge, Dublin* by James Malton. Reproduced by courtesy of Photo Images Ltd.